PURCELL

Music advisor to Northeastern University Press

GUNTHER SCHULLER

Jonathan Keates

PURCELL
A BIOGRAPHY

Northeastern University Press

BOSTON

Copyright 1995 by Jonathan Keates

Published in Great Britain in 1995 by Chatto & Windus Limited, a
division of Random House UK Limited, London. Published in the
United States of America in 1996 by Northeastern University
Press, by agreement with Random House UK Limited.

Library of Congress Cataloging-in-Publication Data
Keates, Jonathan, 1946–
Purcell : a biography / Jonathan Keates.
p. cm.
Includes bibliographical references and indexes.
ISBN 1-55553-287-X (cloth)
1. Purcell, Henry, 1659–1695. Composers—England—
Biography. I. Title.
ML410.P93K4 1996
780'.92—dc20
[B]   96-26031
MN

Printed and bound by Maple Press, York, Pennsylvania. The
paper is Renew Antique Recycled, an acid-free sheet.

MANUFACTURED IN THE UNITED STATES OF AMERICA
00 99 98 97 96   5 4 3 2 1

To Christopher Rowe

Contents

Illustrations

Preface

Unlike many of his contemporaries or near-contemporaries, Henry Purcell had the good fortune never to sink without trace from the musical horizon during the two hundred years in which Baroque music was either misunderstood, treated as an antiquarian curiosity or else despised and ignored completely. He was not restored to greatness in the manner of composers such as Vivaldi and Marc Antoine Charpentier, because he had never entirely forfeited his position as the gifted author of a voluminous oeuvre, at least some of which, in however exiguous a portion, was always available for performance, listening and study. Purcellian scraps, whether in the form of anthems and canticles, theatre music or even such a charming little nonesuch as the part-song 'When the cock begins to crow', were performed throughout the eighteenth century. The Victorians, from patriotic as much as artistic motives, began digging deeper into the mine, dusting off works like *Dido and Aeneas* and developing the idea of the composer not so much as a musical Shakespeare (the term was first applied in 1789 by Charles Burney) as an equivalent Chaucer, a sturdy if often outlandish founding father. When the young Arthur Sullivan, defending his decision to enter the Chapel Royal, protested to his parents: 'But Purcell was a Chapel boy!', the invocation was of an established English musical household god, however imperfectly envisaged.

By the 1950s, when I first heard Purcell's music ('I attempt from love's sickness to fly', sung by my mother at the drawing-room piano) the picture had greatly altered. The tercentenary celebrations in 1959 set the seal on a re-evaluation of the composer as an original genius worthy to be set beside Handel, his fellow subject for commemoration that year, and fully justified in receiving homage from modern English composers, led by Benjamin Britten and Michael Tippett. Our musical Shakespeare had become the national Mozart, a youthful genius gathered too early, but not before he had astonished everybody by his fecund, protean brilliance in an outpouring of music unrivalled in its sheer diversity by any of his immediate European contemporaries. We can all name a historically more important late seventeenth century composer than Purcell – Lully, Corelli, Buxtehude and Stradella spring instantly to mind – but none of these has his phenomenal virtuosity distributed with such effortless grace among multiple genres, and none quite reaches into the well-springs of our essential humanity in the way that Purcell, balancing his musical learning and expressive profundity with masterly manipulations of 'the common touch', can always contrive.

A biography of the composer is an impossible exercise, since we know so little about his antecedents, personal life, domestic surroundings or intimate acquaintance. Hardly any anecdotes exist to fill out the blurred background, made vaguer still by the almost total absence of lettters or private papers. The manuscripts, so neat and confident, with hardly a suggestion of a backward glance, tell us something. Otherwise we have to rely, whatever our Micawberish hope that something more positive will turn up, on those largely chimerical aids to the biographer, ambience, period detail, hypothesis and sheer guesswork.

My aim in this book has therefore been to provide a context for the earliest performances of Purcell's works, relating it to the sketchy details of his professional life. As in my earlier biography of Handel, I haven't stepped back from commenting on individual pieces and expressing personal preferences. I'm conscious that in certain areas, especially as regards the debut works in various fields (the *Theodosius* music, the elegy on Matthew Locke, for example) I have said rather too much, and that in others, such as Purcell's official positions in the court and ecclesiastical establishments, I have sketched in the outlines more thinly. The total picture, however, will perhaps convey something of my undying affection for the composer and his age.

The roots of this love date from 1959, when my enlightened prep school headmaster John Engleheart, himself a pioneer in the

Baroque music revival, introduced me to *Dido and Aeneas* and took me to a remarkable series of tercentennial concerts, in which the experience of hearing *My beloved spake* and *My heart is inditing* was literally a case of 'since then I never looked back'. My first acknowledgment must always be to him.

Most of the work for this biography has been carried out in the congenial surroundings of the Bodleian Library's Music Reading Room in Oxford. My thanks to its staff, and to those of the London Library and the British Library for their continuing helpfulness.

My editors Jenny Uglow and Sarah Holloway have been endlessly encouraging. Jonathan Burnham, originally responsible for commissioning the book, conducted it expertly through an uneasy initial phase.

The following gave various kinds of help or showed interest in the project: Kathy Chubb, Mrs G. Fallows, Anthony Gould, Robin Lane Fox, Gerard McBurney, Alison Millar, Nick Morgan, Roger Parr, Jon and Carol Rayman, Michael Rose, Valerie St Johnston, Mary Sandys, Emma Tristram.

Prologue: The Unfriendly Time

During the fiercely hot summer of 1656, a season of 'so great a drought that hay was £40 the load', Thomas Tomkins, last of the great Tudor composers, died at his son Nathaniel's house in the parish of Martin Hussingtree, a few miles north of Worcester. The city in whose cathedral he had served as organist and master of the choristers for almost fifty years had suffered severely for its loyalty to the crown in the Civil War, and the great church itself, burial place of King John, had been desecrated on several occasions by Parliament's troops. In 1643, when Tomkins's own dwelling was hit by a cannon ball, the organ, installed under his supervision by the leading Jacobean organ-builder Thomas Dallam, was ravaged and the stained glass smashed, following established Puritan practice. Three years later, after a successful siege, the same forces imposed their presence by dismantling what remained of the instrument altogether, while 'some Parliamenters, hearing the music of the church at service, walking in the aisle fell a-skipping about and dancing as it were in derision'. With considerable courage 'a merry lad (about ten years old)' reminded them that when the organ had first been vandalized by the troopers, one soldier had broken his neck, 'and they will not prevent the like misfortune'. The final Anglican service was an evensong three days afterwards, when loyal worshippers crowded to receive Bishop Prideaux's blessing. Tomkins, retreating to his turret study on the south side of the cathedral, turned to the writing of keyboard music, including an eloquent memorial in 1649 for the recently executed King Charles I, entitled 'A Sad Pavan: for These Distracted Times'.

Born in 1572, the composer had grown to manhood in the age of William Byrd and Thomas Morley, and like them had excelled

1

in the period's chief musical genres, the church anthem, the consort song, madrigals and keyboard pieces. Early in his career Tomkins contributed a madrigal to *The Triumphs of Oriana*, the anthology published in 1601 to honour Queen Elizabeth I which Morley himself had edited, and in the *Songs of 3, 4, 5 and 6 Parts* (1622) he revealed a wide acquaintance among the finest English musical talents of the age, dedicating individual works to composers such as John Dowland and Orlando Gibbons. In the setting of sacred texts he had few rivals during the early decades of the seventeenth century. 'Very elaborate and artful pieces' was one contemporary judgment on his anthems and services, 'the most deserving to be recorded and had in everlasting remembrance'.

The musical world whose values Tomkins and his works had so vividly emblematized now lay to all intents and purposes in ruin. Worcester was not alone in having suffered at the hands of the pious reformers, concerned as they were to purify divine worship of the various forms of sensual delight held out to the worshipper by musical, ritual and visual adornments. At Westminster Abbey the Parliament soldiers 'brake down the rayl about the Altar, and burnt it in the place where it stood . . . They put on some of the Singing-men's surplices, and, in contempt of that canonicall habite, ran up and down the Church; he that wore the surplice was the hare, the rest were the hounds.' At Exeter they taunted the choristers, crying, 'Boys, we have spoiled your trade, you must go and sing hot pudding pies.' In Canterbury they despoiled the splendid array of funerary monuments, stripped the lead off the cathedral roof and, encouraged by the preacher Richard Cullmer who announced that he was 'rattling down proud Becket's glassy bones', they knocked out several of the more 'idolatrous' medieval windows. Troopers at Winchester marched into the cathedral with drum and colours, ripped out the altar and rails and burned them at a drunken revel in a nearby alehouse . . . 'and in that fire burnt the Books of Common Prayer, and all the Singing books belonging to the Quire'.

These same Civil War years which saw the destruction of cathedral worship witnessed an inevitable dispersal of the extensive musical establishment gathered around the royal court of the Stuart monarch. Charles I had been noted for his love of music and had given employment to some of the choicest spirits of the period. These included Tomkins himself, Orlando Gibbons, the brothers William and Henry Lawes, the viol player John Cooper whom a visit to Italy had transformed into Giovanni Coprario,* and the inspired theatrical song-writer Robert Johnson, composer of the earliest settings of Ariel's songs in Shakespeare's *The Tempest*. Once the war began, though the King retained certain musicians in attendance at Oxford, the chief Royalist stronghold until 1646, a regular provision of music in chapel and chamber which contributed towards the dignity and 'seemliness' so admired in the English court was no longer appropriate or affordable.

Gone too were the masques, whose elements of dance and song enabled talented amateurs among the courtiers to exhibit their skills alongside professional performers without compromising the social position which many in that parvenu aristocracy were all too conscious of having won very recently. The public playhouses, what is more, had closed their doors in 1642. This prohibition was confirmed six years later by sanctions decreeing that the stages and seating were to be demolished and forbidding all forms of dramatic spectacle on pain of whipping for the players and fines for the audience. As the war drew to a close and the period loosely referred to as 'the Commonwealth' began, during which Oliver Cromwell ruled the nation under the euphemistic title of 'Lord Protector', it must have seemed to many musicians that their sole chances of employment lay either in the lowly capacity of city waits, to provide entertainment at mayoral feasts, or else in attaching themselves to the household of some country landowner with a turn for music, to whose benevolence they could trust until the dawn of a more auspicious political climate.

It would be wrong, however, to see 'the unfriendly time' as being a kind of musical wasteland patrolled by the thought police of Puritan joylessness in an attempt to suppress anything that sounded too suspiciously unlike a psalm tune. The true picture is both more fragmented and more fascinating. If, in the eighteen years between the outbreak of war in 1642 and the restoration of

* He was born John Cooper around 1570, but italianised his name after a journey to the continent, and is often referred to as John Coprario.

3

Charles II in 1660, there was no obvious sense of an established community and hierarchy of English musicians required to furnish composers and performers for court and church, then the void was filled up instead with a whole range of miscellaneous creative activity bearing witness to the nation's unquenchable passion for making and listening to music.

Cromwell himself led the way. His love of music, formed doubt-less during his childhood among the good families of his native Huntingdonshire and neighbouring counties, and developed during his years as a Cambridge undergraduate, found its deepest echo, not, as might at first be thought, in metrical psalm-singing, but in the Latin motets of *Cantica Sacra*, the work of Richard Dering, a Papist convert who spent much of his creative life on the Continent before returning to England in 1625 to become a composer in the Catholic chapel of Queen Henrietta Maria. At the wedding of the Protector's daughter Frances in 1657, the feast was enlivened with '48 violins, 50 trumpets and much mirth with frolics, besides mixt dancing (a thing heretofore accounted profane) till 5 of the clock yesterday morning'.

However others may have condemned dancing, Cromwell and many of his contemporaries clearly saw no harm in it as a formal exercise, linked perhaps with concepts of order and decorum inherited from the liberal pedagogic traditions of the Renaissance which the intrusive religiosity of Puritanism had been unable to destroy. As his ambassador to Queen Christina of Sweden, Cromwell had wisely chosen Bulstrode Whitelocke, a cultivated and accomplished lawyer whose most notable achievement before the Civil War had been to organize the production of a masque *The Triumphs of Peace* to a text by James Shirley, which was presented by the Inns of Court in honour of Charles I with scenery designed by Inigo Jones. The music was provided by the much admired William Lawes and by the versatile Simon Ives, 'an honest and able musician, of eccellent skill in the art'.

Christina, preparing to abdicate the Swedish throne and retreat to Rome, the most musically sophisticated city in mid-seventeenth-century Europe, was curious to know something of English manners under the Commonwealth regime and asked Whitelocke whether dancing was forbidden. 'Some there are that do not approve of it' he answered, 'but it is not prohibited by law, and many there are that do use it'. As if in earnest of this, and 'lest I should be judged too severe and morose, and too much to censure', he accepted the Queen's invitation to a court ball, where an orchestra of violins, bass viols, flutes and citterns first played French dances (including the once-popular but increasingly obsolescent 'branles', known in England as 'brawls') and then performed English country dances. Whitelocke and his fellow diplomats, let it be said, not only joined in the former, but actually taught some new versions of the latter to the Swedes.

Oliver Cromwell plainly saw no harm in this: when the Ambassador told him that they had beguiled the long northern winter nights with dancing for the purpose of exercise and harmless amusement, in addition to Latin debates and orations, he merely observed, 'These were very good diversions and made your house a little academy.' Neither does he seem to have identified anything especially inappropriate in the performance of two pastorals at the wedding of his daughter Mary to Lord Fauconberg at Hampton Court barely a week after her sister's bridal feast, on 19 November 1657. Here the married couple actually took part in a court masque, the groom playing Endymion and his wife Cynthia, though whether, as has been suggested, her father himself appeared as Jove is not firmly established. The other entertainment was a dialogue between three country folk on the nuptials of 'Marina' and 'Damon', though here the couple stayed mute.

It seems clear that as so often under a dictator – and in its overall character and psychology, Cromwell's reign irresistibly embodies various important aspects of a modern dictatorship – a double standard prevailed. While the general tone of public life was that of a theocracy, its rhythms dictated by various kinds of religious observance and pious exercise, the ruler himself – a cultivated member of the Caroline upper classes, who employed the music-loving Italophile John Milton as his Latin secretary – understood the value of sustaining the appropriate amenities of a princely court for the purpose of impressing foreign ambassadors. In 1653, for example, the Portuguese envoy Dom Domingos de Vasconcelos was entertained with a specially composed masque (the first on such a scale to be performed for over a decade) entitled *Cupid and Death*, on a text derived by the dramatist James Shirley from Aesop's fables and using material from two of his earlier masques written for Whitehall in the 1630s.

Telling the story of a disastrous prank played on Cupid and Death when their arrows are exchanged while both are staying at an inn, the piece is divided, after the French fashion, into five 'entries', involving progressive stages of the spoken drama enlivened with songs and choruses set to music by Christopher Gibbons (son of the more famous Orlando) and Matthew Locke, whose career as one of the most accomplished of seventeenth-century English composers was to blossom at the Restoration. In addition each entry featured dances, specially choreographed by Luke Channen, whom Samuel Pepys later referred to in jocular admiration as 'the hop merchant'.

What the audience of *Cupid and Death* were seeing – and had indeed a chance to see again in 1659 when the work was revived – was the nearest equivalent England had yet produced to the operatic form now evolving so exuberantly in the various cities of Italy. In the extended passages of recitative Locke displayed a pliant sensitivity to verbal nuance and to the changes of mood ordained in Shirley's poetry, as well as making some attempt to link the characters, Cupid, Death, Mercury and Nature, to distinctive keys, which in any case determined the governing structure of the scenes he was assigned to set.

Perhaps inspired by this example, no less a figure than Sir William Davenant, epic poet and ingenious dramatist and masque-maker under Charles I, now sought to circumvent the ban on stage plays altogether by mounting dramatic performances clothed in music, according to the Italian mode. In 1656, under the aegis of a group of senior lawyers which included Bulstrode Whitelocke, he presented *The Siege of Rhodes*, a play transformed into an opera libretto and published with the elaborate excuse that it was 'Made a Representation by the Art of Prospective in Scenes, And the Story sung in Recitative Musick'. Neither the vocal items, by Henry Lawes and Henry Cooke, nor the instrumental music, by Charles Coleman and George Hudson, have survived, but the piece by its very nature attracted attention even from Davenant's more sophisticated contemporaries, familiar with the Italian operatic style at its native source. The diarist John Evelyn (whose description of the genre, after attending a performance of Giovanni Rovetta's *Ercole in Lidia* at Venice in 1645 as 'one of the most magnificent and expensive diversions the wit of man can invent' has been quoted to death) witnessed a presentation either of *The Siege of Rhodes* or of its successors *The Cruelty of the Spaniards in Peru* and *The History of Sir Francis Drake*.

> I went to visit my brother in London; and, next day, to see a new opera, after the Italian way, in recitative music and scenes, much inferior to the Italian composure and magnificence; but it was prodigious that in a time of such public consternation such a vanity should be kept up, or permitted. I, being engaged with company, could not decently resist the going to see it, though my heart smote me for it.

This mixture of self-reproaching gravity and natural aesthetic inquisitiveness is typical of Evelyn, and we would give much to know what exactly he heard which made him judge the work so unfavourably. From these original performances, which took place at Rutland House 'in the upper end of Aldersgate Street', beside the former Carthusian monastery of the Charterhouse, all that has come down to us beyond Davenant's texts is the splendid set of scene designs which Inigo Jones's pupil John Webb created for *The Siege of Rhodes*. From these we can see that the work was presented in a visual context by no means unlike that of contemporary Italian opera, with an ornamental proscenium arch framing a stage picture, which could be changed through a sequence of different backdrops. The limited space allowed by the improvised acting area at Rutland House meant that the wings remained fixed throughout, but Webb was able to compensate for this by the decorative elegance of his painted scenes, including a view of Rhodes with the Turkish fleet, the besieged town with tents and guns, and the pavilion of Sultan Solyman the Magnificent, who himself appears in the play.

The Siege of Rhodes proved so popular that after the Restoration Davenant added a sequel and eventually, jettisoning the operatic element altogether, 'caused it to be acted as a just drama'. If the work, with its two companion pieces, did not succeed in establishing a vogue for English opera, it had undeniably made an impact in its original form. Seventeenth-century London would see further attempts at grafting the newer continental musical styles on to the robust traditions of vernacular drama, a *mélange* which Davenant had initiated as a practical means of circumventing the Commonwealth's blanket ban on theatrical performances.

It was not in London alone that musical activity weathered the storms of civil war, theocracy and dictatorship, and the doctrinal bullying which accompanied them. The venerable and entirely praiseworthy English tradition of amateur musicianship – reflected in today's choral societies, school orchestras and *ad hoc* chamber groups – was already well established, and skill on the viols, the violin, the organ or the lute was an accepted indicator of cultivation and gentility. Throughout England noble families welcomed, and when necessary sheltered, visiting professional musicians, and in certain cases such figures were retained in the household either as superior servants or, in at least one instance, honoured guests. Before the Civil War the Kytsons of Hengrave Hall in Suffolk, whose domestic inventory featured sackbuts, hautboys, four lutes, six violins, a chest of viols and 'one payer of great orgaynes', had received the madrigalist John Wilbye, who lived with them for over thirty years until the widowed Lady Kytson's death in 1628. At Kirby in Northamptonshire, home of the Hatton family whose fortunes had been established by Queen Elizabeth's favourite, the personable Sir Christopher, the singular talents of George Jeffreys found a welcome. Until the collapse of the Royalist war effort in 1646, Jeffreys had been a successful composer of secular vocal and instrumental music and organist to Charles I at Oxford. Only when he joined the Hattons as their house steward, conscientious in the management of the day-to-day affairs of the family and the drawing up of accounts, did Jeffreys turn at all seriously to religious compositions whose distinctly Italianate caste reflects an absorption of continental styles not found elsewhere in English music of his immediate period. As an isolated experimenter in an alien mode liturgically ill-suited to a climate of institutionalized plainness in worship, he has been almost completely ignored by musical historians (the latest reputable account of seventeenth-century English music makes two brief references to him), but anyone hearing his anthems will at once be struck by their complex artistic individuality.

The most remarkable case of a composer whose achievement as one of the age's most inventive instrumental writers, not merely in England but throughout Europe, was set against a background of country-house visits and residence with noble families, is surely that of John Jenkins, whose work breathes forth as no other the authentic voice of refined, expressive musicianship among cultivated amateurs in the age of Cromwell. The son of a prosperous carpenter of Maidstone in Kent, Jenkins had joined the household of the Countess of Warwick as a musician around 1603 when he was only eleven. Later entering the service of Sir Thomas Derham of West Dereham Abbey in Norfolk, he came into contact with the family of Sir Hamon L'Estrange of Hunstanton. Both households loved music so much that 'service' is probably the wrong word to use in reference to Jenkins's time with either. In any case, those who knew and admired the composer are at pains to stress his social acceptability among the East Anglian gentry. His friend the Oxford antiquarian Anthony à Wood tells us that 'though a little man, yet he had a great soul', while the invaluable memorialist of English seventeenth-century music Roger North describes him as 'a very gentile and well bred gentleman, and was allways not onely welcome, but greatly valued by the familys wherever he had taught and convers't'.

Jenkins's young pupil Roger North developed an affectionate respect for him. The most versatile of instrumentalists, in 1654 Jenkins came to live at Kirtling Park in Cambridgeshire, where Dudley, third Lord North, Roger's grandfather, had turned his own musical obsession to excellent account by building up an entire household of performers, either dilettante or professional. Not only was the 'good old lord' himself a practitioner on 'that antiquated instrument called the treble viol', but his son and grandchildren all played, as well as 'the servants of parade, as gentleman ushers, and the steward, and clerck of the kitchen'. There was a domestic organist, who accompanied Sunday night singing, there were 'symphonys intermixt with instruments' and 'solemne musick 3 days in the week', let alone open-air concerts with accompanying picnics in a nearby wood called Bansteads, which Lord North had redesigned with glades and arbours as 'a parcel of delectable grounds', nicknamed Tempe after the Grecian vale celebrated by ancient poets.

This utterly irresistible vision of a community of melomanes, gentle and plebeian, beguiling their idle hours with singing and viol consorts is completed by the presence of Jenkins himself, a figure valued evidently as much for his wit and charm as for his skilful musicianship. Dudley North's comment that 'Spirit, Garb and Air shine in his first appearance' applied as much to the man as to his works, and Roger says of him that 'he was ever courted and never slighted, but at home wherever he went; and in most of his friends houses there was a chamber called by his name. For besides his musicall excellences, he was an accomplisht ingenious person, and so well behaved as never to give offence . . .'

Jenkins's popularity underlines the impression, easily gathered elsewhere, of a musical world during the Commonwealth period in which, whatever the essential fragmentation and lack of institutionalized employment for professional performers and composers, the irrepressible musicality of the English guaranteed the endurance of essential traditions and skills and created a continuity on which artists and enthusiasts of a succeeding generation could build. By particular irony, it was the very existence of Puritanism and the lack of a cosmopolitan royal court which contributed towards the survival of robust vernacular forms such as the viol fantasy and the unaccompanied anthem among those who had enjoyed them in times of peace. As Roger North famously observed, 'when most other good arts languished Musick held up her head, not at Court, nor (in the cant of those times) profane Theaters, but in private society, for many chose rather to fidle at home, than to goe out and be knockt on the head abroad . . .'

In 1658 Cromwell's musicians, including John Hingeston, who had petitioned him the previous year for the establishment of a 'corporacion or Colledge' to supply the deficiencies resulting from 'the late dissolution of the Quires in the Cathedralls', and the fiddler Davis Mell, 'a prodigious hand on the violin', followed the procession to his grave. The Lord Protector's death had apparently been accompanied by a violent storm, afterwards known as

'Oliver's Wind' and inevitably interpreted by the more super-
stitious among Royalist sympathizers as the arrival of the Devil
himself to hail the dictator down to hell. However portentous this
may have appeared, few can have foreseen the speed with which
the Puritan dispensation collapsed or have gauged the extent to
which the nation, unimpressed by godly army officers or
Cromwell's son Richard as his possible successors, was ready to
welcome the glamorous, still youthful Charles II, who had
languished in shabby exile for almost a decade since his defeat at
Worcester in 1651.

On 26 May 1660, already proclaimed king by Parliament,
Charles landed at Dover, making a triumphal entry into London
at the end of the following week. Attended by immense troops of
cavalry and infantry 'brandishing their swords and shouting with
inexpressible joy', the restored sovereign rode through the city
along streets strewn with flowers and hung with tapestries, to the
sound of jubilant bell-ringing and acclamations from a crowd
invigorated by the wine pumped through the public conduits. In
his diary John Evelyn, watching the vast procession, whose progress took seven hours, recorded simply: 'I stood in the Strand
and beheld it and blessed God.'

During these years of ending and beginning again, the greatest
of all English musicians was born. We cannot grasp the significance of Henry Purcell's achievement without relating it to the
unique historical perspective of music in England during an age
when to many thoughtful observers the threads of cultural continuity seemed, superficially at least, in danger of breaking. The
swift and apparently painless reinstatement of the monarchy and
the Church of England at 'His Majesty's happy return' did not
mean, on the other hand, that everything was as it had been twenty
years earlier for the musicians who regained their places at court,
in the cathedral organ loft or in the band at the theatre. A new
cosmopolitanism wafted from France and Italy made the English
uneasily aware, not just in music but among the sister arts, of their
own narrowness and parochialism, while a rising tide of patriotic
enthusiasm, reaching its height during the 1690s, inspired a readiness to challenge foreign practitioners in their own forms and
idioms. Tensions like these ordained Purcell's professional destiny

and helped to dictate many of his most important artistic decisions. His genius, both embracing and transcending the variable moods of late seventeenth-century England, gave the period and the culture an unforgettable voice.

I

A Peculiar Readiness of Fancy

Research has never succeeded in establishing the exact date or place of Purcell's birth, and even his parentage is still a matter of conjecture as opposed to hard fact. We know from his memorial inscription in the north aisle of Westminster Abbey that he was thirty-seven on the day he died (21 November 1695) and the title page of his *Sonnatas of III Parts*, published in 1683, records his age as twenty-four, so perhaps – and the Purcellian life record is strewn with such perhapses – he was born at some point during the latter half of 1659. Until a baptismal register should turn up, that is all we can establish, and the same source, whenever it appears, will almost certainly clarify the shared mystery of his father and mother.

The Purcells were one of many English families which assumed a right to a coat of arms, though the various branches – we cannot be certain that they were all necessarily related by much more than a name – ran the social gamut from minor gentry to the humblest of artisans. What the Oxfordshire Purcells and their Shropshire cousins, together with the Irish Purcells who went over to Kilkenny with Strongbow's Norman barons, all had in common was their surname. Stressed on the first syllable (the 'el', which picked up a doubling somewhere along the line, is simply a diminutive suffix), the word means 'little pig', porcel, not unlike the old name 'porcelet' given to the common woodlouse. The canting heraldry of the composer's coat of arms displays three boars' heads, and this porcine allusion was made elsewhere on their family escutcheons by bearers of the name.

It is the presence of this coat of arms underneath Purcell's portrait, forming the frontispiece to his *Sonnatas of III Parts*, which has led one of his most recent biographers to conclude that he was descended from the Purcells of Shropshire, to whom the arms were granted in 1597 as lords of the manor of Overgather on the county's border with Montgomeryshire. Since there is no further evidence from his own meagre life records to establish this connection, we are left wondering whether he might not simply, like many before or since, have assumed the blazon as a guarantee of respectability in launching his first major publication. Just as probably, young Henry, whatever lustre he might have drawn from Salopian squires, from Irish origins or from the lordship of Newton Purcell in Oxfordshire, derived from a lowlier background altogether.

Between Buckingham and Aylesbury, in the villages of Thornborough, Oving and Wing, there dwelt a family of Purcells whose menfolk worked principally as carpenters and, in their various generations, bore the names Henry, Thomas and Edward, all of which figure in the composer's immediate family tree. Thornborough is not far from Claydon, the house belonging to the Verney family, loyal supporters of the King's cause in the Civil War. Sir Edmund Verney had died at the Battle of Edgehill in 1642, clinging to the royal standard which it was his privilege to carry. In 1656, when his son Sir Ralph was busy petitioning Oliver Cromwell in order to avoid sequestration of the estate, the housekeeper Joanna Westerholt, sending a pasty of forty-one pigeons to regale him while absent in London, accompanied this with a letter about some tiresome building workers at Claydon. She wrote,

> This last week cam Pursell the carpenter and his men, he only himselfe sate in the house, but all his men come in for their beere, and that not seldome nor in small proportions; and by theire example al the workmen doe soe worry me for drinke, that though I many times anger them, and hourly vexe myselfe with deniing one or other of them, yet we spend a great deale of beer . . .

Was this 'Pursell the carpenter' our musical Henry's grandfather? His candidacy is reinforced by a Buckinghamshire tradition, recorded without attribution by the composer's first authoritative modern biographer, which asserts that the elder Henry and his brother Thomas were kidnapped to serve as choristers in the Chapel Royal, presumably during the early 1630s. The practice of pressing choirboys into the King's service dated back to the Middle Ages – in 1440 Henry V had commissioned the Dean of Westminster John Croucher 'to take throughout England such and so many boys as he or his deputies shall see fit and able to serve God and the king in the said royal chapel' – but we may wonder whether parents always surrendered their children willingly and whether the story of the young Purcells being carried off to London may not in fact be entirely genuine.

Whatever the truth, the names of both Thomas Purcell and his brother appear regularly in lists of court musicians made during the early years of Charles II's reign. Thomas is noted as a member of the Private Musick, providing domestic entertainment for the royal family, under the heading 'For lutes and voyces, theorboes and virginalls', and in 1662 figures as one of the 'composers for the violins', taking the place of Henry Lawes. The elder Henry Purcell, meanwhile, took over briefly in a similar capacity from the aged Italian Angelo Notari, a survivor from the era at the beginning of the century when the Monteverdian style known as the *seconda prattica* was starting to make its influence felt on English monody. Joining the choir of Westminster Abbey in 1661, Henry was registered two years later among the Gentlemen of the Chapel Royal, alongside his brother Thomas, in a roster apparently drawn up with the intention that the choir should not benefit from the grants made to the restored monarchy by Parliament.

Scholarly opinion is still divided as to which of these two musical Purcells was Henry the composer's father. On the evidence of a letter written to the virtuoso bass singer John Gostling on 8 February 1679 and containing an explicit reference to 'my sonne Henry', it has been reasonably concluded that the signatory 'T. Purcell' is the most likely candidate for the honour. Just as reasonably, it has been pointed out that since the elder Henry died in 1664, when his son was five years old, Thomas would have assumed control of the boy's upbringing *in loco parentis* and could easily have referred to him as 'my sonne', though he had four of his own.

The elder Henry's widow Elizabeth, of whom we know hardly anything, certainly not her maiden name, lived on until 1699, and it is her status as his wife which supplies a crucial piece of evidence. When the musician John Hingeston, a figure of great importance in the mid-seventeenth-century musical establishment, died in 1683, he left a will including among its provisions a legacy of £5 to his godson, identified as 'Henry Pursall (son of Elizabeth Pursall)'. Any doubts as to who this was or the possibility that there might have been another Henry Purcell entitled to this not altogether negligible sum can be counterbalanced by two references to other members of the clan which clarify their relationship to the composer. When Daniel Purcell, himself an extremely accomplished master, became organist and *informator choristarum* at Magdalen College, Oxford, in 1689, he was later entered in the college register as 'son of Henry Purcell, Gentleman of the Chapel Royal ... He was brother of Henry Purcell ...' The fact is confirmed both by a newspaper advertisement of 1717, in which the composer's son Edward refers to 'his uncle Dr Daniel Purcell', and by an obvious family likeness between Henry and Daniel, the latter eminently better looking but sharing his brother's unmistakable aquiline nose, one of those features through which kinship is most often traced.

Assuming then that in a family where the choice of Christian names was scarcely original – the generations we are concerned with featured four Edwards, four Katherines, three Elizabeths and three Thomases – Henry was the son of Henry and Elizabeth Purcell, we can also suppose that he grew up in London, more precisely in Westminster, where his parents lived in the area (for it could hardly be called a street) known as Great Almonry, lying at the west end of the Sanctuary of Westminster Abbey. The Sanctuary, as its name indicated, was a place originally sought out by fugitives from justice, or simply from those seeking to kill them, its limits indicated by a huddle of houses stretching north from St Margaret's church. On one side of this safety zone, whose privileges had been progressively abolished during Queen Elizabeth's reign until James I in 1624 cancelled them entirely, the alms collected during Abbey services were distributed to the poor. In this 'Almonestrye' William Caxton had set up the first English printing press, and during the same period Henry VII had founded an almshouse here for twelve poor men, a priest and three nuns.

His mother, the saintly Lady Margaret Beaufort, established a similar charity at the Almonry's lower end, which was later converted for use as lodgings for adult members of the Abbey choir. It was probably in one of these houses, no longer surviving, known as Choristers' Rents, that the Purcell family lived during the last years of the Commonwealth.

Westminster Abbey stood on the very edge of London's narrow urban spread along the northern curve of the Thames, beyond the official limits of the city. To the west lay open country embracing the royal park of St James's, the marshy area of the manor of Ebury (which would soon fall via an advantageous marriage into the lap of the Grosvenor family), and the broad expanse of Tothill Fields, where during the Middle Ages trials by combat had been staged and those accused of sorcery had been made to watch as their magical paraphernalia was publicly burned. Famous for growing parsley and for the sand indiscriminately quarried from them, the fields had formed part of the defensive works thrown up by the Parliamentarians in 1643, when fear of a Royalist attempt to seize control of London had prompted the building of a line of forts stretching in a semicircle from Shoreditch to 'Tuttle Fields'. More ominously, the place contained a pest-house in the form of a row of wooden sheds, a house of correction where prisoners were employed in beating hemp, and a cemetery in which, after having been driven to London following the Battle of Worcester in 1651, over a thousand Scottish prisoners were buried.

The streets around Great Almonry, far from benefiting from the health-giving airs blowing in off the adjacent fields, formed one of the seedier, less salubrious corners of seventeenth-century London. Outbreaks of plague decimated the area during Charles I's reign and the overseers and church-wardens were constantly fretting over the state of the various sewers. A legacy of the old sanctuary rights, apart from the local street name 'Thieving Lane', was the number of louche, if not downright dangerous characters noted as living in the streets clustered around the Abbey and the old Palace of Westminster in which Parliament sat. The district was also popular with foreigners, from its closeness to Whitehall where many of them were employed. A census drawn up just before the Civil War had recorded some 800 of them, mostly

French and Dutch, working principally as painters, engravers, silversmiths and musicians.

It was as part of a small local community of native English musicians that the Purcells lived in this quarter of London. Next door dwelt Henry Lawes, whose brother William, before being killed at the siege of Chester in 1645, had been the doyen of early Stuart instrumental composers. Henry, who provided the music for John Milton's Ludlow masque *Comus* and earned the poet's praise in a sonnet for his 'tuneful and well-measur'd song', was the master most sought after by the so-called 'Cavalier' lyricists, Thomas Carew, Edmund Waller, Richard Lovelace and others, when it came to providing a musical idiom which would adequately render the sense and flow of their lines through its extreme plasticity. Near him in Westminster lived John Banister, the violinist and subsequent promoter of the first of London's public concerts, as also did another noted instrumental composer whose elegy Purcell later composed, Thomas Farmer. Dean's Yard, under the shadow of the Abbey's west end, was the home of John Wilson, one of the period's most original song-writers, whose name had appeared as 'Iackie Wilson' in a list of actors attached to the First Folio edition of Shakespeare's works. As a boy singer at the Globe Theatre, he must have known the playwright personally, and later wrote an appropriately melancholy setting of 'Take, O take those lips away', the song which introduces the forlorn Mariana in *Measure for Measure*.

A year after the young Henry Purcell was born, the lives of all these musicians were dramatically transformed by the Restoration. The royal court returned to Whitehall, and with it the need for a fully fledged musical establishment to provide dances, songs and the appropriate festive dimension for palace entertainments, let alone to furnish a complement of singers and instrumentalists for the Chapel Royal. Charles II, whatever his public protestations, was not religiously inclined. Even the famous deathbed conversion to Catholicism had as much to do with exhausted resignation and the promptings of family loyalty to a devout wife, an over-zealous brother and the memory of a beloved sister, as with any indwelling spirituality. He had, however, an inordinately strong sense of what was due to him as king in terms of status, exaggerated no doubt by his years in exile, living on handouts from the kings of France and Spain. A monarch must have a court chapel, and though he could not command as much revenue as his father, whose regal state was the most elaborately maintained in Europe during the 1630s, Charles was determined to re-establish as much as possible of the former order and 'seemliness' among his musicians.

At Whitehall the chapel building itself had suffered considerably from ideologically motivated assault by the Puritans. The painted-glass east window was knocked out and replaced by plain lights, the cross was pulled down and all pictorial decoration ruthlessly plastered over or scraped off by carpenters specially employed for the purpose. In the same year that this spoliation took place, 1644, the organ was dismantled and later found a temporary home at Magdalen College, Oxford, before ending up in the Northamptonshire church of St Nicholas, Stanford, where it remains to this day.

Complete refurbishment was clearly of immense symbolic importance, therefore, in establishing the presence of a restored episcopalian Church of England with the monarch at its head as an indisputable reality. Throughout the early 1660s the work went steadily forward. In 1662 Purcell's godfather John Hingeston, officially appointed 'tuner and repairer of organs, virginals and wind instruments', installed a new organ, probably the first to be built in England by Bernhard Schmidt, 'Father Smith', recently arrived from Germany. The following year the loft, hung with crimson damask, was fitted with rooms for the chapel sub-dean, 'the organist in wayting' and the 'keeper and repayrer of his majesty's organs', each with a fireplace and shelves for storing music. On holy days the altar was covered with 'a Carpet partly Velvet, and partly white Gold flower'd Sattin' and the splendid array of newly made communion plate and silver-gilt candlesticks set out.

Meanwhile the Anglican liturgy itself had been reinstated through the revised prayerbook of 1662, and the musical component of the various services restored to its proper place. It was here that King Charles's own taste played its part, with notable consequences in the development of a style in which Purcell himself would eventually excel. At the French court of Louis XIV,

Charles had had plenty of opportunity to appreciate the playing of the royal string band, the famous 'Vingt-quatre violons', which he was now determined to emulate in England. Easily bored, as monarchs often are, he could hardly be expected to embrace with enthusiasm the complex imitative structures of the native fantasia style as practised by composers like John Jenkins and William Lawes, in which the linear design of each piece was emphasized by having a single player to each part. Instead he preferred something he could tap his feet to, with a clearly defined rhythm and melody and a strong formal outline, something which should remind him, in contexts sacred or secular, of dance forms like the gavotte, bourrée and minuet, all newly popular in Paris. Looking back on the change in musical taste, that invaluable witness Roger North was generally cynical. 'He had lived some considerable time abroad,' he says of Charles,

> where the French musick was in request, which consisted of an Entry (perhaps) and then Brawles, as they were called, that is, native aires and dances. And it was, and is yet a mode among the Monsieurs, always to act the musick, which habit the King had got, and never in his life, could endure any that he could not act by keeping the time; which made the common andante or else the step-tripla the onely musicall styles at Court in his time. And after the manner of France, he set up a band of 24 violins to play at his dinners, which disbanded all the old English musick at once.

Noting the King's 'utter detestation of Fancys', North adds that he used to rally Sir Joseph Williamson, one of his chief ministers, on too much enthusiasm for the fantasia style, 'and he would not allow the matter to be disputed upon the point of meliority, but run all downe by saying, Have I not ears?'

The inevitable result was that at Whitehall not merely the court dance music but that of the Chapel Royal as well attempted to keep pace with the royal fads. As a matter of course during certain services, especially those for important feast days or on occasions connected with great public events such as naval victories over the Dutch, anthems were sung, often specially written by court composers, and the style chosen humoured the King's pleasure.

Thomas Tudway, who began his career as a Chapel chorister before going on to be a Cambridge music professor and an important collector and editor of sacred compositions by his contemporaries, tells us:

> some of the forwardest and brightest Children of the Chappell, as Mr Humfreys, Mr Blow etc. began to be masters of a faculty in composing: This his Majesty greatly encouraged by indulging their youthful fancys, so that every month at least, and afterwards oftener, they produced something New of this Kind; in a few years more, severall others, Educated in the Chappell, produced their Compositions in this style, for otherwise it was in vain to hope to please his Majesty.

From what Tudway observes elsewhere, it seems that Charles himself actually ordered the Chapel composers to add 'Symphonies etc. with Instruments' to their anthems. The novelty increased the Chapel Royal's popularity with that sermon-fancying public in Restoration London which moved from church to church on Sundays across the city, sampling the preachers and enjoying or criticizing whatever music happened to be on offer. The restless Samuel Pepys, who began his diary while living in Axe Yard a few streets away from the Purcells, was a case in point. Turning in at the Chapel Royal on 8 September 1662, he recorded afterwards 'a most excellent Anthem (with Symphony's between)' and the following week 'a Symphony between every verse of the Anthem, but the Musique more full then it was last Sunday, and very fine it is'. His friend and fellow diarist John Evelyn, of a more sober cast and perhaps not quite so musically enraptured, was altogether less impressed. 'Instead of the antient grave and solemn wind musique accompanying the Organ was introduced a Consort of 24 Violins betweene every pause, after the French fantastical light way, better suiting a Tavern or a Playhouse than a Church'. Evelyn lamented besides the disappearance of 'the Cornet, which gave life to the organ, that instrument quite left off in which the English were so skilful', but this merely reflected the radical shift throughout Europe during the late seventeenth century in the role and importance of the various members of the string and wind families, a change to which the cornet, formerly a significant presence in works of composers like Giovanni Gabrieli, Monteverdi and Schütz, fell a major casualty.

Under its new master, Henry Cooke, referred to as 'Captain Cooke' from the rank he held in the Royalist army during the Civil War, the Chapel Royal became a major focus of musical life during Charles II's reign. Cooke himself was a composer, though not an especially gifted one, who had contributed pieces to Davenant's *The Siege of Rhodes* and furnished some of the King's coronation music in 1661. His major achievement, however, was to establish the Chapel as a centre of professional excellence among singers, instrumentalists and composers, training the choir to a standard it had probably never attained before, encouraging the choristers to write their own anthems, and ensuring, even in the always uncertain financial climate of a court whose pretensions and extravagance wildly outstripped its resources, that the material wellbeing and status of the singers, both boys and men, were adequately guaranteed.

Receiving £30 annually per child for 'diett, lodging, washing and teaching', Cooke was expected in return to give the boys lessons on the organ, lute and theorbo, to provide proper heating in the practice room, to arrange when necessary for the attendance of doctors and nurses, and to make annual tours of the various cathedrals, trawling for talent among choirs at Lichfield, Canterbury, Rochester and elsewhere. In addition he had been appointed in 1660 composer for lutes and voices, theorbos and virginals, to replace the Frenchman Nicolas Duval who had originally arrived from Paris with Queen Henrietta Maria thirty-five years previously.

Henry Purcell the elder did not live long to enjoy his position as a Gentleman of the Chapel Royal and a member of the King's music. On 28 October 1664 we find a warrant being made 'to swear John Goodgroome musician in ordinary to his Majesty for the lute and voyce, in the place of Henry Purcell, deceased', but the actual appointment had been noted in the Lord Chamberlain's accounts in August, and the Cheque Book of the Chapel Royal records that Henry had died on the eleventh of that month. Buried two days later on the east side of the Westminster Abbey cloisters, he was appropriately laid in a grave beside that of his fellow musician and former neighbour Henry Lawes.

His widow Elizabeth, by now the mother of six young children, moved out of Great Almonry to a house rented from the Dean and Chapter of Westminster in Tothill Street, where she was granted a forty-year lease 'under the old rent and usual covenant'. She seems to have survived on various payments from the Chapel Royal and the money received from taking in lodgers (a certain 'Frances Crump' is mentioned in St Margaret's Vestry Book, though the clerk adds the caveat, 'it is ordered that the business be very well examined before any money is paid').

Tothill Street still exists, running west out of Broad Sanctuary towards Petty France, where the poet John Milton had once lived in 'a pretty garden-house, next to Lord Scudamore's and opening into the Park'. The thoroughfare, debouching, as its name implies, into Tothill Fields, had been one of the smartest in the area, the residence of various noblemen during Tudor times, whose large gardens stretched northwards as far as St James's Park. Here had lived William Lord Grey of Wilton, 'greatest soldier of the nobility', who had managed not to lose his head after the abortive rising on behalf of Lady Jane Grey in 1554, in which he was directly involved. Here too there had formed a little pocket of Elizabethan recusant families, the Dacres, the Stourtons and others, whose houses still bore their names, and here also was the Office of the Revels, where court entertainments were projected and scrutinized under the hypercensorious eye of old Sir Henry Herbert, restored to the position of Master of the Revels he had first enjoyed under Charles I.

The unhealthy condition of low-lying Westminster, with its bad drainage, 'nuisances' and overcrowding, was a continual source of worry to the citizens, who were aware of the reality of these health hazards without knowing quite how diseases were spread. In 1665 London was visited by the worst outbreak of bubonic plague in its recent history, during which 100,000 people died. In the parish of St Margaret's Westminster, where the Purcells dwelt, 3,000 lives were claimed by the epidemic during the terrible summer and winter of 1665–6, and an area was specially cleared for plague burials in the cemetery in 'Tuttle Fields', separated from the main graveyard by a wall and ditch, with a bridge across it. We know a good deal about the response of the local authorities to the incidental problems created by the plague in Westminster, thanks to a report by the indefatigable Earl of Craven, famous for having served with King Gustavus Adolphus of Sweden during the Thirty Years War and for his quixotic devotion to Charles I's daughter Elizabeth, Queen of Bohemia. 'The streets are dayly cleansed,' he observes, 'and the filth carried away by the Raker who brings the carts every morning and giveing notice thereof to the inhabitants by the sound of his Bell to the end that every Perticular house alsoe may be cleared of its filth.' The various dunghills or 'laystalls' proved more of a difficulty 'by reason of titles in law wch the proprietors had therein', but the persistence of the magistrates was gradually managing to clear them away. Pest-houses, meanwhile, needed enlarging, but the necessary intiative, thought Craven, could scarcely be undertaken while so many of the 'middling sort of persons' were themselves suffering from the effects of 'the late Calamity' and while the nobility were reluctant to take up residence again in plague-stricken Westminster.

This last detail is of interest when we survey the growth of London during Henry Purcell's boyhood. Retreating from the noxious riverside airs, those who could afford it or who had providently acquired lands on which to build moved uphill towards Piccadilly and the Tyburn Road (modern Oxford Street). During the late 1660s and 1670s the serious development of May-fair and St James's as elegant residential suburbs began, much to the irritation of the City of London, which saw itself losing a valuable source of revenue by this aristocratic westward drift.

The Purcells were of course in no position to follow, and it is remarkable that the entire family, Henry, his elder brothers Edward and Charles, his sister Katherine and the two youngest children Joseph and Daniel, together with 'the Widow Pursel' herself, managed to survive the plague unscathed. Perhaps still more noteworthy, in an age of high infant mortality, is that all six of the Purcell children attained adulthood, three of them, like their mother, outliving their famous sibling.

It was almost inevitable that Henry, inheriting his father's musical gifts, should enter the Chapel Royal as one of the twelve children under Captain Cooke's tutelage. We know nothing as to the exact date at which he joined the establishment, but it would seem likely that he was around seven or eight, even if the earliest members of the newly founded choir in 1660, including future composers such as John Blow, Pelham Humfrey and Michael Wise, had all been somewhat older. The children, as mentioned previously, were provided with board, lodging and education – though perhaps Purcell, living locally, was able to return home each evening – and, as part of the royal household, were allotted the official livery, which has remained more or less unchanged to the present day. 'For each of them', says the Lord Chamberlain's warrant, 'one cloak of bastard scarlett cloth lyned with velvett, one suit and coat of the same cloth made up and trimmed with silver and silk lace after the manner of our footmen's liveries.' With this went shirts, shoes, stockings, two hats, three handkerchiefs, three pairs of gloves and 'two pieces and a half of rebon for trimming garters and shoestrings'. In the summer the uniform changed to a satin-lined cloak and doublet with scarlet trunk-hose.

Cooke's exceptional teaching skills were based on his own experience as the possessor of what Samuel Pepys, who knew him personally, called 'the best manner of singing in the world'. The diarist was somewhat less enchanted by his bumptious, know-all manner, exhibited one evening in February 1667 at the house of Dr Pierce, surgeon-general to the navy. Having berated Pierce for the dinner itself, 'an ill and little mean one, with foul cloth and dishes and everything poor', Pepys went on to criticize Cooke himself, who

> had the arrogance to say that he was fain to direct Sir W. Davenant in the breaking of his verses into such and such lengths, according as would be fit for musick, and command him that way, when W. Davenant would be angry, and find fault with this or that note – but a vain coxcomb I perceive he is, though he sings and composes so well.

Cooke had taken part in *The Siege of Rhodes* and provided some of its music, and the experience to which his remarks testify, that of trying to influence poets to write fluid, settable texts, is surely not uncommon, but the 'bragging' manner on which Pepys comments elsewhere does seem to have been an authentic feature of Cooke's personality.

Educating the Chapel choristers to a high standard was altogether less of a problem than maintaining them in the proper style, given the continuing financial embarrassments of the court, at times so strapped for cash that according to Cooke the children were scarcely able to set foot out of doors owing to the general raggedness of their liveries. As well as being taught writing and arithmetic, the boys were encouraged to compose from the outset of their musical training, and it comes as no surprise to find that several of Purcell's most respected contemporaries, including Blow, Humfrey, the theatre musician Robert Smith and William Turner, who dedicated his entire career to service with various cathedral choirs, began composing while still children of the Chapel Royal.

It would be tempting to imagine that Henry Purcell's unique sensitivity to nuance and linguistic subtlety in the English texts he set, as well as his evident sensitivity to Latin, evinced by a small but significant clutch of sacred works, was entirely spontaneous and owed nothing whatever to his schooling. There is evidence however – and as always in the case of Purcell's life this is extremely tenuous – that he received more than a basic grounding in the non-musical aspects of a Chapel boy's education.

Since 1670 his cousin Charles, son of Thomas Purcell, had been a pupil at Westminster School. In the Abbey Treasurer's accounts for 1678, we find the name of Charles Purcell scratched out and that of Henry substituted, and both of them appear in the school registers for the following two years. A further hint that this was indeed our Henry Purcell is offered by the mention in a will made by the composer's widow Frances in 1706 of 'a mourning ring of Dr Busby's'. There is no proof that the famous and terrifying headmaster of Westminster actually left this ring to Purcell himself, but since he too died in 1695, predeceasing his young contemporary by six months, the deduction seems promising. The two may have become acquainted when Purcell reached adulthood, but the not uncommon desire of a forward pupil at a good school to keep up with his old teachers after leaving may just as well have cemented the friendship between them.

If the Henry Purcell who figures in the Westminster roll was the composer, then the same source indicates that he attended the school as a 'Bishop's Boy' like the cousin Charles whom his name replaced. The bishop in question was the highly controversial John Williams, the archetypal Welsh careerist of the period, who had risen from humble origins in Caernarfonshire to become a fellow of St John's College, Cambridge, and university proctor, afterwards being made Bishop of Lincoln, Lord Keeper of the Great Seal of England and Archbishop of York. Having made himself unpopular with Charles I for urging a more conciliatory approach to Parliament, he was sent to the Tower and eventually retired to Wales, where his Royalist countrymen shrewdly selected him as the ideal mediator with the Parliamentarians after the decisive Battle of Naseby in 1645.

Heartily loathed as he was by more orthodox Anglicans (who frequently derided him for his obesity), Williams was conspicuously eager to do well by the various foundations with which he was linked. Besides enriching and rebuilding his Cambridge college, he created, while Dean of Westminster, a series of four scholarships endowed from the Middlesex manors of Sudbury and Stanmore, whose fee-farm rents he had acquired in 1623. Two of the scholars were to be Welsh natives and the others were to have been born in the diocese of Lincoln. Once their Westminster education was completed, they were to be 'from thence elected and transplanted into St John's College, Cambridge'. If boys from Wales and Lincoln were not forthcoming, those born within the liberties of Westminster could be chosen instead. To consolidate the arrangement more substantially, Williams bought the patronage of four rich livings to which the boys, in an ideal world, would eventually succeed after their period of university study. The scheme soon ceased to work as intended: though the four scholars went on sporting the violet gown prescribed in Williams's original document, St John's confiscated its share of the scholarships and the Bishop's Boys were finally rendered obsolete in 1872.

Eighteen was a somewhat advanced age to enter Westminster, but few pupils in the seventeenth century would have been foolish enough to decline the chance to receive what was then the best available education in England. Under Busby's long headmastership, spanning some fifty years from his election in 1640, the school became an astonishing nursery of national talent among lawyers, the clergy and college fellows at the two universities, not to speak of poets, scientists, historians and philosophers. John Locke was one of Busby's pupils; so too was the pulpit virtuoso Robert South, whose sermons, with those of Archbishop Tillotson, set the tone for the best preachers in an era when sermons constituted a performance art as magnetic as stage plays. A stormier cleric altogether was Purcell's direct contemporary Francis Atterbury, famous as a leading Tory churchman during the reigns of Queen Anne and George I, and a friend of Pope and Swift. While Dean of Westminster he made himself popular with the school's pupils by building them a new dormitory.

Perhaps the strongest proof that Purcell spent some time under Busby's tutelage is offered by the appearance of various Old Westminsters as associates with him at different stages of his career. With one of the school's most famous pupils, John Dryden, he was to work closely during the 1690s at Drury Lane and Dorset Garden playhouses, and there was a similar theatrical connection with Elkanah Settle, one of the candidates for authorship of the anonymous text for Purcell's *The Fairy Queen*. For a school kept by another of Busby's pupils, Lewis Maidwell, the composer wrote one of his best odes, *Celestial Music Did the Gods Inspire*.

Among churchmen too the Westminster connection enhanced Purcell's success. Nobody has ever found much to say, either in praise or denigration, of Nicholas Brady, best known as collaborator with Nahum Tate (himself the librettist of *Dido and Aeneas*) on a metrical version of the psalms which remained in use throughout Protestant churches of every shade for some two hundred years. He left Westminster for Oxford in 1678, so Purcell, who joined the school that year, may well have overlapped. They were to meet again in 1686, by which time Brady had been appointed vicar of St Katherine Cree in the City of London. He not only invoked Henry's help in testing a new organ for the church, but subsequently provided him with the text for the great St Cecilia ode of 1692, *Hail, Bright Cecilia* one of Purcell's most popular works among his contemporaries.

Almost every pupil of Dr Busby's with any claim to real celebrity and success acknowledged his impact as a teacher and disciplinarian. Though never particularly loved – he was far too free with the birch rod and the flogging block for that – the headmaster was respected for his ability to find out the best qualities in his scholars and bring them to the sharpest possible pitch. Richard Steele, the Augustan journalist and dramatist, though never taught by him, was sufficiently impressed by those who had been to declare himself, 'confident I could discover a stranger who had been such with very little conversation; those of great parts who have passed through his instruction have such a peculiar readiness of fancy and delicacy of taste, as is seldom found in men educated elsewhere, though of equal talent'.

Busby had, what is more, as Steele says, 'a power of raising what the lad had in him to the utmost height', which, however obliquely, must have made its mark on the young Henry Purcell. That standards, however, were slipping somewhat during the boy's time at Westminster is attested by an alarming incident which took place in the summer of 1679. In a little street behind Dean's Yard, a bailiff took possession of one of the houses and arrested the owner. When the boys got wind of this supposed infringement of ancient sanctuary rights, they seized whatever clubs and cudgels they could lay hands on, and raced to visit vengeance on the wretched officer, whom they eventually battered to death. Dr Busby, returning from spending the day at Chiswick, rounded up the whole school and singled out eleven culprits among the King's Scholars. Though Charles II immediately issued a royal pardon for these, three elected to stand trial, but Busby finally perjured himself in giving an alibi for one of them, while against the others there was insufficient evidence. The parents of the young malefactors were required in addition to stump up the substantial sum of £23 1s 8d each as a share of the general indemnity.

Purcell was not, so far as we know, involved in this inglorious episode. His musical talents were by now evident enough for him to be taken seriously as a pupil, or at any rate as a protégé, by various composers who had themselves either been Children of the Chapel Royal or else furnished music for Captain Cooke and his choristers. One of these teachers was almost certainly the Westminster Abbey organist Christopher Gibbons, son of the great Orlando, whose playing John Evelyn had admired on a visit to Oxford in 1654, but whose instrumental compositions were described by Roger North as 'very bold, solid and strong, but desultory and not without a litle of the barbaresque'. Gibbons scarcely led an exemplary life: Anthony à Wood, the Oxford antiquary, calls him a 'grand debauchee' who 'would sleep at Morning Prayer when he was to play on the organ', and one of his voluntaries carries a note 'drunke from the Catherine Wheale, Christopher Gibbons'.

Another of Cooke's pupils from whom Purcell absorbed much was the precociously gifted Pelham Humfrey, most tragically short-lived of those who gave an unmistakably idiomatic voice to the Restoration anthem, a voice echoed and sophisticated by another young prodigy on whom his mantle most easily fell. Probably born in London in 1648, Humfrey joined the Chapel around 1660, perhaps part of the first intake of boys at the choir's re-establishment with the return of King Charles. He may well have been the composer mentioned by Samuel Pepys in 1663, who noted on 22 November that 'the Anthemne was good after the sermon, being the 51 psalme – made for five voices by one of Captain Cooke's boys, a pretty boy'. This was surely the rather self-consciously mannered first version of *Have mercy upon me, O God* (the Bible significantly heads the psalm with the words 'To the chief Musician') which Humfrey took up again more successfully some years later.

By the time he left the Chapel choir on Christmas Day, 1664, Humfrey had evidently become a prized asset among younger English musicians. His importance was underlined by the fact that whereas Cooke was given the usual retrospective £30 for the maintenance of John Blundeville and John Blow, the two other outgoing choristers, 'Pelham Humphryes' was worth £10 extra. Plans had plainly been made already to provide the eighteen-year-old boy with the best possible musical training then available by sending him to France and Italy. Payments from Secret Service funds were issued over the next three years, and though no exact details are known as to where he went and whom he studied with, we can guess from his later style, with its allusions to Lully and Carissimi, that he may have spent significant periods in Paris and Rome, perhaps as a pupil of both these enormously influential composers.

Care was taken to provide Humfrey, in his absence, with appropriate official positions in the hierarchy of English court musicians. He was made a member of the King's private music as a lutenist in 1666, and the following year saw him named a Gentleman of the Chapel Royal. Could there have been a lingering suspicion that without these incentives he might not have returned? Certainly when he did, it was with a vastly inflated notion of his own superiority. Pepys, recording 'a fine Anthemne, made by Pellam (who is come over)' on 1 November 1667, met him a fortnight later in a tailor's shop and was able to confirm his worst fears of Humfrey's vanity and boastfulness. 'Little Pellam Humphrys, lately returned from France' was

> an absolute Monsieur, as full of form and confidence and vanity, and disparages everything and everybody's skill but his own. The truth is, everybody says he is very able; but to hear how he laughs at all the King's music here . . . and that Grebus the Frenchman, the King's Master of the Musique, how he understands nothing nor can play on any instrument and so cannot compose, and that he will give him a lift out of his place, and that he and the King are mighty great, and that he hath already spoken to the King of Grebus, would make a man piss.

Humfrey was being grossly unfair to Louis Grabu, newly appointed Master of the Private Musik, a nomination which created understandable resentment among native-born musicians. A pupil of the mediocre Robert Cambert (who had fled to London from Paris as a result of Jean-Baptiste Lully's intrigues against practically anybody else who could rule a stave or pen a row of crotchets), Grabu has been consistently traduced by writers on the Restoration musical scene, but he was a perfectly competent if not particularly inspired practitioner in his field. By granting

31

him an official appointment, what the King seems to have been attempting, as with increasing the number of his string band, was to inject a little more of the Versailles atmosphere into the musical world of Whitehall and Windsor.

Following the royal lead, the tyranny of French taste in the London of Purcell's boyhood was all pervasive. We have only to look at a play like Sir George Etherege's *The Man of Mode*, first produced in 1676, to see how completely its eponymous beau, Sir Fopling Flutter, affects the latest Parisian styles. Described as 'a great Critick ... lately arriv'd piping hot from Paris', he is the total fashion victim, from his suit by Barroy and his 'garniture' by Le Gras to his Chédreux periwig and Orangerie gloves – 'You know the smell, Ladies!'

As in clothes, so in music, the French style made its indelible impact. Few composers have appeared more profoundly unattractive than Jean-Baptiste Lully in their personal dealings with fellow musicians, but his influence should not be estimated purely in proportion to a lack of effective rivals. It is true that a comparatively recent reappraisal of the achievement of his great contemporary Marc-Antoine Charpentier, whom Lully ruthlessly marginalized, has brought us to acknowledge the former rather than the latter as the most potently expressive and versatile French master of the seventeenth century. Considered purely in terms of musical history, however, the relationship between Charpentier and Lully is rather like that of Handel to the mainstream composers of Italian *opera seria*. One is undoubtedly the more rewarding and original artist, but it is the other with whom the sequential textbook development of European music is mainly concerned.

French influence had not been altogether unknown in England before the Civil War: Charles I married a sister of Louis XIII, Henrietta Maria, who brought with her several Parisian musicians, their names – Etienne Nau, Nicolas Picart, 'Mons. de Flelle' and others – appearing in court lists of the period. Roger North underlines the important influence of French lutenists on the layout and style of instrumental suites or 'setts' which became fashionable among Caroline music lovers, especially in the deft hands of William Lawes and John Coprario. 'The lessons', he tells us, referring to the individual movements, 'had a spice of the French from whom wee had the lute, and most of the composers were lutinists, and it is the mode for gallants and ladys to learne on the lute.'

The major wave of Gallicism was to break over English composers and audiences with the importation of Lully's manner, as well as of actual pieces composed by him, during the late 1660s and 1670s. Young King Louis XIV prided himself on his prowess as a dancer, and the spectacular *ballets de cour*, framing the Sun King as their hero, demanded a sequence of tuneful, rhythmic, crisply outlined movements, corresponding to the various dance forms, minuet, bourrée, chaconne or gigue, whose steps were carefully learned by everyone with any pretence to good breeding. Lully, however much his adoption of France might have made him more French than the French themselves, was born a Florentine as Giovanni Battista Lulli, and his Italian inheritance makes itself felt in the predominance of a consistent melodic line giving shape and direction to the piece in hand. 'Baptist's vein', as North famously called it, soon permeated every aspect of music in London: dances and overtures from the composer's latest operas and ballets were transcribed and published soon after their various premières; new forms like the gavotte, the rigaudon and the rondeau (the last two sometimes misleadingly anglicized as 'Rigadoon' and 'Round-O') found their way into instrumental suites; and Lullian *ballabili* even made an incongruous appearance at such solemn occasions as the annual Oxford University degree ceremony.

This sense of a universal appropriateness and adaptability at the heart of the French court style made its presence known in the music Pelham Humfrey provided for the Chapel Royal following his return from the Continent in 1667. He had almost certainly heard and learned from Lully's motet *Miserere mei Deus*, with its brilliantly contrived synthesis between dramatic expressiveness and meditative solemnity, and was to make use of French idioms in the string symphonies and ritornellos which introduced the various episodes making up his verse anthems. The fact is, nevertheless, that whatever Pepys's scornful reference to 'little Pellam Humphrys' as 'an absolute Monsieur', his music was rooted just as strongly in native English traditions of alertness to the weight and nuance of words and in the already well-established formal outlines of the verse anthem – that standard feature of seventeenth-century Anglican ceremonial, first evolved by Orlando Gibbons and Thomas Tomkins and eventually brought to its perfection in the hands of Humfrey's pupil Henry Purcell.

The word 'pupil' here needs to be used with caution. We do not know for certain that Henry had lessons with Humfrey, but it would seem rather odd, given Humfrey's supervisory position in the Chapel, if he had not transmitted some of his professional expertise to the boy. What might the young master have taught his forward scholar? It is easy to listen to a performance or look at the score of one of Humfrey's eighteen anthems and describe it airily as 'Purcellian', but the influence reaches more deeply than that of a common idiom, a set of stylistic tricks and devices coldly acquired for the purposes of technical accomplishment. Humfrey's muse was a melancholy one – only two of his anthems are in major keys – and his particular fondness was for texts expressive of grief, suffering and repentance. Though he never wrote a full-scale theatrical work (despite contributing two 'masques' to Thomas Shadwell's 1674 adaptation of Shakespeare's *The Tempest*), he clearly understood the dramatic potential embodied in the verses chosen for setting and exploited it to the full. A piece such as *By the waters of Babylon* pushes these histrionic, representational qualities – one might almost call them 'operatic' – to the full in its overwhelming evocation of the miseries of the captive Jews, expressed in Psalm 137. We catch from the very beginning the sense of hopelessness expressed in the descending intervals of the introductory symphony, and a mounting unease in the music climaxes in the conflict between Babylonians, bumptious and scornful in triple measures, and Israelite exiles, angular and chromatic in duple time. We can hardly imagine that Purcell could have remained unresponsive to this kind of pictorial eloquence in the design. Although he by no means confined himself to penitential texts in his own sacred works (avoiding them altogether in the case of his symphony anthems, where the mood is always decidedly upbeat), he made several copies of Humfrey's music for his own reference.

When Purcell left the Chapel Royal choir in 1673, his destiny was clearly indicated by the terms of a warrant issued on 17 December: 'to provide outfit of clothing for Henry Purcell, late child of His Majesty's Chapel Royal, whose voice is changed and gone from the Chapel'. It ordained 'the sum of £30 by the year' which we know was paid to Pelham Humfrey, now Cooke's successor as Master of the Children, for teaching various ex-choristers, a job he seems sometimes to have farmed out to other musicians. Purcell's schoolfellow Henry Hall, later organist at Exeter and Hereford and composer of an elegy on his friend's death in 1695, had been granted a similar bursary the previous Christmas, and his clothing allowance was carefully itemized. 'Two suits of plain cloth, two hats and hat-bands, four whole shirts, four half shirts, six bands, six pairs of cuffs, six handkerchiefs, four pairs of stockings, four pairs of shoes and four pairs of gloves'. Presumably Purcell received the same wardrobe, and a bill made out by the Lord Chamberlain's office the following year specifies extra handkerchiefs for him.

His forwardness, that quality so much admired in children (more particularly boys) during an age of often brutally swift mortality, is demonstrated for us in the fact that even before he quitted the Chapel, a warrant had instituted him assistant to the elderly John Hingeston as 'keeper, maker, mender, repairer and tuner of regals, organs, virginals, flutes and recorders and all other kind of wind instruments whatsoever'. A salary for this was only to be paid to him on Hingeston's death 'or other avoidance of the latter'. No details are afforded as to the actual work involved, but the experience of dealing with the technical aspects of individual instruments must have been invaluable, and the inclusion of flutes and recorders in the list reminds us of his extraordinarily sensitive use of the latter especially in his odes and dramatic works.

On St George's Day, 1674, when the court went to Windsor for traditional celebrations, Pelham Humfrey had stayed in London to make his will. Perhaps exhausted by his recent heavy involve-ment in Shadwell's *Tempest* performances, which incorporated Chapel Royal singers, he may well have been conscious that his days were numbered, and on Tuesday, 14 July, he died at the age of twenty-seven. Later generations were to see Purcell as his direct heir, and it was this mantle of artistic inheritance to which Henry Hall alluded in his 1695 elegy, calling 'young Humphries',

Our first reforming Music's Richelieu
Who dying left the Goddess all to You.

For a new teacher Purcell turned to another Gentleman of the
Chapel, sworn in as Master a week after Humfrey was buried in
the south-east corner of Westminster Abbey's cloisters. Born
in 1648, John Blow was well established as a court musician, with
official posts as a royal keyboard player, an organist at the Abbey
and a composer for the Private Musick. After Purcell he emerges as
the most productive and versatile English musician of the period, a
remarkably able, expressive writer of songs and anthems and the
author of one major dramatic work, the so-called 'masque'
of *Venus and Adonis*, through-composed opera along the lines
familiar to us from *Dido and Aeneas* which it helped to
inspire.

In this case the relationship between master and pupil was a
good deal less straightforward than it had been where Humfrey
was concerned. The two surviving educational outlines Blow com-
piled, one for learning keyboard thoroughbass, the other for
composition, show him to have been a precise and methodical
teacher, and Henry Hall, once again in his capacity as amateur
poet, paid tribute to him in some verses printed in *Amphion
Anglicus*, an anthology of fifty songs by Blow published in 1700.

'Britain's Orpheus', says Hall, 'learned his art from you.' Doubtless he did, but the learning process seems to have worked equally
well in the other direction, with the mature Purcell making his
mark on Blow's style, both sacred and secular, even if the older
composer hung on to his own unmistakable idiom, mixing grandeur and gravity with something a good deal more skittish and
wayward, revealing the robust sense of humour he shared with
his pupil. A favourite story tells us that Purcell's succession in
1679 to the post of Westminster Abbey organist which had been
occupied by Blow was a result of the latter's admiring resignation
in his favour. No shred of evidence supports this idea: Blow may
simply have moved aside because his other court posts were more
attractive or perhaps, as has been suggested, because pressure was
put on him to do so by those eager to advance Purcell's career.
Whatever the truth, no hint of animosity or rivalry clouded their

relationship, and they went on taking hints from one another throughout Purcell's life.

The London musical scene during the 1670s had a liveliness and variety holding out infinite stimulus to a young professional performer and composer. In 1674 a major revival took place at the Duke's Theatre in Dorset Garden of the version of *The Tempest* originally prepared in 1667 by Sir William Davenant and John Dryden. Davenant, who made much of his supposed kinship with Shakespeare – the playwright, if we are to believe John Aubrey, fathered him on an Oxford innkeeper's wife on his way back to Stratford – was a highly successful dramatist and poet at the Caroline court. It was his idea, according to Dryden, that Miranda should be given a male counterpart in the form of Hippolito, 'a man that has never seen a woman'. This sexual innocent, who marries Miranda's equally uncanonical sister Dorinda, typifies a Restoration desire to spice up the drama with libertine sophistication of the sort which would have appealed to King Charles and the more rakish element at court, including the Earl of Rochester and the young Duke of Monmouth, whose outrageous, sometimes violent escapades kept town tongues wagging.

The 1674 *Tempest* revival, with Thomas Shadwell's additions and new music, was a fascinating hybrid. A drift towards incorporating more musical elements in productions of spoken drama had been apparent for some years. When *Macbeth* was revived in 1673, the tragedy was described as 'being drest in all its finery, as new Cloath's, new Scenes, Machines, as flyings for the Witches; with all the Singing and Dancing in it . . . being Excellently perform'd, being in the nature of an Opera, it Recompens'd double the Expence'. The revived *Tempest* too was 'in the nature of an Opera', as Shadwell's fustian prologue was at pains to emphasize:

> We have machines to some perfection brought,
> And above 30 Warbling voyces gott.
> Many a God & Goddess you will heare
> And we have Singing, Dancing Devils here.
> Such Devills, and such gods, are very Deare.

A concluding 'Masque of Neptune & Amphitrite' in Act V was intended to provide an effective fusion of song, dance and scenic machines, and an extended description of the sets and disposition of the orchestra implies that the whole performance was one of the grandest spectacles yet witnessed on the London stage.

The artistic resources of the court musical establishment were all channeled into the production. A printed quarto mentions 'the Band of 24 Violins with the Harpsicals and Theorbo's which accompany the Voices', and most interestingly specifies that they were 'plac'd between the Pit and the Stage', instead of being located in the gallery above the proscenium arch, where the theatre musicians usually sat. Members of the Chapel Royal choir also took part, as we know from a memorandum issued by the Lord Chamberlain on 16 May 1674, headed 'Chappellmen for ye theatre', telling 'Mr Turner and Mr Hart or any other men or boys belonging to his Majesty's Chappell Royall that sing in ye Tempest at His Royal Highnesse Theatre' to 'remaine in towne all weeke (dureing his Majesty's absence from Whitehall) to performe that service'. The same document specifically refers to the show as 'ye opera', one of the earliest recorded uses of the term in official records of the period, revealing that this was how the Dorset Garden production team wanted the work to be understood.

Having already left the choir, Purcell is not known to have taken part in these *Tempest* performances, but this is no reason to assume that he may not have seen one of them, more especially since his teacher Pelham Humfrey was so closely involved in the project, contributing a masque in Act II, in which a chorus of devils threatens the shipwrecked courtiers, and music for the Neptune and Amphitrite episode at the close of Act V. Other composers lent their talents, including Pietro Reggio, a singer from Genoa who worked closely with Shadwell, and the elder John Banister, who until 1666 had directed the royal string band and whom Roger North tells us 'had a good theatricall vein and in composition had a lively style peculiar to himself'.

Most important among this *Tempest* team where Purcell was concerned was Matthew Locke, a major link between the musical world of John Jenkins and the Lawes brothers before the Civil War and the more diffuse energies of the Restoration, during which his creative talents were fully stretched in every direction. Locke is always looked at askance by some of the earlier modern writers on seventeenth-century music, as a sort of bad-boy composer who began by carving his name so deeply into the stone coping of the Exeter cathedral organ loft that you can find it there to this day, ran away to the Low Countries during the war and perhaps converted to Popery, since he became organist of the chapel at Somerset House specially appointed for Charles II's Portuguese queen Catherine of Bragança and her devoutly Catholic household.

Locke was at home in every musical vein. He earned Roger North's praise for composing 'a magnifick consort of 4 parts, after the old style, which was the last of the kind that hath bin made, so we may rank him with Cleomenes King of Sparta who was styled ultimus herooum'. The arch fogey adds a disapproving note by saying: 'He conformed at last to the modes of his time, and fell into the theatricall way and composed to the semioperas divers pieces of vocall and instrumentall enterteinement, with very good success.' Last of the heroes he may have been in harking back to old-established English instrumental forms, but he was just as self-motivated in the modernism of his immensely colourful, individualistic anthem style. This is reflected in works ranging from the chamber intimacy of *How doth the city sit solitary* to the monumentally grandiose architecture of *Be thou exalted, Lord*, written to celebrate a victory over the Dutch in 1666. Thus far the most ambitious anthem ever conceived for use in Anglican worship, it demands eight solo voices, three choral groups and contrasting instrumental ensembles of viols and violins.

When Locke died in the late summer of 1677, Purcell was deeply affected. Though a purported letter from the older to the younger composer is patently a Victorian forgery, Locke's influence on the youthful Purcell's style had made itself felt in works such as the so-called 'Stairre-Case Overture', whose earliest source is an eighteenth-century transcription now in the Bodleian Library. This short French overture, which presumably took its nickname from the broadly spaced intervals of the opening prelude, seems to have been written around 1676 when the *Tempest* music was still fresh in the boy composer's memory, and pieces like the solemn Act II curtain tune, with its hauntingly improvisatory structure, in which the movement seems to alter its shape and direction with each succeeding bar, were bound to have left their mark.

The depth of Purcell's emotion at the loss of such a mentor, let alone his wish to speak on behalf of the entire community of English musicians, can be measured from the elegy on Locke, 'What hope for us remains now he is gone?', written in 1677 and published two years later. While we know for certain or can hazard a convincing guess at the identity of most of the poets who furnished the composer's texts, the authorship of this brief sequence of lines, in the irregular Italian *versi sciolti* style often favoured for such compositions, has always remained mysterious. Given the uniformly intelligent and sophisticated approach to word setting and choice of material which distinguishes Purcell as a vocal composer, and considering the advantages his Westminster schooling were likely to have given him, we need hardly doubt that he wrote these lines himself. The little portrait they enclose of an artist endowed with positively numinous skill in the exercise of his gifts, a man

> whose skilful harmony
> Had charms for all the ills that we endure

and who

> knew such mystic touches that in death
> Could cure the fear, or stop the parting breath,

is a genuinely searching tribute from one musician to another, yet the poetic technique, the handling of rhyme, syntax and grammar, are emphatically not those of a professional writer.

In spirit the work belongs to an archetypal seventeenth-century tradition of funerary verse, a sort of verbal equivalent of the splendid marble and alabaster tombs raised during this time in churches throughout England, a poetry astonishing in its intensity and range. We may think for example of Milton's *Lycidas*, the noblest exemplar of the genre, of Bishop King's heartfelt *Exequy* on his wife's death, of Sir William Davenant's exquisite little dialogue between a philosopher and a lover over a dying mistress, or of Thomas Carew's masterly elegy on John Donne, a critical essay at the poet's graveside.

A Peculiar Readiness of Fancy

By the time Purcell came to write his 'On the Death of His Worthy Friend Mr Matthew Lock, Musick-Composer to His Majesty and Organist of Her Majestie's Chappel, Who Dyed in August 1677', the vogue for such poems was on the wane. Restoration authors, with the notable exception of Dryden, who had learned his craft in an earlier age, tended to shy away from death as something altogether too solemn for their cynical banter. Even some of the poems written at Purcell's own demise are scarcely more than decorous shadows of a once vital poetic form. Thus music becomes a primary element in validating such works during the later Stuart period. It is hard to imagine poems like Carew's triplet sequence on young Mary Wentworth or Andrew Marvell's classic send up of the funerary mode in 'To His Coy Mistress' needing or receiving musical accompaniment. By the 1670s however, a text like Purcell's, though in itself a perfectly adequate 'copy of verses', carrying a respectable flavour of classical learning in its allusion to the emotive powers vested in musicians, becomes inconceivable without the clothing of notes, voices and instruments.

Purcell set his lines as a monody for high voice with a continuo accompaniment, introducing a second vocal line in the little chorus ending the piece with a vision of Locke's soul flying heavenwards. The style is often loosely referred to by musicologists as 'recitative', but this requires clarification in view of our modern tendency to apply the word solely to passages of linking dialogue and reflection between the individual aria or ensemble numbers in dramatic and sacred works. More widely interpreted, the term implies a free-moving vocal line, unguided by the structural limitations of melody or the punctuations of instrumental accompaniment, in which the music strictly follows the outline of the text.

Intensely word-conscious as English culture has always been, the *stile recitativo* of the Italian Baroque was bound to be seized upon avidly by composers of the early Stuart period as an ideal vehicle for the weightier sort of meditative or amorous discourse. The challenge in such music was twofold: on the one hand the composer must try not to let the longer verse lines slacken into rambling aimlessness; on the other he needed to avoid a potential rhythmic tedium in the repeated iambic trot of the chosen metre.

'What hope for us remains' is Purcell's earliest essay in this style, which he was to return to constantly throughout his creative life. By the late 1670s it had been considerably influenced by the adventurousness of Italian continuo writing, but essentially this elegy's dramatic impact is owed to the young English composer's own extraordinary alertness to the interpretative possibilities of the text. On the line 'From pointed griefs he'd take the pain away', for example, a series of hard-edged chromaticisms underpins the descending voice part, while 'His lays to anger and to war could move' has a deliberately trumpeting aggressiveness on both levels which is then skilfully mellowed by the layout of the following line, 'Then calm the tempest they had rais'd with love'. The ear is perpetually engaged, both on this level and in terms of the music's rhythmic inventiveness, so that the work's sheer fluidity, its organic nature, let alone its confident harmonic independence, provide the best imaginable tribute to Locke's genius from his incomparable heir, simply because, we cannot help feeling, it is what Locke would have wanted Purcell to write for him.

'What hope for us remains' represents its composer's first major musical achievement. Its publication in 1679, two years after it was written, must have indicated to London musicians, supposing they were not already aware of the fact, that an impressive new talent had arrived on the Restoration scene. The elegy appeared in the second of five collections issued between 1676 and 1684 under the title *Choice Ayres & Songs to Sing to the Theorbo–Lute or Bass–Viol* by the publisher John Playford, who, with his sons Henry and John junior, was the capital's most important music seller. Born in Norwich in 1623, Playford had started his London career as a publisher of political tracts during the unsettled period following the defeat of the Royalist army at Naseby in 1645. The subsequent attempt by Charles I to reach some sort of advantageous settlement with the triumphant Parliamentarians, had culminated in his imprisonment, but there was still a strong monarchical groundswell among various elements even in so markedly Puritan a city as London, and Playford's willingness to enter the war of words on the King's behalf made him an immediate object of suspicion to a nervous Parliamentary regime. While the King himself was still in control before the war began, the Court of Star Chamber had tightened press censorship with a special decree, and though the hated tribunal was itself abolished in 1641, the Puritans were so discomfited by the ensuing torrent of pamphleteering that two years later an ordinance was passed against unlicensed books and printing presses. Those infringing the act were to have their houses searched, the offending publications were to be confiscated, the presses broken up and the malefactors were to be brought before Parliament.

Against this very same law John Milton had so memorably thundered in his *Areopagitica*, subtitled 'a speech for the liberty of unlicensed printing, to the Parliament of England'. As it turned out, this classic defence of intellectual liberty was futile in the face of reactionary terrors. Parliament was not composed of sage and severe Athenian judges, London scarcely merited the poet's exuberant accolades of 'a city of refuge, the mansion house of liberty', and the situation noticeably worsened with the King's execution in 1649. A warrant was issued for John Playford's arrest for the publication of seditious pamphlets, and though the law did not pursue him very far, he seems to have preferred to concentrate on music publishing as a safer option.

Playford's shop stood in the spacious porch of the Temple Church, of which he was noted as an extremely assiduous clerk, raising the overall quality of services through his attention to detail. The distinction of his wide-ranging publications, which included books of music theory, instruction manuals for different sorts of instrumental technique, anthologies of songs, sets of instrumental part-books, psalm collections and dancing methods, lay in the seriousness with which he approached his chosen role as a musical encourager and enabler. There was rather more to Playford than the mere commercial acumen of a publisher with a keen eye for the latest craze and for opportunities of exploiting it. He clearly enjoyed writing the prefaces which opened many of his volumes, and these often reflected his own didactic awareness of a professional and amateur public, keen and interested but perhaps too self-conscious as to its lack of sophistication in comparison with other European musical cultures. In his collection of part-songs *The Musical Companion, in Two Books*, issued in 1673, when talking of 'the so much cry'd up Italian and French ayres being here imitated, if not equallized in this kind', he adds, 'nor could I ever yet be convinc'd but that we have at this day as able professors of musick of our own nation, as any foreigners: For the musick is the same (abating the language) both for cords, discords, passions, spirits and humours: Where then is their excellency? Were we not generally too apt to disesteem the labour & parts of our own (though otherwise elaborate and ingenuous) countrymen?' Playford doubtless meant 'ingenious' rather than 'ingenuous'. Purcell, barely out of his teens, must have been both of these things, but it was as just such an 'able professor of musick' that he was to be associated for the rest of his life with the firm and family of the Playfords.

The successive issue of Purcell's songs in Playford's editions was one means of promoting professional reputation, but just as convenient a showcase for the young composer's talents was offered by the Chapel Royal and Westminster Abbey. In 1679, the year in which 'What hope for us remains' was published and in which he assumed Matthew Locke's place at court as composer for the violins, he was appointed as organist at the Abbey. This was the very position from which John Blow was always said to have moved aside in Purcell's favour, but, as we have noted earlier, the exchange may well have been advantageous to the already overworked 'Dr', as his famous pupil calls him. In any case, the exact terms of the appointment are not clear. All we know is that Purcell's name appears in place of Blow's in the Abbey treasurer's accounts, and that the duties themselves were probably not very demanding.

What is significant, however, is the outpouring of sacred works which began as the composer found an individual style for himself during the late 1670s. The reintroduction of music into English church worship at the Restoration was not simply designed to humour the tastes of Charles II; Purcell's anthems need to be heard, if possible, in the Anglican liturgical context for which they were composed and to whose solemn authority they were an essential adjunct. We know little about the exact circumstances in which many of the early anthems were performed, beyond occasional manuscript notes as regards a particular date in the ecclesiastical calendar, but we should bear in mind the forces at

Purcell's disposal: a well-trained choir assisted on many occasions by members of the royal string band, with continuo support provided by the organ and the large lute known as the theorbo, 'which likewise', as the Cambridge musician Thomas Mace wrote in 1676, 'could Humour the Consort properly and evenly with the Pedal'.

Some of the earliest pieces Purcell wrote for the choirs with which he was now working were in the old 'full anthem' style whose technique he could have learned from careful study of the rich literature of Tudor and Jacobean church music. When we compare a work such as the first setting of *Hear my prayer*, a probable fragment of a longer composition, and *O God, the king of glory*, perhaps also simply a cut-down portion of a more ambitious concept, we can see at once how adept the boy Purcell had already become at grafting his own idiom on to an established tradition. In each case, the first a heart-wrenching tangle of false relations, the latter a radiant paean to divine ascendancy, it is the athleticism and plasticity of the word-setting which write Purcell's name on the score, though each demonstrates his characteristic determination that the individual work should create its own distinguishing rhetorical colour.

It seems a pity that Purcell wrote so few full anthems, but he was able to find a compromise with the more popular 'verse' style, alternating solo and choral passages, by means of works fusing both genres. The most exhilarating of his early 'full-with-verse' anthems is surely *Blow up the trumpet in Sion*, one of those Purcellian creations which have the proverbial effect of making the hair on the back of the neck stand up whenever we hear it. Taken from the book of Joel, the text, with its notes of warning, an admonition to 'call a solemn assembly' and a prayer that God should spare his people, may well have been chosen with some political reference, at a time when court and church felt themselves menaced by the machinations of Lord Shaftesbury and the earliest stirrings of the Popish Plot hysteria.

If it was written in 1678, then *Blow up the trumpet* is a remarkable accomplishment for so youthful a composer. The setting is in ten parts, opening with a brilliantly deceptive air of triumph on stirring vocal trumpet calls, before the real mood, essentially grim and relentless, establishes itself. The harmonic theatricality of the piece is continuously exciting, as the invention tacks about like a skilful yachtsman from the sturdy C major at the start to E flat in 'sanctify a fast', thence to the agonized subtleties of 'Spare thy people, O Lord', to culminate in an extended sequence of entries by soloists and choir on the words 'Wherefore should they say among the people: Where is their God?' Thus the anthem ends, not with one of those positive conclusions, a bouncing 'Alleluia' or an ineluctable 'Amen', to which acquaintance with Purcell's church music accustoms us, but on this note of grave, unresolved spiritual doubt. It is perhaps that very feature, rather than the work's inherent expressive complexity, which has discouraged frequent performance by cathedral choirs of what, from any analytical standpoint, must emerge as a brilliant validation of Purcell's imaginative approach to his medium.

Such a validation needs making now and then by his admirers. Surprisingly, in view of the pleasure his early church music offers to the listener and the performer, it has not always been approved by the critics, several of whom seem to find Purcell's creativity too hectically engaged, too eager to make a memorable impression through harmonic daring or pictorial word setting, and insufficiently concerned with overall integrity of outline and structure. The simple answer to this ought to be that some indulgence is due to a young man trying to impress. In any case, closer attention to these first compositional essays for the Chapel Royal will reveal a much less superficial intent behind many of them, inspired as several are by Purcell's frankly competitive alertness to the stylistic mannerisms of his mentors Locke and Humfrey, and by his genuine concern with exploiting to the utmost the flexibility and associative resonance of his texts.

Humfrey's beneficial influence on the Purcellian idiom is at its strongest in some of the verse anthems written between 1677 and 1680. There are moments when, in listening to the individual voices in Humfrey's anthems, we are almost tempted to give them names, so dramatic is their expressive commitment to the words. The same is true in a piece like Purcell's *Blessed be the Lord my Strength*, whose earliest source is a Cambridge manuscript dating it to 1679. We can sense the Humfredian slant, not just in the careful fragmentation of portions of the psalm text among the individual soloists, cast as affirmers, questioners or respondents, but in the composer's deliberate option, at the opening 'Blessed be the Lord my strength, who teacheth my hands to war and my fingers to fight' for a restrained dignity in preference to blustering aggression.

This intensity of intervention in the dialogue whose outcome will be of real spiritual concern to us as members of a believing congregation is yet more notable in two similar verse anthems from this period, *Bow down thine ear* and *Who hath believed our report?* By now Purcell had liberated himself from the rather frigid formal outlines in which he had begun composing, exemplified in *Lord, who can tell*, with its faint feeling that the young Henry is looking over his shoulder to make sure he has got everything right. Here the question is not so much one of mastering the tricks of a certain style as of establishing the clear outlines of his own personal idiom, compounded of allusions to the established tradition of English cathedral music, overlapping with something more blatantly rhetorical and Italianate in the solo episodes, but distinctively Restoration in the freedom of harmonic language. *Who hath believed our report?* makes a particularly powerful impression in all these respects because of the structural unity Purcell imposes, both in the sharply defined contrast between choral passages and those for single voices, and in the expansion, through successive sections, of ideas propounded at the beginning of the piece. The text here is the famous 'passion' sequence from Isaiah chapter 53, some of which Charles Jennens later chose for Handel to set in *Messiah*, and since Purcell's anthem was written in 1679, a turbulent time politically, it is tempting to wonder whether these 'suffering servant' verses were deliberately selected as implying a parallel with Charles II.

It would be easy to imagine that Charles himself had jogged a clerical elbow to persuade Purcell to set the erotic poetry of the symphony anthem *My beloved spake*, if we did not also know that at this period, and for a long time afterwards, the official interpretation of its source, The Song of Solomon, was as an allegory of Christ's love for Holy Church. Since with only a few exceptions the rest of Purcell's sixty-odd anthems were written to psalm texts, the choice was a singular one, the more so since it is now believed that the work marked his debut as a church composer.

Equally interesting is the fact that having established his claim to attention with an anthem in the most elaborate of the period's accepted genres, he did not seriously concentrate on further experiments with symphony anthems until 1682, five years after *My beloved spake* is thought to have been composed in its earliest form. It was obviously written to impress the King himself, who, as Thomas Tudway tells us, came to the Chapel, 'only upon Sundays in the morning, on the great festivals, & days of Offerings'. By 1677, a small band of the Twenty-Four Violins, set up at court under John Banister's direction early in the reign, was already a dependable feature of royal attendance at the Chapel. The arrangement seems to have been that five or six of them, placed in a gallery close to the organ loft, played one to a part, with the addition of a theorbo continuo, as mentioned earlier. The 'symphonies' they played to introduce or vary the course of the anthems were exactly those kind of instrumental embellishments which flattered the royal taste in church music, and older contemporaries such as Locke, Blow and Humfrey had been swift to capitalize on the new trend.

As Purcell's exordium in a style of which he was later to prove himself an accomplished master, *My beloved spake* represents a formidable achievement, and has deservedly remained among his best-loved works. Even if Humfrey is the model here, in such features as the central reprise of the opening symphony and the way in which the various segments are clearly delineated, the overall profile is that of a new composer with something of his own to say and with his glance trained confidently on a beckoning horizon. Whatever the doctrinal interpretative overlay of The Song of Solomon, the young man's response here is frankly to its sensual beauty. No special irony dictates that his music should turn out to be more faithful to the spirit of the Jewish love poem than its superimposed Christian exegesis, The lyrical exuberance of that initial summons to 'rise, my love, my fair one and come away', the jubilant chorus to the words 'And the time of the singing of birds is come' and the exquisite slipperiness of the harmony in 'The voice of the turtle is heard in our land' all conspire to shape a musical discourse which experiences rather than merely enacts the words. The spring, with its green shoots, blooming grapes, birdsong, and awakening to the impulses of renewed existence, which rises to greet us from *My beloved spake*, belongs not just to the poet of ancient Israel, but to Purcell himself. His own season of early promise, so abundantly fulfilled, had just begun.

2

Court, Chapel and Stage

If Purcell really had been numbered among the audience for those handsomely equipped *Tempest* performances of 1674, or had even perhaps taken some part in the proceedings, then it was almost inevitable that sooner or later he would gravitate towards composing music for the theatre. It is no particular irony that makes an opera his best-known work, and *Dido and Aeneas* was scarcely an isolated one-off in a musical career distinguished for its extreme versatility and diversification. Where a constituency existed for music of a special character during this period, Purcell was there to compose it. Among the most impressive aspects of his overall artistic achievement is that he should have found it so easy to excel in whatever form he turned his hand to.

The traditional image of the Restoration theatre, which has prevailed since the revival of interest in its playwrights began during the late nineteenth century, is compounded of a uniquely English amalgam of snobbery, highmindedness, prurience and nostalgia. We like to conjure up a world of ogling and orange wenches, with Old Rowley himself, ensconced amid his courtiers, sizing up the charms of Nell Gwynn's *décolletage*, while at the same time we smugly damn the plays themselves to perdition, refuse to take the tragedies of playwrights such as Dryden, Otway and Lee at all seriously and voice a righteous horror at the coarseness of the dialogue in the comedies of Wycherley, Shadwell and Aphra Behn. Possibly we are starting to move away from critical positions of a kind voiced by L.C. Knights (who ended a devastating article on Restoration comedy, couched in the authentic vein of Leavisite puritanism, with the generic verdict that the plays were 'trivial, gross and dull'), but a true understanding of the complexity and variety of late seventeenth-century English drama has been very slow in coming.

Purcell's age had accepted the challenge of reconstructing a dramatic tradition broken by the Civil War and the theocratic dominance of Protestant extremism, though this acceptance, however enthusiastic, had not been tempered with practical wisdom. The history of London theatres during the reigns of Charles II, James II and William and Mary, a history in which the composer played a central part, is one of overreaching, mismanagement and thoughtlessly squandered aesthetic resource. Any notion of being able to return to a situation like that familiar to Shakespeare and his contemporaries, in which several dramatic companies contrived to exist side by side, regularly employing in-house playwrights to provide scripts directly addressed to the talents of individual members of the troupe, was out of the question, but this did not stop managers trying to foster a supply of theatrical talent for which a demand did not always exist.

During the first two decades of Charles II's reign, London's playgoers were offered a choice between a pair of major theatres, together with a number of one-off entertainments which offered their rival attractions in successive years. In 1661, under the directorship of Thomas Killigrew, a courtier with ambitions in the playwriting line, the new Theatre Royal in Bridges Street off Drury Lane was opened. Its troupe, featuring actors such as the elegant comedian Charles Hart and 'Major' Michael Mohun, so admired in the tragedies of Nathaniel Lee, became known as 'the King's Company'. Its rival playhouse lay further east in Lincoln's Inn Fields, where Sir William Davenant, irrepressible in his initiatives where any theatrical enterprise was concerned, had opened what was referred to as an 'opera' in a converted tennis court with a company focused on Thomas Betterton, the most magnetic English actor of his generation. Betterton's career, beginning in 1660 when he was twenty-five, extended into the next century and undoubtedly influenced the way in which contemporary dramatists conceived certain stock character types of Restoration theatre.

By 1671 Davenant's company, the Duke of York's Players, were preparing to move from Lincoln's Inn Fields into a superb new theatre, the largest so far built in London, at Dorset Garden off

Fleet Street. The land on which it stood had originally belonged to the bishops of Salisbury, and an old theatre at Salisbury Court close by had been kept open until recently under the management of William Beeston, a survivor like Davenant from the previous theatrical age. The Sackvilles, dukes of Dorset, had purchased this episcopal estate, and the new playhouse took its name, Dorset Garden, from their grounds running down to the shore of the Thames.* Its frontage, essentially that of a grand Stuart merchant's house to which a classical portico had been added, gave obvious hints as to the handsomeness within. The stage area of the 140-foot building was noted for its depth, which, as in the case of spectacles like *The Tempest*, allowed plenty of opportunity for the kind of perspective illusions beloved by Baroque scene-painters and theatre-goers. A set of engravings accompanying Elkanah Settle's *The Empress of Morocco* shows, as well as the various set designs themselves, the extremely grand proscenium arch, with the royal arms framed by a pair of seated putti, carved swags of fruit and leaves in the Grinling Gibbons mode on either side. The twin figures of Comedy (half naked and holding a mask) and Tragedy (sporting buskins and a crown) flank what appears to be an upper room with windows, an area whose purpose is still not clear to theatrical historians since it could hardly have been integrated with the performance going on beneath.

The French traveller François Brunet, visiting Dorset Garden about five years after its opening, tells us something of the impression made by the new theatre. Going to see 'la Comédie de la trouppe de M^r Le Duc Dyorcq ou nous n'entendismes que baragouines', he was struck by the provincial shabbiness of the actors' costumes in comparison with the magnificence of the auditorium itself. He wrote:

The place where they act is incomparably finer and more clean than those where our own comedians play ... in the parterre, which is

---

*The theatre eventually became a timber warehouse and the site, later occupied by the City of London School, now lies under an American bank. Excavations during the present century unearthed portions of the Dorset Garden building's foundations, but nothing more substantial survives.

shaped like an amphitheatre, there is no inconvenient noise. There are a mere seven boxes, each containing twenty people, with a similar number above and a gallery on top ... for the servants who are admitted for nothing.

Brunet could hardly avoid noticing the consistent mockery of French fashions in which the comedies constantly indulged, and he also remarked the disdain for the Aristotelian unities, on whose observance the dramatists of his own country so piqued themselves. But even though he hardly understood anything of the play itself, he found the audience arresting and attractive enough.

The design for the Dorset Garden playhouse, known formally as the Duke's Theatre, is often attributed without good authority to Sir Christopher Wren. We know that he was responsible for the new Theatre Royal in Bridges Street, and when that burned down soon after completion in 1672 he supplied another plan, but the state of the King's Company finances was such that loans had to be raised from among the actors themselves and the ground on which the playhouse stood was mortgaged. Things were made worse by what seems to have been a collapse of discipline and morale among the Theatre Royal players during the 1670s. Restoration audiences were notoriously capricious, and empty houses had been a problem since the company's inception, yet a more judicious manager than Thomas Killigrew could surely have held his actors together with proper attention to their material well-being and collective spirit. As it was, riven by arguments and lawsuits, the company lurched slowly but perceptibly towards disaster.

At Dorset Garden, though the atmosphere was less fractious, similar financial difficulties beset the theatre throughout the 1670s. Lavish productions of *The Tempest*, *Macbeth* and other plays with extensive musical elements were intended to allure the kind of novelty-seeking London audience which would run after anything from a Punch and Judy show to the Duke of Modena's Italian comedians acting *Scaramouchi and Harlekin*. It has been calculated that a full house for the theatre, which held approximately 1,200 spectators, would have netted box office takings of £110, but contemporary evidence suggests that the management was lucky to receive half that sum from a day's performance.

It was at this critical time in the fortunes of London theatre that Henry Purcell wrote his earliest music for the playhouse. All Restoration plays were fitted out with musical items, providing a framework for the performance, though not necessarily for the content of the play in the illustrative fashion familiar to us from works like Mendelssohn's incidental music to *A Midsummer Night's Dream*. Composers, some of them professionally attached to the two companies, would supply a set of introductory pieces, tunes to follow each act except the last and songs to be sung by the actors themselves, many of whom were noted for their good voices. Occasional items were added, designed to highlight crucial dramatic moments such as love scenes, the appearance of ghosts and dream figures, the recitation of soliloquies or incidents involving disclosure and discovery.

The initial 'first and second music' were contrasting movements intended as much as anything to quieten the audience and indicate the start of the play. After these one of the cast stepped in front of the curtain on to the broad apron jutting beyond the proscenium arch and spoke the prologue. This was sometimes written by another hand at the author's request and was nearly always couched in a tone of straightforward banter with the audience, spiced with topical allusion to current news items, fashion, scandal and politics. An overture or 'curtain tune' followed, after which the two looped halves of the green curtain were drawn up to present a series of stage pictures whose components were changed in full view of the audience. At the end of the fifth act the epilogue was spoken, often by the most attractive of the company's actresses or sometimes by a little child, whose infant piping lent comic incongruity to the ribaldry and double entendre of the playwright's heroic couplets.

To what extent spectators bothered to listen to the music being played is not clear. Many songs became popular favourites, but the impact of the instrumental numbers was substantially lessened by the general noise and restlessness of the Restoration audience, with its beaux seated obstructively on the stage itself, its 'vizard masks' or prostitutes plying for trade in the pit, its little gusts of quarrelling, its distracting ribbon of chatter and its acceptance of that longstanding irritant to actors and managers, the custom of the 'free act', whereby it was possible to saunter into the playhouse and watch a single act for nothing.

Against this ostensibly unrewarding background Purcell was to write some of his most engaging music. A taste of what audiences with more than half an ear might expect was provided in his first theatrical commission, the songs and instrumental music for Nathaniel Lee's tragedy *Theodosius or The Force of Love*, produced at Dorset Garden in the spring or summer of 1680. The fine cast included Mary Betterton, wife to the great tragedian, an actress highly commended for her truth to nature in Shakespearean tragic roles (her Lady Macbeth was distinguished by 'those quick and careless strokes of terror, from the disorder of a guilty mind' presented 'with a facility in her manner that render'd them at once tremendous and delightful'). She played one of the two heroines, Pulcheria, while the other, Athenais, who commits suicide by drinking poison during a melodramatic soliloquy, was assigned to Elizabeth Barry, the age's most compelling tragedienne. Barry's character was as freely besmirched as Mrs Betterton's was spotless. According to one contemporary, she was quite capable of spending the whole night with a man, taking all his money and then refusing to acknowledge him the next day unless he could produce a further five guineas. It was she for whom the dramatist Thomas Otway, hopelessly enslaved by her beauty, created two of the finest Restoration tragic roles, Belvidera in *Venice Preserv'd* and Monimia in *The Orphan*, while John Dryden, not in love with Barry but enraptured by her astonishing vocal flexibility and majestic stage presence, shaped the part of Cassandra in his *Cleomenes* specifically to capture her talents.

Without Otway's romantic fervour or Dryden's grandeur and refinement, Nathaniel Lee had achieved success as a writer of tragedies through his resolve to push the declamatory, high-flown, 'ranting' manner (borrowed from the French dramas of the Corneille brothers and their fellow Norman Jean Rotrou) to the absolute limit and sometimes beyond. His eye for dramatic situations and thrilling episodes was consistently strong. Whatever the contemptuous assessments made of his verse style by modern critics, a glance at his best plays, such as *Lucius Junius Brutus* or the robustly stageworthy treatment of Alexander the Great's amorous Indian adventure in *The Rival Queens*, reveals a dramatist with a genuine awareness of what actors enjoyed speaking and what audiences wanted to hear.

Theodosius was one of Lee's most successful plays: as late as 1750 we find it included in a projected repertoire for a theatrical troupe setting off on a tour of the American colonies. Like much else on the Restoration stage its composition entailed recycling an earlier work, Philip Massinger's tragedy *The Emperor of The East*. This had been written forty years earlier, and Lee had injected a more blatant element of melodrama while simultaneously heightening the tension between religion and sex on which the original play depends; a tension which, as Dryden's barnstorming *Tyrannick Love or The Royal Martyr* had earlier proved, was a dependable draw with London audiences.

Briefly, the story tells of the Emperor Theodosius trying to find refuge in religion from his unholy desire for a young girl whom he has seen bathing. He has entrusted the imperial government, in Constantinople where the play is set, to his sister, the strong-minded Pulcheria, and persuaded two younger sisters Marina and Flavilla to enter a convent. The Emperor's unknown love turns out to be Athenais, daughter of the philosopher Leontine, herself in love with the Persian prince Varanes. It is Leontine whose pride and ambition drive Athenais to her death. Having persuaded Varanes to renounce her on the grounds that

> Sure the World would blush to see the Daughter
> Of a Philosopher on the Throne of Cyrus

he subsequently gives the nod to her marriage with Theodosius, even though she herself has sought to break free from the Emperor's obsession by becoming a nun, baptized with the name of Eudosia. Offered an agonizing choice between Varanes and Theodosius she obeys her father's wishes by accepting the latter, but frustrates his plans for a secret midnight wedding by taking

Into my Veins a cold and deadly Draught,
Which soon would render me, alas, unfit
For the warm Joys of an Imperial Lover.

Varanes too commits suicide (offstage) and this bleak chronicle of human frailty and betrayal ends with Athenais's death before the eyes of a horrified court.

It has been convincingly argued that the music Purcell produced to accompany *Theodosius* is more closely integrated with the drama than we might at first suppose. How far Lee was in direct contact with the composer during the writing and rehearsal periods we cannot know, but it is undeniable that without its musical component this cleverly constructed tragedy, with its interlocking subplots and careful balance of characters and relationships, would lose important elements of pathos and solemnity. The first act depends on the musical 'book-ends' of the priest Atticus's opening invocation, 'Prepare, prepare, the rites begin', and the extended *scena* towards its close, after he and his fellow ministers challenge the two princesses to renounce the world, an essentially operatic episode owing something doubtless to the masque sections of earlier Dorset Garden successes.

Those familiar with Baroque artistic idioms will have learned that an overture in a minor key does not necessarily herald a tragedy, but the G minor introduction to *Theodosius* (identified as recently as 1950 after having been parted from the score along with two other items which have not survived) has the kind of angular, brow-furrowing seriousness exactly suited to establishing the tone of the play. Lee took considerable care in specifying a detailed setting for the first scene (interestingly none of the other acts has a named location): 'A stately Temple, which represents the Christian Religion, as in its first Magnificence... The side Scenes shew the horrid Tortures with which the Roman Tyrants persecuted the Church; and the flat Scene, which is the Limit of the Prospect, discovers an Altar richly adorn'd...' He seems to have intended 'Prepare, prepare' as 'A Chorus heard at a distance', to herald the entrance of Atticus 'the Chief of all the Priests... the Waiters in Ranks bowing all the way before him'; Purcell, however, wrote it as a bass solo with two voices, tenor and alto, joining in a reprise and accompanied with recorders, used to induce an atmosphere of mystic gravity and otherworldliness.

The priests' spiritual examination of Marina and Flavilla as they prepare to renounce the world falls into a sequence of skilfully differentiated sections. In their musical setting Purcell shows himself still strongly marked by the influence of Locke and the Caroline court composers of his father's generation, though the repetition of the word 'never', in the line 'And sin shall never charm you more', is an archetypally Purcellian trademark. Is the harmonic edginess and nervous chromaticism in this scene indicative of the girls' uncertainty, given the role which their brother has thrust upon them for his own dubious motives? It certainly seems so, and Purcell plainly sought to exploit the episode's dramatic possibilities still further by gently suggesting, in Flavilla's musically more bland response to her interrogation, that she will go more blithely than her sister into the life of material privation awaiting them both.

No act tunes for *Theodosius* have survived, so presumably four of the five extant songs Purcell composed for the play were meant to take their place. Here too there is an obvious connection between their various themes and the stages of the drama at which they occur. 'Now the fight's done', with its bawdy contrast between death in battle and the far preferable 'death' by orgasm, ushers in the bluff warrior Marcian, a cheery pagan whose success in winning Pulcheria's heart strikes the only positive note in the play. In 'Sad as death at dead of night', whose bass line seems at first to be heading towards the melancholy ground pattern familiar to us from many of the composer's best laments, the music rises splendidly to the promise – if that is the correct word – of Lee's vision of Athenais's approaching fate, summed up in the lines:

Curse the night, then, curse the hour
When first he drew thee to his arms,
When virtue was betray'd by power
And yielded to unlawful charms.

Its companion piece, 'Dream no more of pleasures past', enforces the same gloomy image of woman as victim of faithless, exploitative man.

It is when we come to 'Hail to the myrtle shade' at the end of Act III that the mood changes. The fetching artlessness of this song, with its lilting B♭ melody, shows Purcell's skill in being able to move without the least apparent effort from music of 'science' and 'learning' or dramatically emotive declamation to something like a folksong that coachmen might whistle or kitchenmaids hum at their work, though the rhythm and structure of the melodic line are as much French as English. The song's function is surely to provide a moment of relief before we plunge once more into the deepening emotional confusion which overwhelms the central characters.

Oddest of all these pieces is the song assigned to Athenais's maid Delia in the fourth act. At her mistress's bidding she leaves the stage to fetch her lute, allowing the prospective Empress, already dressed in royal robes, a moment of solitude in which to drink off the bowl of poison placed beside her, and to declare with a certain pardonable smugness that,

> tho' my Birth's unequal
> My Virtue sure has richly recompens'd
> And quite out-gone Example.

What then follows is a set of lyrics on the theme of suicide, telling us how Phyllis (the same name used in 'Hail to the myrtle shade'), for love of Philander who had forsaken her, stabbed herself and watched unmoved as 'her Blood ran streaming down the Floor'. Taking a hint from Lee's rhythms, Purcell eschews the obvious opportunity for anticipatory mourning suggested by the words and once again turns to a folk idiom for his inspiration. This time he gives us what was always called, during the English Baroque, 'a Scotch tune', a quasi-Strathspey in a pert G major, whose admirable unexpectedness underlines Athenais's positive feelings about what she has just done, and offers a foretaste of the irony with which Theodosius's presumption will be punished at the close of the play. The apparent incongruity between macabre text and bouncing melody is so marked that it is impossible to believe that the effect was not deliberately calculated by both composer and dramatist.

Even if it failed to assure the rickety fortunes of the Duke's

Players at Dorset Garden, *Theodosius* was a decided success. 'All the Parts in't being perfectly perform'd, with several Entertainments of Singing, compos'd by the Famous Master Mr Henry Purcell . . . made it a living and Gainful Play to the Company: the Court, especially the Ladies, by their daily charming presence, gave it great Encouragement.' As well as producing a skilfully plotted and vigorously dramatic piece of theatre, Lee had given his tragedy a touch of that topicality which was essential if a play was to win favour with the Restoration audience. So far from offending royal susceptibilities, the theme of the amorous monarch was a favourite with poets and audiences, before whom Charles II freely paraded his seraglio of mistresses, Lady Castlemaine, the Duchess of Portsmouth, Nell Gwynn and the rest. The historical context of early Christianity, what is more, flattered the prevailing Anglican orthodoxy, which liked to claim that the Church of England was far closer than its Romish rival to the primitive religion of the early fathers.

It is on this religious issue that we can perhaps catch Lee hedging his bets. The grand ceremonial at the beginning, with 'Ministers walking busily up and down', must surely have held a savour of Popery for some spectators, while those who knew something of the young Duchess of York's family history would have recalled that, like Theodosius, her grandfather Duke Alfonso III of Modena had abdicated his throne and sought a holy life in a monastery. Against such details, the Emperor's blatant hypocrisy in cloaking his lust for Athenais under the guise of devotion stands out, as do the robust objections made by the pagan Marcian to the new Christian religion.

This havering on Lee's part was doubtless not without its point. Some two years earlier, in the late summer of 1678, news had been brought to King Charles of a grotesque conspiracy, in which he was to have been respectively shot by two Catholic laymen, stabbed by a brace of Jesuits and poisoned by his wife's Papist physician, while his brother James, Duke of York, stood by as an accomplice. Elsewhere, various cities in Britain were to be fire-bombed with incendiary devices known as 'mustard balls', and a wholesale slaughter of Protestants was projected, outdoing by far the notorious Massacre of St Bartholomew perpetrated against the

Huguenots by Catherine de Medici and the Duc de Guise. A secret army of 50,000 troops was already forming, it was said, with reinforcements expected from France, and leading Catholic noblemen were rumoured to be preparing to welcome an immense throng of Spanish pilgrims, to be landed on the coast of Wales.

The initial promoter of this extraordinary farrago was Titus Oates, a failed Catholic ordinand of spectacular ugliness who had been cast out of the seminaries at Valladolid and St-Omer for suspected sodomy. His backers were a group of political malcontents led by the dangerously brilliant and ambitious Anthony Ashley Cooper, Earl of Shaftesbury, later to be immortalized in all his demonic phosphoresecence by John Dryden in *Absalom and Achitophel* as a man

> For close designs and crooked counsels fit,
> Sagacious, bold and turbulent of wit.

Using Charles II's eldest bastard son, the glamorous Duke of Monmouth, as a popular figurehead, Shaftesbury seized his hour to set in motion a shameful exercise in deliberately induced political hysteria, playing on the worst aspects of English xenophobia, religious bigotry and nationalist paranoia.

From the solemn search of the cellars of the Houses of Parliament by Sir Christopher Wren to the mysterious murder of the magistrate Sir Edmundsbury Godfrey on Primrose Hill, the wilder details of the 'Popish Plot' scare bear a sinister *avant-la-lettre* resemblance to ideas of a 'Red menace' promulgated so successfully in postwar America by Senator McCarthy and his associates. Godfrey's ghost was supposed to haunt Queen Catherine's chapel at Somerset House; a maid accused of setting fire to her employer's home claimed that she had done it at the instigation of a Popish priest; and Jack Ketch the hangman was ordered to preside over a public burning of assorted 'massing trash' from Catholic households. The Duke and Duchess of York retreated hurriedly to Brussels, while Charles, in a cynical gesture of self-preservation, allowed a number of entirely innocent Catholics to undergo trial and execution.

As we shall subsequently see, Purcell could hardly remain untouched by the inquisitorial anti-Catholicism set in place by a hysterical government and ruthlessly exploited by Shaftesbury and his loyal followers, concentrated as many of them were in London itself. He was always first and foremost a working musician, however, and was thus unlikely to refuse the prestigious commission to supply the music for the court ode *Welcome, Vicegerent of the Mighty King*, which acclaimed Charles's return to London, in September 1680, from his annual visit to the races at Newmarket.

The production of congratulatory odes to celebrate royal birthdays, weddings and homecomings was a custom dating at least from the reign of Charles I, and its revival during the 1660s and early 1670s had been pioneered by composers as distinguished as Matthew Locke, Pelham Humfrey and John Blow. Occasions of this kind were an opportunity for courtiers to demonstrate their loyalty and a chance for those with adequate funds to show off their newly acquired finery. Quite when the expression 'in a birthday suit' began its use as an ironic euphemism for total nudity is not known, but the joke is obvious, given that the original 'birthday suits' were the most expensive and elaborate affairs, their ornate tailoring often not capable of surviving more than one exhibition of such finery.

London itself participated fully in the rejoicings. The shops were shut, and apprentices and servants given the day off, the bells of the different churches were rung and the King attended a service at the Chapel Royal. The various regiments of horse and footguards were reviewed in Hyde Park, a forerunner of today's Trooping the Colour ceremony, and, as still happens on the royal birthday, a salvo of cannon was fired. In the afternoon the sovereign held a court drawing room, and on the same evening guests attended a grand banquet. It was at one or other of these receptions that the specially composed ode, congratulating the monarch on having come safely through another year, was performed by musicians from the Chapel Royal and the Private Musick, together with others brought in expressly for the occasion.

By its very nature the poetry of these celebratory addresses was conspicuously unmemorable and sometimes downright bad, condemned like so much writing of this kind to an insincerity which the hack versifiers and dim laureates who provided it were not skilful enough to conceal. Even taking their political loyalties into account, it is still impossible to believe that Nahum Tate, Thomas D'Urfey, Thomas Flatman and other suppliers of the fulsome and the flattering really saw the Stuart monarchs as refulgent semi-divinities or that the glitter they claimed to apprehend derived from anything more numinous than the purse of guineas which rewarded their various panegyrics. The convention here was as well established as that which, in painting and sculpture, apotheosized the ruler as an antique hero dressed in kilt, buskins and artificially muscled cuirass. We need to look at these texts therefore not with the scornful eye of a modern aesthetic demanding absolute integrity before it gives the nod to artistic achievement, but with a sense instead of their appropriateness to the moment and above all to their suitability for musical setting.

Nobody knows who wrote the ode *Welcome, Vicegerent of the Mighty King*, but its tone is entirely consistent with the sort of blind obsequiousness with which Charles evidently felt at home, if only because it must have reminded him of the continuous torrents of flattery which the poets and musicians of France caused to roll before his cousin Louis XIV. The anonymous bard shows no reluctance in underlining the 'divinity which doth hedge a king', and given the threats currently offered to this by Shaftesbury and his hell-raisers, the point probably needed emphasizing among those loyal to the sovereign's interest. Significantly, London, noted for its contumacious Whiggery and the ease with which the anti-Popish faction could play upon the aggressiveness of its mob, is identified as conspicuously faithful,

> this head city, this imperial town,
> The seat and centre of the crown,

and stricken with sadness at the royal absence. To the King are attributed the power to make the stones of the city walls sing, as the god Apollo contrived to do with those of Thebes, and the ability to convert an unusually inclement early autumn into something resembling spring. Conjuring long life 'by the power of the Une and the Trine' the poet, in a vein of up-front vulgarity which suggests that he has really had enough of the whole thing, concludes:

Then all that have voices, let 'em cheerfully sing,
And those that have none may say, 'God save the King'.

Purcell did not include *Welcome, Vicegerent* in the manuscript, now in the British Library, into which he gathered most of his other early works in this form, perhaps because he felt it was still an apprentice work, announcing his authentic voice but in a somewhat limited, foursquare fashion, showing plenty of promise but still formally constrained. The welding of the overture's fast-section repeat on to the opening chorus is a skilful touch, as is the characteristically exuberant string ritornello which follows the chorus 'But your blest presence now'. But in the two duets, 'Ah! Mighty Sir' for alto and bass and 'When the summer' for two sopranos, there is a curiously short-breathed quality, as if the young composer were on the edge of delineating a clear individual profile but was still afraid to let himself go. The same is true of the final choruses, none of which is adequately extended, though there are abundant signs of an inventiveness seeking to break the rigidity of the verse forms. The development of Purcell's style in vocal music was inevitably linked with his broadening perceptions of flexibility in the lines of text he set, so that music empowers and elucidates language, dictating its own paragraphs, punctuations and inflexions. This little ode, touched with moments of wit and harmonic subtlety, marks a notable if still rather tentative début in a genre he was soon to make his own.

At some stage during this year of 1680, when he turned twenty-one, Purcell was married – or at least, we think his marriage may have taken place, though the one piece of evidence which seems to point towards this as the year of the wedding remains partially conjectural. On 9 July 1681 a certain Henry Purcell, infant son of Henry and Frances Purcell, was baptized at the church of All Hallows the Less, in the City, and is recorded as having been buried in the churchyard nine days later. Were the parents our composer and his wife? Since we know that he did not move to the parish of St Margaret's Westminster until 1682, it is quite possible that the newly married couple lived with Mrs Purcell's family in the City, at their house in Thames Street.

Until the relevant documents are recovered, we must accept the consensus of informed opinion, which seems to be that Frances Purcell's maiden name was Peters, that the J. B. Peters who witnessed Purcell's will was her brother, and that his name was John Baptist. Further evidence brought to light by Purcell scholars includes the presence, among Peters's children, of a girl named Frances and a boy christened Henry. None of this absolutely proves that Purcell's wife was Frances Peters, but the accumulated detail makes the identification more than likely.

The first John Baptist Peters, Frances's father, had arrived in London from Flanders at some stage during the mid-seventeenth century, and still gave his name with the Flemish spelling 'Pieters' in the document of denization which made him the King of England's subject in 1663. What trade he followed is not clear, but the mention, in an inventory made at his death in 1675, of a hundred skins of gilt leather in one room of his house suggests that he may have been a merchant of the kind of stamped and gold-tooled leather so popular with Restoration decorators and furniture makers.

His widow Amy, who lived in the Thames Street house with her two unmarried daughters, another married daughter and her husband, three apprentices and two maids, evidently sold wine from the premises. Since the inventory also mentions twenty dozen napkins and thirty-six tablecloths, twenty dozen plates and fifteen chamberpots, we can deduce that the handsomely furnished premises were probably managed as a tavern. This is certainly the conclusion reached by a recent Purcell biographer, Maureen Duffy, the earliest to examine the relevant records, and it may be that Henry's first meeting with Frances took place when he came here for refreshment, perhaps after playing the organ in one of the nearby churches.

John Baptist Pieters had registered himself in the 1663 document as conforming to the Church of England, but this may only have been nominal, since he had been baptized a Catholic in his home town of Ghent. To what extent the rest of the family were actively Papist is by no means clear, but the suggestion that Purcell's anthem *Beati Omnes*, one of only two he wrote to a Latin text, was composed for his own wedding seems entirely plausible, given that its verses include the reference to the 'fruitful vine' traditionally used in marriage services, and the adoption of Latin may have been intended as a sop to Frances's family susceptibilities.

Nothing is known of Frances Purcell beyond what we can deduce from her assiduity in publishing several of her husband's works after his death, including the so-called *Ten Sonatas of IV Parts* and the great *Collection of Ayres Compos'd for the Theatre*. In 1698, when *Orpheus Britannicus*, a major anthology of Purcell's songs, was issued by Henry Playford, Frances supplied a moving preface to the book in the form of a dedicatory epistle to the composer's pupil Annabella Howard. The language of this address implies a genuine wifely attachment. Mrs Purcell writes of 'those strong impressions of grief which have continued upon me ever since the loss of my dear lamented husband' and speaks of herself as somebody who 'must own my self fond to a partiality of all that was his'.

Even if the dedicatory preface to *Orpheus Britannicus* was written by someone else at Frances's request, its validity as evidence for the closeness of the marital relationship and for her real conviction of her husband's genius can hardly be in doubt. There may be some truth in the story told during the late eighteenth century by Sir John Hawkins, which represents Purcell as a typical Restoration toper, lurching home after a drinking bout to find his wife ready to lock him out of doors on a particularly rainy night, but it seems in excess both of facts and probability to represent her as a shrewish Xanthippe, indirectly responsible for the composer's death by causing him to catch a mortal chill. The same story has been told of Pergolesi, and in any case the figure of the meekly suffering artist's bullying wife, even in such substantial avatars as Frau Strauss yelling 'Richard, jetzt gehts komponieren!', always nurtures an element of myth on which the great man's admirers delight in elaborating.

The early 1680s, whatever the additional social *cachet* given to Purcell by his marriage and growing celebrity as a young composer in demand amid a wide variety of musical milieux, seem to have been a time of distinct unease for him, the period when he sat down to write some of his most dark-hued works, especially as regards the setting of religious texts. It may be that he was more deeply perturbed than we now realize by the worsening political situation, which to loyal servants of the court, whose livelihoods depended on a measure of order and stability, must have seemed to threaten total anarchy or perhaps a return to Puritan republicanism. One of the Chapel Royal anthems belonging to this gloomy interval may well be *I Will Love Thee, O Lord*, which selects verses from Psalm 18 'To the chief Musician, A Psalm of David, the servant of the Lord, who spake unto the Lord the words of this song in the day that the Lord delivered him from the hands of his enemies, and from the hand of Saul'. In his capacity as one of the King's chief musicians, Purcell was well placed to appreciate the beleaguered atmosphere surrounding both the monarch and his power. The dramatic opening to the psalm, with its references to 'the sorrows of hell' and 'the snares of death' and its picture of the earth shaking and trembling – 'the foundations also of the hills moved and were shaken, because He was wroth' – threw Charles's predicament into lurid relief. Presumably responsible for choosing his own text (though there must often have been consultations with the Dean of the Chapel and other clergy as to suitability), the composer ignored the extensive sections dealing with God as a vengeful deity equipping David for combat against his enemies. It was these verses to which he turned a decade later when writing his last anthem, the disappointingly jejune and rhetorical *The Way of God Is an Undefiled Way*, to celebrate the military prowess of King William III.

I Will Love Thee, O Lord provided yet another showcase for the talents of the remarkable John Gostling, 'that stupendious bass' as Evelyn called him, a minor canon of Canterbury cathedral who had been personally summoned in 1679 by the King himself to join the Chapel Royal choir, with an inducement of £50 a year to cover his expenses in the various journeys he would have to make between London and his home and family in Kent. Gostling's range spanned more than two octaves, and Purcell showed himself fully determined to exploit this astonishing vocal resource in a whole series of works for the Chapel in which the bass soloist is the dominant feature and in which the driving spirit is a collusion between creator and interpreter in the cause of the wittiest and boldest use of the voice. Gostling became a great admirer of Purcell's talents and the manuscript into which he gathered his own copies of the various sacred works is an important early source. It may indeed be that *I Will Love Thee, O Lord* acted as one of the inducements for him to settle his affairs in Canterbury and hurry to join the Chapel choir, since there exists a letter to him from Purcell's uncle Thomas, warning that ''tis very likely you may have a summons to appear among us sooner then you Imagin: for my sonne is Composing wherein you will be cheifly consern'd'. That reference to 'my sonne' is of course one which continues to give us trouble.

What probably did most to establish the image of Charles II as David, as in this anthem – whether as steadfast hero surrounded by predatory enemies in his flight from Saul to the cave of Adullam, or as the doting father of a brilliant, beautiful and ultimately damned rebel son – was the publication in 1681 of Dryden's classic satire *Absalom and Achitophel*. In this, biblical parallels are explicitly made with the King, the Duke of Monmouth, Shaftesbury and a host of other contemporary figures. Purcell's own presentation of his royal master in the guise of the King of Israel emerges at its most intensely dramatic in *Jehovah, Quam Multi Sunt Hostes*, the magnificent setting of the Latin Vulgate text of Psalm 3, 'Lord, how are they increased that trouble me', which in the Authorized Version bears the subtitle 'A Psalm of David when he fled from Absalom his son' and whose use at this time scholars have legitimately taken to apply to Monmouth's ascendancy as the popular Protestant champion, hoisted high by Shaftesbury and his followers. The verses of the Hebrew poem depend for their effectiveness on an alternation in mood between the psalmist's apprehension at the sheer numbers ranged against him and his complete assurance of God's protection. We shall probably never know how the ancient Israelites originally sang this psalm, but it would be fascinating to discover whether David, accompanied by the very harp which soothed Saul's melancholy, made any attempt in music at differentiating these two atmospheres of unease and confidence.

To achieve this contrast in his own setting, Purcell made careful use of the structure of the verse anthem, by now established as a standard Anglican form. The layout of such pieces owed much to the popular Elizabethan genre of the consort song, in which, accompanied by an instrumental ensemble of viols and keyboard, a group of singers would now and then divide into solo or duet 'verses' before uniting in a final chorus. In the verse anthems of late Tudor and Jacobean composers such as Orlando Gibbons and Thomas Tomkins a similar technique is followed, but care is always taken to preserve an overall polyphonic framework.

By the Restoration, however, the inevitable influence of continental styles, whether in French *grands motets* or in Italian church music in the tradition of masters like Claudio Monteverdi and Alessandro Grandi, had started making its impact. Contrapuntal cohesion binding together the work as a whole had given way to a sequence of distinct episodes, marking the alternation between solo and full choir more strongly, and often reducing the function of the choir to the provision of choruses signposting the course of the work. The advantage to anthem writers with the slightest sense of drama, like Locke and Humfrey, was obvious. Both composers extended the expressive possibilities of the redeveloped form to limits which displayed the full range of a pictorial imagination in the service of breathing fresh immediacy into the sacred texts.

The verse anthem never lost its popularity with English cathedral musicians and examples of it are still being produced for modern choirs. For composers of Purcell's generation the impetus to remodel the form came largely from the Chapel Royal, but it was not really until the late 1670s that a new and clearly defined style began to take hold. Since, however, a Latin motet such as *Jehovah, Quam Multi Sunt Hostes* could not have been given as part of an Anglican vernacular service, there is a faint possibility that Purcell may have written either for performance in Queen Catherine's Catholic chapel or else in a private house, perhaps that of his wife's family.

Whatever the circumstances of its first performance, it is difficult not to feel that in this, one of his finest, most tautly constructed sacred works, a perfect welding of the cerebral and the impassioned, Purcell was making a conscious gesture in the direction of that Italian style absorbed through his early study of Monteverdi and Carissimi. The piece opens with a ghostly obliquity, the treble line peering nervously about, as it were, for hidden enemies over an upward-sliding scale, before an almost tangible sense of menace and hostility is created by the jagged-edged setting of 'quam multi insurgunt contra me' and the earliest of a series of choral climaxes pinning the anthem's declamatory paragraphs together.

The first of these is given to the tenor, floridly declaring that God is his shield and then launching into a deceptively cheerful passage of arioso, answered by the temporarily heartened full choir. With astonishing suddenness the mood then shifts to embrace the descriptive potential of the next lines, the words meaning 'I laid me down and slept; I awaked; for the Lord sustained me', with the choir evoking the muted softness of a secure sleep. As for the ensuing bass solo verse, 'Non timebo a myriadibus populi', those who continue to maintain that Purcell was entirely unaffected by contemporary Italian music should listen again to this superlative essay in international Baroque and ask themselves whence, if not from the young composer's sophisticated awareness of Venetian and Roman styles, the entire multifaceted episode arises. The concluding chorus, in the triple time favoured by Restoration composers for their anthem closes, merely sets the seal on our overall impression of a youthful Henry Purcell firmly in control of mannerisms which, foreign as they were to English church music, he would successfully harness to his own confident eclecticism.

'Confident' is nevertheless a dangerous word to use regarding Purcell's state of mind during the early 1680s. There are no letters, journals or testimonies from friends upon which we can draw from this period to reconstruct a personal life: that problem is a continuous one for the biographer at every stage of Purcell's career. What we can use, albeit with the greatest caution, is the evidence offered by the kind of texts he was choosing to set at this time and by the music with which he clothed them. Taking these elements into consideration, together with the tense political atmosphere and what may have been a certain material insecurity (*Theodosius* had not generated any further theatrical commissions for the immediate future), we may be tempted to see Purcell as being plunged into a moment of gloomy uncertainty which his religious works from 1680 and 1681 reflect.

Two anthems written for the Chapel Royal are particularly

eloquent in this respect. *Bow Down Thine Ear*, harking back stylistically, in its poignantly bleak opening, to the world of late Tudor church music, was probably composed around 1680 and its selection of verses from Psalm 86 may well point towards the composer's own mood at this time, even if phrases such as 'for I am poor and in misery' need not be taken too literally. The whole deftly organized work represents a miniature emotional drama, in which the suffering soul, calling upon God, revives through its own determination to follow His holy will. In *Be Merciful Unto Me*, later – but not that much – in date, the text, bristling almost to paranoia with encircling enemies and stressing a need to seek refuge in the divine word, is assigned largely to three solo voices, brought together at crucial moments in passages of eloquent harmonic complexity to which the cheerful 'Alleluia' flourishes of the full choir at the end seem merely an incongruous footnote.

The most obvious expression of this sombre, introverted aspect of a massively comprehensive musical personality is to be found in a group of settings made around 1680 of metrical psalms, biblical paraphrases and sacred poems, all of which Purcell may have intended to publish or circulate as a single collection. Taken together, they provide one of the most intense reflections of his spirituality, though their evidently more intimate small-scale character in comparison with the Chapel Royal anthems has allowed many commentators to ignore them altogether.

Even if the kind of devotional profundity which characterized early seventeenth-century English Protestantism was fast disappearing, and the likelihood of another George Herbert, Henry Vaughan or Thomas Traherne was hardly to be entertained, the tradition of domestic piety and meditation was still strong among those old enough to remember the gravities of the world before the Civil War or else not too hopelessly infected with the present age's whore-and-bottle hedonism. Written with one voice to a part over a plain continuo line, these little motets may well have been intended by Purcell for use in 'private devotions'. We may imagine them as being sung to a chamber organ and viola da gamba in some wainscoted parlour of the period, by amateur performers mindful of that decorum and solemnity which in their youth during the 1640s had made the house as seemly a place for godliness as the church.

There is another intriguing possibility as to the context of this music's first performance. Most of the texts for these pieces derive from *A Century of Select Psalms*, metrical paraphrases published in 1679 by John Patrick, appointed eight years earlier as Preacher to the Charterhouse on the northern edge of the City. Like his brother Simon, later Bishop of Ely, Patrick, son of a Lincolnshire merchant, was a formidable controversialist. He weighed in against the Church of Rome with a series of polemic pamphlets, sermons and essays during a period of disquiet among Anglicans following the settlement of English ecclesiastical affairs at the Restoration. Enormously popular, especially with dissenting congregations, his psalms went into many editions, though their original title page makes clear that he had simply intended them 'for the use of the Charter-House'.

The Carthusian monastery known, like its sister foundations throughout England, as the Charterhouse had survived more or less intact as a building, though its monks were of course dispersed at the Reformation. In 1611 the rich philanthropist Sir Thomas Sutton, having purchased the property from the Earl of Suffolk, shifted here his original establishment at Hallingbury in Essex of an almshouse or 'hospital' for eighty poor men and a school for forty-four boys. Founded by royal warrant in the teeth of opposition from, among others, Sir Francis Bacon, the Charterhouse prospered, partly through successful management of its endowments, but also through the precision with which its original statutes were set out. Samuel Herne's *Domus Carthusiana*, a laudatory account of the charity and its munificent donor published in 1677, details the exact sums to be paid to everyone from the schoolmasters to 'the Matron', 'the Landress', 'the Cook, besides his accustomed Kitchin Fees', 'the Clock keeper', 'the Scavenger' and 'the Scrape Trencher'. Particularly interesting where Patrick and perhaps also Purcell are concerned is the stipulation that 'the Master and Preacher shall have Superintendancy over the Chappell Clerk, Organist and Sexton, to see if each of them carefully perform the Duties of his place . . . the second [i.e. the organist] in teaching the poor Scholars to Sing, and playing on the Organs at set times of Divine Service'. The organist's wage, incidentally, was £13 6s 8d, with an extra allowance of forty shillings.

There is no evidence that Purcell acted as organist at the Charterhouse, though nothing completely rules out the possibility that he might have given musical assistance at chapel services. The anthem *Lord, Who Can Tell How Oft He Offendeth*, a very early work dated to 1677 and hauntingly redolent of the composer's profitable absorption with the style of his Elizabethan and Jacobean predecessors, may perhaps have been performed there, and we know that *Blessed Is the Man that Feareth the Lord* was expressly provided as a 'Psalm Anthem for ye Charterhouse sung up [sic] ye Founders day' in 1688 (when John Patrick, according to custom, preached the sermon), though it is probably an adaptation of a piece composed several years before. Another Carthusian connection may have been through Purcell's publisher Henry Playford, who acted as one of the foundation's auditors.

With the notable exception of the wondrously exuberant *O All Ye People, Clap Your Hands*, one of Purcell's most captivating expressions of sacred rejoicing, all of what we might daringly label 'the Charterhouse motets' are essentially deep-shadowed, sombre-hued works, their harmonies and vocal lines playing upon our sense of the psalmist's tortured anguish and despair. Even the texts not taken from Patrick's *Century* – two versions of passages from Job by the much-commended translator and Levantine traveller George Sandys and a poem by Thomas Flatman, the able imitator of Cowley's Pindaric manner – are concerned with wretchedness and suffering.

Such is the pliancy with which the medium is handled that the vein so deeply mined here never exhausts itself in monotony or empty repetitiveness. Each of the twelve compositions shapes its own world within the overall homogeneity of Purcell's chosen idiom. Sometimes, as in *Plung'd in the Confines of Despair*, he offers us what is really a verse anthem, with a clearly aligned episodic layout, dramatically alternating interventions by solo and ensemble voices according to the shifts in direction made by the poem. Elsewhere, in pieces such as *Hear Me, O Lord, the Great Support*, the more fluid structure incorporates wholly unexpected elements, as when the tenor, to the lines

Thy love more cheers my heart than when
Their corn has wish'd increase:
Or when a happy vintage makes
Their wine o'erflow the press

launches into something like a Scotch song in one of the theatrical scores or, more relevantly, given what is being sung about here, the anacreontic 'Tis Wine Was Made to Rule the Day', published in *Orpheus Britannicus*.

Purely in terms of his professional career, Purcell can have had little to complain of during 1681. To this year belongs the second of his court odes, *Swifter, Isis, Swifter Flow*, which is subtitled in the original manuscript 'A Welcome Song in the Year 1681 for the King'. Scholars are not in agreement as to where exactly Charles was being welcomed from. Franklin Zimmerman believes that the piece was written to celebrate the court's return from Windsor to Whitehall in the autumn. A later Purcellian, Robert King, in the notes to his complete recorded edition of the odes, states that 'it seems to have been composed to celebrate the return to London of Charles II from his annual visit to Newmarket', quoting the diarist Narcissus Luttrell's comment on 12 October that 'at night, for joy, were ringing of bells and bonefires in severall places'.

A more plausible suggestion is surely that the anonymous poem and Purcell's score were furnished to commemorate the occasion of the sovereign's homecoming after one of the most significant episodes of his kingship, when for once he used his sense of royal dignity and authority in a thoroughly positive fashion, calculated both to secure his throne and to establish the rule of law against the menaces of Shaftesbury and Monmouth. Briefly, during the early spring of 1681, realizing the power of popular feeling on which the Whig politicians could play while Parliament sat in London, Charles had invoked an ancient royal privilege, not used by any of his forebears since the fifteenth century, which permitted him to summon the Lords and Commons to assemble in any place he might choose.

Charles's selection of Oxford for a session of Parliament was a masterstroke of political manoeuvring. His father's capital during the Civil War, the city had sustained its loyalty to the crown through a shrewd series of appointments among college heads and local clergy, and the foundation had been laid for that staunch Toryism to which the university was to adhere well into the following century. In their carriages the nobility and gentry converged upon the city during the second week of March, and the session began on the 21st. It must have been obvious to anyone with the slightest awareness of the situation's potentially volatile components that Charles's move was intended to isolate the Whigs from their power-base. But his appearance before the assembled House of Lords a week later, dressed in his full regalia of robes and crown in order to dissolve Parliament, which had barely commenced its operations, fell upon everyone as a complete surprise, overtaking Shaftesbury just at the moment when he fancied himself able to force the King's hand in adopting Monmouth as a successor and immeasurably heartening the embattled Tories.

The section of the Thames which flows through Oxford is known as the Isis, from which it seems a possible deduction that Purcell's ode, *Swifter, Isis Swifter Flow*, was composed to welcome the King back to London after Parliament concluded its deliberations. Charles had not bothered to survey the results of his bold assertion of royal prerogative, simply mounting to his coach and setting forth at once for Windsor, from which it seems he returned to Whitehall that same evening. Since he had not left for Oxford in secret, and since it must have been reasonably assumed that he would be absent for some time, the unnamed poet had doubtless already supplied Purcell with the text, as a court ode was not something to be whipped up at breakneck speed. It was therefore probably written in February or early March 1681, and its performance doubtless took place soon after the King's return on 28 March.

The poetry of this welcome song is no more inspired than that of its predecessor. Since they feature several of the same ideas and close in exactly the same way, with the final chorus leading inexorably to a 'Long live/God save the King', it is possible that they are by the same author. Once again he alludes to the seasons – comparisons with the spring are of a nature, in this case, to underline the likelihood of composition earlier rather than later during 1681. This time, however, the prevailing political crisis is directly referred to, and stress is laid besides on London's loyalty, called into question during recent months and soon to be summarily dealt with by the recall and regranting of its charters. Interestingly, in view of Charles's amorous inclinations, the city, personified as 'Augusta', is represented, as on Caius Gabriel Cibber's relief sculpture adorning the Monument (Christopher Wren's Corinthian column commemorating the Fire of London), in the guise of a woman favoured by the royal attentions.

> Though causeless jealousy
> May by the faction be broach'd,
> Your Augusta will never be
> From your kinder arms debauch'd.

Structurally *Swifter, Isis* is a more expansive and confident work than *Welcome, Vicegerent*. Once again overture and opening vocal sections are welded together, the tenor soloist and then the chorus taking up the descending figure in the orchestra, whose repetitions imitate the flowing of Isis. This time Purcell contrasts the sonorities of his band of string and continuo players with a pair of recorders, introduced to give a plangent sensuousness to the bass solo 'Land him safely on her shore'. It was the first of various occasions when these instruments were linked by the composer with poetic references to love, for the air speaks of the King's arrival filling London's walls with joy,

> As lovers' hearts with happiness,
> Tender lovers when return'd
> To those dear arms whose loss they mourn'd.

Presumably one of these recorder players also played the oboe for the eight bars doubling the violin part in the closing ritornello to the agreeably varied tenor air, 'Hark, hark! just now my listening ears', and afterwards heard no more. This too was a Purcellian first, and he soon showed that he could use the instrument, growing in popularity with composers throughout the late seventeenth century, to create haunting effects in his stage works as well as to enrich his court odes.

In a work with so many exciting anticipations of the maturer, more nonchalantly experienced artist – ground bass, that ultimate

Purcellian signature, makes two noteworthy appearances – it is not surprising to discover a final chorus whose glimpses towards the future surely lead to *Dido and Aeneas* and *King Arthur*. The composer has a field day with the lines

> May no harsher sounds e'er invade your blest ears,
> To disturb your repose or alarm our fears

in which the music's breezier serenities are deliberately troubled by a sudden harmonic shift towards a mood of jarring insecurity. The subsequent entries for the voice parts in the dismally banal couplet

> No trumpet be heard in this place or drum beat,
> But in compliment or to invite you to eat

show a greater assurance than is displayed by *Welcome, Vicegerent* as regards Purcell's management of the choir in a secular piece of this type.

During the late summer and early autumn of 1681, another compositional form, one in which he had never worked before, began to absorb his energy and inspiration. The Anglican liturgy incorporates a whole series of canticles in its morning and evening services, and it was a sequence of these, together with a Kyrie and setting of the Nicene Creed for Holy Communion, which Purcell now assembled. The task required a different style from those adopted in the fashioning of anthems, whether full or verse, and the comprehensive nature of this B♭ service suggests that he was consciously aiming at something substantial, if not monumental, in which he could both test his skill in a new medium and by doing so establish himself yet more firmly in the tradition of English cathedral music stretching back to the great services of Tomkins, Gibbons and Byrd.

In these canticles, particularly in the Benedicite, whose formulaic repetitiveness might challenge the ingenuity of any composer, Purcell uses the full choral sound as an almost abstract medium. Although there are plenty of episodes designed to blend and contrast the different voices, we are not conscious, as in the anthems, of the choir merely as onlookers, commentators or postscript writers, like the chorus in a drama. Instead, the impacted textures, moving easily between different rhythms, take on a bone-less, reptilian quality, rescued from monotony by deftness in the counterpoint rather than obsessive attention to word-painting of the sort we expect elsewhere in Purcell. The overall idiom is carefully controlled throughout by the need to provide the sort of complete liturgical apparatus to which any well-trained English cathedral choir could gain instant access.

From the Westminster Abbey accounts we know that the B♭ service was copied out by Michaelmas (29 September) together with the anthem *O God, Thou Art My God*, one of Purcell's most popular sacred works. The reason for its success is perhaps that very same approachable quality which distinguishes the canticles, and the piece, manuscript evidence implies, was composed as a pendant to them. An initial sturdiness of affirmation in this anthem is never afterwards shaken, even in passages such as 'My flesh also longeth after thee in a barren and dry land where no water is', and the festive triple-time Halleluia dances to so infectiously cheerful a tune that it has since been seized upon by hymnbook compilers as the melody for 'God is made the sure foundation'.

When Purcell returned to the stage that autumn, it was to the Theatre Royal in Drury Lane, rather than to Dorset Garden. Restoration dramatists, as we have noted in the case of Lee and *Theodosius*, were always keenly alert to the appeal of topicality, and somebody had the idea of reviving, at this politically volatile season, the old historical tragedy of *Richard II* by Shakespeare. The play, which in our own day has been given a series of memorable revivals, whether as a vehicle for Sir John Gielgud or as the basis of an unforgettable Parisian production by Ariane Mnouchkine, was emphatically not an audience favourite during the seventeenth century. Theatre managements may well have recalled the occasion in 1601 when Shakespeare and his fellow actors were packed off to prison for having staged the play as part of a propaganda effort on behalf of Queen Elizabeth's favourite, the Earl of Essex. The Queen herself, fully aware of the political under-tones, had famously exclaimed: 'I am King Richard, know ye not that?'

Once again the work was doomed to founder amid scandal and embarrassment. The poet chosen to adapt it for its 1681 revival was Nahum Tate, whose later association with Purcell as librettist of *Dido and Aeneas* has ensured him a fame which he would hardly have acquired on his own account. If not an especially gifted poet, he was a versatile one, turning his hand to anything from the carol 'While Shepherds Watched' to a long poem on the virtues of tea-drinking and a collaboration with Dryden on the second instalment of *Absalom and Achitophel*.

His reworking of *Richard II* is a hugely cut-down version of the original, with additional scenes using the Jack Cade episode from *Henry VI, Part 2*. The political expediency of these additions is obvious, and Bolingbroke is clearly intended to represent the Earl of Shaftesbury, who could pique himself on being portrayed as a demagogue, rabble-rouser or grotesque pantomime villain in at least a dozen plays of the period, including Thomas Otway's *Venice Preserv'd* and Dryden's *The Duke of Guise*. Some of Shakespeare's best poetry is suppressed in the process: though 'Of comfort no man speak' is included, poor John of Gaunt never gets to utter his 'This England' speech. Tate also vulgarizes the Duke of York, turning him into a typical Restoration pantaloon.

Purcell's contribution to the performance was the single song 'Retir'd from any mortal's sight', printed in the original playbook after the title page as 'Song for the Prison SCENE in the last ACT'. Tate's rewriting skills had been at work in this, one of Shakespeare's most poignant episodes, introducing a mysterious disappearing banquet designed to delude the wretched king in his dungeon at Pomfret. The song, an additional torment for him, occurs soon after this, and like the lyrics assigned to Athenais's suicide scene in *Theodosius*, the poem is a sad one, telling of shepherd Damon who exclaims:

> Some ease . . . some respite give,
> Why, mighty Powers, ah! why
> Am I too much distrest to live,
> And yet forbid to die?

This time, however, the key is a gloomy G minor, and the tempo anything but buoyant, let alone a Scotch dance. Though the song is strophic, Purcell nevertheless manages to fit a twelve-note melisma into the penultimate bar of each verse, which can be used to stress the pathos of Damon's predicament, resolved as this ultimately is by his death (clinical rather than sexual, despite the obvious double entendre).

The published quarto edition of the play features another song, 'Love's delights were past expressing', which Purcell seems not to have set. Either way it scarcely mattered, for *Richard II* the play was unacceptable in its original form, and Tate was forced, to get it past the Lord Chamberlain, to change the title to *The Sicilian Usurper* and alter the names of the various characters. Even this measure was unsuccessful, and to the poet's chagrin the play was taken off after its third performance. In his vindication, attached to the printed text, he objected that 'Every Scene is full of Respect to Majesty and the dignity of Courts, not one alter'd Page but what breaths Loyalty, yet had this Play the hard fortune to receive its Prohibition from Court', but such claims were evidently unavailing against the official horror of anything which even hinted at sedition.

Purcell was probably on safer ground with another play which glanced at contemporary politics, Thomas D'Urfey's farce *Sir Barnaby Whigg or No Wit Like A Woman's*, produced at Drury Lane in 1681. D'Urfey, later to work closely with the composer on various theatrical projects, evidently felt entirely confident in deriding the supporters of Shaftesbury and Monmouth as unreconstructed Roundheads. The Theatre Royal audience was probably Tory for the most part, and the comedy was intended as a riposte to Shadwell's anti-Catholic *The Lancashire Witches*, produced some months earlier at Dorset Garden. Littered with jibes at the Whigs, including the prologue's reference to 'the Numerous, Buzzing, Crop-ear'd Crew' and the hero Wilding's furious denunciation of 'ye soulless Insects, ye rotten sheep, that ... infect a Nation', *Sir Barnaby Whigg* is otherwise a typical Restoration mixture of cuckoldry and intrigue. Purcell's contribution was a sea song 'Blow, Boreas, blow', sung in Act I at the invitation of Captain Porpuss, 'a blunt Tarpawlin Captain', veteran of the battle of Solebay in the wars against the Dutch. 'I had then a Lieutenant aboard, a little Dapper fellow, but as stout as Hercules; and when we met a-nights in the great Cabbin over a jolly bowl of Punch, the Rogue wou'd sing us the finest Sea Songs and so Roar 'em out: I think I've a fellow can remember one of them. Sing, sirrah'. And so he does, a stirring musical evocation of an ocean tempest.

By the end of the year Purcell and his wife were living in Great St Anne's Lane, Westminster, in the parish of St Margaret's, where his name is included in the rate-book as a new arrival. The surrounding area seems to have been particularly popular with musicians. Among the Purcells' neighbours were the composers John Blow, Robert Ramsey and John Banister, the Abbey precentor Stephen Crespion and the publisher John Carr, who was to collaborate with Playford two years later in issuing the *Sonnatas of III Parts*.

The move to Great St Anne's Lane may well have signified increasing stability and prosperity for Henry and Frances, and if there was still any lingering depression it must have been substantially lifted by the commission for a new court ode, the welcome song *What Shall be Done in Behalf of the Man* to mark the homecoming of the Duke of York from an unofficial exile in Scotland.

Having fled overseas to Flanders when the first wave of anti-Popish hysteria broke over London, James had begged his brother the King for leave to transfer himself and his wife Mary of Modena to Scotland. The request was granted on condition that they went there by sea, but the crossing from Holland proved so stormy that there was nothing for it but to complete the journey by land from London. Settled in Holyrood Palace, the couple found themselves pawns in an elaborate political game being played by the King, the exiled Monmouth who had taken refuge in Protestant Holland, and the most devious and coldly calculating of the royal mistresses, Louise de Kéroualle, Duchess of Portsmouth. Though a staunch Catholic, she was content to receive hefty bribes from Shaftesbury and his henchmen to use her influence with Charles as they directed.

First of all, the King allowed his brother and sister-in-law, after three months in Edinburgh, to return to London, purely, it appeared, as a public symbol of his irritation at the rising popularity of Monmouth, who, having turned up suddenly from Holland, was now making a triumphal progress through the West Country, a journey ominous for his future destiny. Then the Duchess of Portsmouth, tempted by a colossal *douceur* of £600,000 from Shaftesbury, began work on the King to get James sent back again to Scotland. He meekly returned with Mary at his side, and they spent the next year in gaining the good opinions of the Scots with games of golf and fashionable tea-drinking, though this most emphatically Protestant kingdom could never quite stomach the couple's fervently displayed Popery.

Ironically, it was another access of Portsmouth's apparently insatiable greed which brought them home once more. When Shaftesbury tried to cut off the revenue from the Post Office which James had been awarded as a perquisite, on the grounds that his control of the service endangered national security, she managed to gain the King's promise that he would make his brother part with an annual sum of £5,000 out of this postal income. With most untypical shrewdness James assented, on condition that he be allowed to sign the relevant documents in England. When he got back to London, his brother once again saw the expediency of using him to embody his official displeasure with the Whig extremists and ordered him not to leave again for Edinburgh. It was only when Mary, five months pregnant and feeling decidedly frail, felt unable to travel south by coach to join him, that James set off to bring her home in one of his own royal naval frigates. The ship struck a sandbank off the coast of Norfolk, and the Duke, with a handful of attendants, took to a lifeboat, leaving over a hundred people, including several royal musicians, to drown as the vessel sank within a matter of minutes. Mary was brought safely back to England in another ship, and the pair, together with James's daughter by his previous marriage, the Lady Anne, finally landed at Erith, on the Thames estuary, on 27 May 1682.

It was this joyful homecoming which surely occasioned *What Shall Be Done in Behalf of the Man*, rather than, as some Purcellians maintain, James's earlier southward journey in March. Since the Duke and Duchess subsequently joined the King at Windsor, it was presumably at the castle that the welcome song was first performed, since we learn from the Treasury accounts that Purcell and his fellow musicians had followed the court there on 17 May, the composer receiving the sum of £11 13s 2d for his attendance. Once more the poet is unknown, but his style and technique seem altogether more polished than those of the ungainly versifier of the two earlier odes. The intention here is more blatantly propagandistic, and the allusion to recent political events very heavily underscored. James, vindictive as he was, must have enjoyed such passages as

> His foes shall all tremble before him,
> His friends little less than adore him,
> And the mobilè crowd
> Who so foolishly bowed
> To the pageant of royalty, fondly mistaken,
> Shall at last from their dream of rebellion awaken,
> And now every tongue shall make open confession
> That York, royal York, is the next in succession.

Amid much flattery of the King himself, doubtless in order to humour his profound sense of decorum, we cannot listen to lines like

> Mighty Charles, though joined with thee,
> Equal in his pedigree
> Noble York by nature stands,
> Yet he owns thy sovereignty
> And readily obeys all thy commands

without recalling the elder royal brother's devastating put-down to the younger: 'They would never kill me, Jamie, to make you king.'

Even if this were true, the Duke ought to have felt honoured by the care Purcell devoted to setting this effusively laudatory text. The ode is unquestionably among his finest early achievements in the genre, its manner purely Purcellian yet at the same time marked by touches showing French and Italian influence, especially in the overture and the tenor air 'All the grandeur he possesses'. His experience in writing for well-trained solo voices in the Chapel Royal came splendidly to his aid in the opulently conceived bass declamation of the 'mighty Charles' verses quoted above, in which the grandeur of the vocal line brilliantly exalts the sense of fraternal duty conveyed by the poet. Best of all is the ensuing chorus, 'But thanks be to heaven', in which a list of admiring adjectives,

York, the obedient, grateful, just,
Punctual, courageous, mindful of his trust

is divided by the composer among individual voices in a moment
encapsulating that authentic late-seventeenth-century wit so prized
in Purcell's London. A wit was somebody who could combine
humour with sensitivity, discernment and the various perspectives
of cultural allusion, somebody whose way with words enabled
them to formulate memorable *bons mots* and epigrams, but who
was also gifted with analytical good taste and intelligence. Purcell
possessed this faculty in abundance, and there is plenty of evidence
to suggest that his contemporaries, especially those who sought
after his death to memorialize and enshrine his achievement as
'our musical Shakespeare', appreciated the adaptability and dis-
crimination with which he employed his creative resources. With
a good education behind him and continual contact with a lively,
cultivated, increasingly cosmopolitan milieu such as that of Restoration London, he must have been sufficiently aware of the shortcomings inherent in some of the ode texts. Yet he never adopted
a cynical or half-hearted approach to the business of giving lyrical
wings to flat-footed numbers. *What Shall Be Done in Behalf of
the Man*, with its careful avoidance of the humdrum or predictable
in the marriage of music and words, and its continuously sensitive
handling of choral and instrumental textures, is the first of Purcell's
secular works to convey without reserve the urbane sophistication
of his musical personality.

Alas, this could scarcely be said of his next court ode. In October, 1682, when the King and the Duke of York returned to
London from the races at Newmarket, Purcell was commissioned
to set the official welcome song *The Summer's Absence Uncon-
cerned We Bear*, to be performed on the 21st. The unnamed poet,
while flattering the monarch as fulsomely as custom required,
dwelt with understandable insistence on the political discontent
currently clouding the royal horizon, ascribing the crisis to a
surfeit of peace and prosperity. Peace herself is envisaged,
perhaps not altogether innocently, as a nymph surrendering to
Charles's embraces. As a result of his constancy, he is assured
that:

Britannia shall now her large empire bestride
And over the seas she unrivalled shall ride,
Sole Empress she the vast flood shall command
And awe the great blustering Hectors at land.

Musically the work shows Purcell consolidating on features he had developed in the earlier odes, but not necessarily improving them. Soloists and chorus are closely integrated as before, and though John Gostling was given some fine virtuoso passages, especially in the opening recitative, there is a certain sense throughout the whole piece of the composer keeping 'hold of Nurse, for fear of finding something worse'. There are two discreet, not especially idiosyncratic experiments with ground bass, and the string writing in the introductory symphony and the ritornelli has a sinewy charm, but the abiding impression is one of embarrassed constraint. Perhaps it was simply that a deeper, more exotic stimulus than the words of a fawning court poetaster had seized upon the composer's restless creative fancy.

3

After the Italian Way

In 1673, while Henry Purcell was still a boy at the Chapel Royal, a royal marriage took place which was to have a significant impact on English musical life. On 20 September that year, in the northern Italian city of Modena, a proxy wedding ceremony was conducted in one of the grander apartments of the dignified but rather gloomy Palazzo Ducale which dominates the southern end of the town. The bride was Maria Beatrice D'Este, fourteen-year-old daughter of the widowed Duchess of Modena, now regent of her prosperous little sovereign state. The bridegroom, represented by the English envoy Henry Mordaunt, Earl of Peterborough, was Charles II's brother, James, Duke of York, an ageing widower with two teenage daughters, both of whom, like their newly acquired stepmother, would eventually become Queen of England.

The marriage had been brokered partly through the good offices of Pope Clement X (who had firmly but tactfully applied spiritual blackmail to the understandably reluctant Maria Beatrice, adjuring her to 'reflect upon the great advantage which would accrue to the Catholic faith' through the match), and partly by diplomatic pressure from Louis XIV of France, at that time the most powerful man in Europe. James had converted to Catholicism in 1669, before the death of his first wife Anne Hyde, and with a proselyte's characteristic zeal was absolutely determined to secure himself a consort in the same faith before Parliament, with its bench of Anglican bishops and its predominantly Protestant membership, should reassemble to thunder its disapproval.

'Mary of Modena', as she is known to English history, was a singularly fortunate choice. Intelligent, charming and resourceful – everything, in short, that her husband was not – she became one of the more regrettable casualties of seventeenth-century politics,

86

and as a queen in exile attracted more or less equal measures of sympathy and admiration from even the most hardbitten of contemporary commentators. To a biographer of Purcell her significance is not simply as a token of Catholicism during an age of intense religious bigotry (which, as we shall see, impinged briefly but seriously on the composer's career). The Este family, from one of whose branches she derived, had become famous for their patronage of musicians. While dukes of Ferrara, until papal greed invoked a technicality to rob them of their domains in 1597, they had at various times welcomed Josquin des Prez, Adrian Willaert and Luzzasco Luzzaschi to their court. Moving to Modena, they continued this tradition by fostering the talents of such fine composers as the madrigalist Orazio Vecchi, Marco Uccellini, whose collections of string sonatas had a profound influence on the development of instrumental chamber music (and, however indirectly, on Purcell's own style), and Giovanni Battista Vitali, a Bolognese master whose violin writing was enormously admired in England after the Restoration.

It was inevitable that, as a member of a music-loving family marrying into a foreign court where, whatever the financial embarrassments, music was encouraged and enjoyed, Mary – or 'Italian Molly' as the English rudely referred to her – should have sought to introduce a touch or two of her own country's sophistication to her adopted land. She maintained close links with her brother, the young Duke Francesco II, who assumed full sovereignty the year after her marriage and promptly established a magnificent court orchestra and choir, attracting some exceptional talents and placing Modena, for thirty years at least, among the major musical centres of Italy. Several of Francesco's musicians from the Modenese ducal chapel found their way to London, where Mary's presence, as part of a royal family centred on a king with an unshakeable sense of the deference due to those associated with him by blood or marriage, must have seemed to guarantee a favourable reception for them all.

The significant factor in any overall view of the London musical world in which Purcell came to maturity is the increasingly marked presence, not just of Italian musicians, but of performers from France, Germany and the lands of the Holy Roman Empire, all testifying to the fact that English culture during the Restoration period was anything but xenophobic. For proof of this we need only turn to the writings of the invaluable Roger North. Disapproving as he remained of the newer Baroque style, with its emphasis on technical display and its strongly marked associations with opera, he grudgingly acknowledged its pervasiveness in the hands of skilful foreign executants.

> Here came over many Germans, cheifly violists [i.e. violinists] as Scheiffare, Voglesang, and of other names to fright one. These introduced many solos for the viol and violin, being rough and unairy devisions, but for the active part they were coveted. The best printed consorts that went about were of one Becker, a Sweed, which doe not deserve to be, as they are, laid aside. And severall little printed consorts came over from Itally, as Cazzati, Vitali and other lesser scrapps which were made use of in corners.

Contemporary manuscripts containing copies of Diedrich Becker's sonatas from his much-admired *Musicalische Frülings–Fruchte*, published at Hamburg in 1668, appear in various British collections. An earlier German violinist, bringing with him that virtuoso style for which composers like Johann Rosenmuller and Johann Heinrich Schmelzer were writing so brilliantly, was Thomas Baltzar of Lübeck, who had arrived in England two years before Cromwell's death. With his exceptional fluency of execution on the instrument, Baltzar was bound to invite the kind of interest which surrounds concert fiddlers with sulphurous and satanic glamour. Old John Wilson, the song composer and erstwhile singer for Shakespeare, hearing Baltzar play in Oxford, feigned to inspect him to find out if he had a 'Huff', a hoof, 'that is to see whether he was not a Devill'. Diabolical or not, Baltzar was listed as 'composer for the viollins' in the Private Musick from 1660 until his death three years later, and it is to him that North attributes the general enthusiasm for the violin which now seized amateur performers in England. Baltzar, he says, 'shewed so much mastery upon that instrument that gentlemen, following also the humour of the Court, fell in *pesle mesle*, and soon thrust out the treble viol, and not without the greatest reason, for the former hath of the latter multiple advantages'.

Baltzar was not the only foreign musician in the royal band. Besides the aged Angelo Notari and the French lutenists already referred to, there was the German string-player Dietrich Stoeffken, who had come to England before the Civil War and whose name the writers of official documents early reduced to 'Steffkins'. The King's harpsichord maker was an Italian, Girolamo Zinti, who had worked for the music-loving Queen Christina of Sweden, and his successor was the assistant he had brought with him from Stockholm, Andrea Testa. Other Italians, the Bolognese violinist Matteo Battaglia and the organist Giovanni Sebenico presided over the services in the Catholic chapel of Queen Catherine at Somerset House, and Locke, also employed there, was held to have absorbed their influence -- 'by the service and the society of forreiners he was not a little Italianized' – though apparently they disliked his style of organ-playing. London meanwhile heard its first Italian castrato in 1664, accompanied by the talented Vicenzo Albrici, a pupil of Carissimi, who worked with Heinrich Schütz at Dresden. Albrici gave lessons to Johann Kuhnau and later become one of Bach's predecessors as organist of Thomaskirche in Leipzig, where, probably more for the sake of convenience than out of conviction, he went over to Protestantism.

The two most highly regarded foreign musical figures in Purcell's London – one of them at least known to him personally – were the harpsichordist Giovanni Battista Draghi, Sebenico's successor at the organ in Queen Catherine's chapel, and the hugely influential violin virtuoso Nicola Matteis. Comparatively little of Draghi's music survives for us to assess the validity of contemporary London's enthusiasm for 'Signor Baptist' as he was often called. The songs and dances he contributed to the 1674 *Tempest* revival have been lost, as alas have the various pieces he supplied for Shadwell's second operatic venture, an English adaptation of Molière's *Psyché* in 1675, with most of the music provided by Matthew Locke. Also due to Draghi was the earliest setting of Dryden's 'Song for Saint Cecilia's Day', 'From Harmony, from Heavn'ly Harmony', best known to us now in the colourful version made by Handel in 1737. A published set of harpsichord suites and some more recently discovered keyboard works, in a manuscript notebook containing pieces by Purcell, go some way towards helping us to understand how much the English master may have owed to the Italian's style.

Nicola Matteis emerges, at least in the pages of North and Evelyn, as a dashing virtuoso, whose wizardry on the violin dazzled English amateurs during the 1670s. He arrived from Naples, where he had played in the orchestra of the Spanish viceroy's chapel, though whether he was a native Neapolitan is unknown, and even the date of his birth is obscure. Roger North keeps calling him 'old Nicola', but since there is evidence that he remained in England until the early eighteenth century he was perhaps only a little older than the musical memorialist himself. Never in doubt, from North's irresistibly opinionated and idiomatic pages, is the sense of Matteis as a fiery innovator, a veritable John the Baptist of Italian taste among British performers and audiences. He speaks at various points of 'the coming over of old Nicola', calls him 'a sort of precursor who made way for what was to follow', and says that he was 'very poor, but inexpugnably proud, and hardly prevailed with to play to anybody'. It was rumoured that he had walked all the way through Germany with his violin on his back. This perfect archetype of the penniless artist nourished on disdain was ultimately, if somewhat laboriously, won over by a group of noble dilettanti. These included the Royalist veteran and press censor Sir Roger L'Estrange, whose family had sheltered John Jenkins during the Civil War, and the government servant William Bridgeman, a member of the 'Musicall Society' to whom Purcell was to dedicate his 1684 ode *Welcome to All the Pleasures*.

Through their careful humouring and persuasion, Matteis, according to North, 'became the most debonaire and easy person living; he came to little meetings and did just what they would have him'. Though Jenkins himself admired Nicola's compositions – 'he touched them over and pulling off his spectacles clapt his hand on the book and declared he had never heard so good a piece of music in his life' – their short-winded, rather facile charm hardly does justice to the idea of the daredevil fiddler who 'could hold an audience by the ears longer than ordinary, and a whisper not be heard amongst them'. This 'very tall and large bodied man', who 'rested his instrument against his short ribbs', used a bow long enough for a bass viol and taught the English to hold it 'by the wood onely and not to touch the hair'.

Poor old Nicola grew prosperous, squandered his money on a big house in Norfolk which he could not afford, 'contracted bad diseases which ended in dropsyes, and so he became poor. And dyed miserable'. His performing style had nevertheless made its mark, as North rightly perceived, and the growing number of nobility and gentry now setting out to make the tour of Italy started forth across the Channel with his exquisite divisions in their ears and an eagerness to probe the native sources of his inspiration among Italian players, teachers, publishers and *cognoscenti*.

From Venice, from Modena, from the circle surrounding the self-banished Queen Christina at Rome, from the decaying Medicean court of Florence or from Turin, that nursery of fine fiddlers, the returning travellers brought home sets of sonatas written in the newest Italian vein, alternating slow and fast sections and making use of various popular dance rhythms of the day, most notably the allemande and the gigue. Some of these were written for solo instrument with continuo, but many followed the growing trend for the kind of four- or five-movement work which employed an ensemble of two principal performers with accompanying bass.

Nobody seems quite certain how the trio sonata, that most engaging, widely practised and long-lived of Baroque musical models, came to be developed, but by the 1640s in Italy something like a standard form had started to evolve. Stringed instruments were favoured for the upper parts, with the bass played on a violone, accompanied – or not, according to taste – by an organ, a harpsichord or a plucked instrument such as a lute or a theorbo. During the mid-seventeenth century the summit of artistry in this genre among Italian composers was probably best represented by Giovanni Legrenzi in Venice, in sets of robustly tuneful sonatas whose movements bore playfully allusive titles, 'la Buscha', 'la Rossetta', 'la Bonacossa', and by Marco Uccellini and Giovanni Battista Vitali in Modena, both of whom incorporated the latest French dance types, minuets and bourrées among them, into their lively, multi-faceted trios.

It was not these composers, however, who found the greatest

91

favour with English violinists and keyboard players, fresh from their lessons with 'old Nicola' and 'Signor Baptist' and clearly delighted (as amateur music-makers in Britain always have been) with the essentially sociable aspect of the trio sonata, a medium in which as many as five players might legitimately take part. One name frequently occurring in manuscript collections of the period, and specifically mentioned by North in connection with the new vogue for sonatas, is that of Maurizio Cazzati, *maestro di cappella* at the basilica of San Petronio in Bologna at a time when several musicians linked with this particular church were beginning to evolve the form known to us as the concerto. Whatever his proficiency as a composer of religious music, he was more highly regarded for his skill in the writing of violin solos and trios, and copies of the latter found their way to England. His was not a particularly inventive or exciting talent (these works are notably lacking in melodic interest), but as far as the layout of the movements and lively instrumental dialogue was concerned, he was an important influence on contemporary writers in the medium.

More arresting than Cazzati, and clearly someone whose style caught the young Purcell's attention at a crucial moment, was the Roman lutenist Lelio Colista. A composer attached to various churches in the papal capital in the mid-seventeenth century, he earned admiration among the keenly discerning Roman audiences of the time, being described by the Jesuit polymath and museum-maker Athanasius Kircher as 'vere Romanae urbis Orpheus' – 'truly the Orpheus of the city of Rome'. An English Papist, visiting Italy in 1661, listened entranced as 'the Theorbo man Lelio Colista played rare volenteryes' at the Spanish Ambassador's chapel.

It seems odd, given the wide distribution of Colista's trios in manuscript throughout England, that nobody here attempted to publish them. The emphasis in these pieces is on clearly defined contrast: North's apt analogy in discussing another composer's trios, of the different stages of an argument, comes at once to mind. An opening slow movement propounds a solemn statement, followed by a contrapuntal canzona, in which individual voices sustain vigorous dialectic. Then, as North so irresistibly puts it, 'comes properly in the Adagio, which is laying all affaires aside, and lolling in sweet repose', after which a further quick movement

92

in triple time, perhaps in the form of a minuet or a gigue, concludes the work.

The obvious danger in compositions of this kind was that the sonata might fragment into a series of diffuse episodes, and it was the business of any competent handler of the medium to avoid this, through holding the individual movements together by such devices as the use of fugue or building over a ground bass. Colista's particular penchant was for a species of echo technique created by sequences of ascending or descending figures across the various voices. This emphasis on the all-important underpinning structure was something the young Henry Purcell learned directly from a study of such sonatas. Ironically however, various pieces he is known to have inspected or made copies of under Colista's name turn out to be by the great Milanese violin virtuoso Carlo Ambrogio Lonati, known as *il gobbo della Regina* – 'the Queen's hunchback' – because he had played for Queen Christina. Perhaps Matteis, who knew him personally, had brought these pieces over, though Lonati himself was later to visit England during the reign of James II.

Was the work of that most illustrious of Queen Christina's musicians, Arcangelo Corelli, also known to Purcell? Early sonatas by Corelli turn up in contemporary English manuscripts, and his *Sonate a tre*, op. 1, the first of those collections which made him the most influential of late-seventeenth-century Italian masters, were published in 1681. But it is likely that Purcell had already begun to compose his own sonatas along lines suggested by Cazzati, Colista and Lonati before the Corellian invasion, which, if North's assessment is correct, 'cleared ye ground of all other sorts of musick whatsoever'.

In his fogeyish fashion North speaks of 'Corellys first consort' when mentioning the op. 1 sonatas. The term 'sonata' took some time to establish itself among the English, who were not the most expert at correctly reproducing foreign musical labels – in various contemporary sources we find 'mennowit', 'borry' and the curiously avian-sounding 'tuckatoo'. The earliest Englishmen to write sonatas under that name were both Catholic expatriates working on the Continent. Henry Butler was a string player for the King of Spain and William Young served the Austrian Archduke Karl

Ferdinand, governor of the Tyrol. Young's collection of eleven
solo and ensemble sonatas was published in Innsbruck in 1653 and
was evidently known in England, but native composers remained
reluctant to pick up the form. Even Nicola Matteis preferred to
label his four collections *Ayres for the Violin*, though in fact they
included sonatas. The violinist, concert promoter and song writer
Robert King wrote a 'Sonetta after the Italion way' which is
essentially a trio sonata, but it was not until 1683 that an English
musician undertook to present to the public the first nationally
composed collection of trios in the newest Italian vein.

In the *London Gazette* for 24–8 May that year there appeared
the following advertisement:

> These are to give notice to all gentlemen that have subscribed to the
> proposals published by Mr Henry Purcell for the printing his sonatas
> of three parts, for two violins and bass to the harpsichord or organ,
> that the said books are now completely finished, and shall be deliv-
> ered to them upon the 11th June next. And if any who have not yet
> subscribed shall before that time subscribe, according to the said
> proposals (which is ten shillings the whole set) which are at Mr
> William Hall's house in Norfolk Street, or at Mr Playford's and
> Mr Carr's shops in the Temple; for the said books will not after that
> time be sold under 15s the set.

The gist of this somewhat confusing announcement, and of a
second in the *Gazette* of 11 June, telling subscribers either to send
in 'the proposal paper they received with the receipt to it when
they subscribed' or else to go directly to Purcell's house to collect
their copies, was that the composer had floated the project of
publishing his trio sonatas by subscription before actually com-
pleting them. The scheme was not uncommon, and became even
more popular in the eighteenth century, when the firm of John
Walsh issued many of Handel's works with lists of subscribers
attached. We do not know, unfortunately, the names of those who
laid out their ten shillings for the initial offer, but we can be certain
that the novelty value of the pieces themselves, underlined by a
further *Gazette* announcement on 29 October 'concerning the
new Musical Compositions called SONATA's lately published by

Mr Henry Purcell', would have commended them to a wide musical circle.

Purchasers of the *Sonnatas of III Parts*, engraved by the music printer Thomas Crosse and published by John Playford and John Carr, were greeted, after the title page, with a prefatory address from the composer himself. Though Playford was given to writing his own commendatory prefaces to the works he published, there is no reason to doubt Purcell's authorship, and sections of this introduction are unusually revealing about his attitudes and intentions, and about his entirely pardonable sense of the momentousness of the publication itself. Waiving the customary 'elaborate harangue on the beauty and the charms of Musick', he goes on to claim that 'for its Author, he has faithfully endeavour'd a just imitation of the most fam'd Italian Masters; principally to bring the Seriousness and gravity of that sort of Musick into vogue and reputation among our Countrymen, whose humour, 'tis time now, should begin to loathe the levity and balladry of our neighbours'. After modestly suggesting, in the manner of prefaces from time immemorial, that others would have done the job much better, Purcell excuses himself for an inadequate knowledge of Italian: 'he is not asham'd to own his unskilfulness in the Italian Language; but that's the unhappiness of his Education, which cannot justly be accounted his fault'. But he declares himself 'not mistaken in the power of the Italian Notes, or elegancy of their Compositions, which he would recommend to the English Artists'. He has scrupulously edited the printing and 'has now thought fit to cause the whole Thorough Bass to be Engraven, which was a thing quite besides his first Resolutions'. The preface concludes with an explanation for 'the English Practitioner' of 'a few terms of Art unusual to him', musical directions such as adagio, grave, largo, allegro, vivace and piano.

Several points are worth emphasizing in this introductory statement, which clearly ranks as something rather more important than the standard-issue 'epistle dedicatory' or 'gentle reader' address with which most seventeenth-century volumes opened, and which writers like John Dryden raised to a fine art during these very same years when Purcell was making his mark as a composer. Its mixture of elegance, seriousness and sly humour is absolutely typical of Pucell and if he did not write it, then the author was evidently somebody who knew him intimately and could capture the essence of his personality.

Various Purcellian scholars have indulged differing degrees of cynicism as to the composer's claim that he had 'faithfully endeavour'd a just imitation of the most fam'd Italian Masters'. Franklin Zimmerman, the doyen of Purcell experts, has gone so far as to doubt that these Italian models ever existed, which seems absurd, both in view of the obviously Italianate design of the sonatas, in the *da chiesa* slow–fast–slow–fast layout (perfected, though not originated, by Corelli) and the different contrapuntal and rhythmic devices taken over from Italian composers whose work Purcell is known to have examined. Even if this was a blatantly commercial device, designed to attract what might be termed musical fashion victims, the allusion to 'fam'd Italian Masters' was not without substance.

Still more arresting is his stated intention 'principally to bring the Seriousness and gravity of that sort of Musick into vogue and reputation among our Countrymen' and the slighting reference to 'the levity and balladry of our neighbours'. The fling at the French must have been clear for all to infer, but did Purcell really mean this? A Gallic accent bit deeply into his musical style, and 'Baptist's vein' – North's famous phrase alludes to Jean–Baptiste Lully rather than Giovanni Battista Draghi – was in any case part of the civilized discourse of Restoration composers. What is more, the dedication of the sonatas published in 1683 was to Charles II himself, so wholeheartedly Francophile that, unbeknown to his countrymen, he had no qualms in selling the kingdom to his cousin Louis XIV in the secret treaty made at Dover in 1670. We may wonder whether Charles ever bothered to read the opening pages of the volume laid at his feet by the young Composer-in-Ordinary.

Other touches in the preface are revelatory of Purcell the man, so tantalizingly blurred a figure when it comes to personal records and the detailed reminiscence of friends and acquaintances. His careful editing is entirely typical: he was always scrupulously neat and meticulous in the layout and presentation of scores, and his manuscripts are a good deal easier to follow than those of certain other Baroque composers. As for his 'unskilfulness' in Italian, this is of course wittily figurative, referring as it does to music rather than the written and spoken idiom. Far too much has been made of 'the unhappiness of his Education' – not a reference to miserable schooldays or inadequate teaching, simply an accepted *façon de parler* of the period, in which the creative artist modestly deprecates his skills at the outset so as to ambush us with his brilliance later on.

The fact is that these dozen sonatas were a selection from a larger number already written. In 1697, two years after Purcell's death, his widow Frances issued a collection entitled *Ten Sonatas of IV Parts*, which must naturally have led to the assumption that they had been composed as a separate set, possibly at a later period in his career. As it happens, they are not in four parts but three, since, as with sonatas by Colista and his Italian contemporaries, the two bass parts, for viol and keyboard continuo, are only semi-independent of one another, and the same is true of Purcell's 1683 set. The 1697 group represents no obvious change or development in their composer's style, apart from some overall revision. The impression that they were in fact written around the same time as the earlier sonatas is borne out by an autograph in the British Library in which all or part of at least eight of these so-called later works appear, with the superscription in his own hand on the title page 'The Work of Hen. Purcell Anno Dom. 1680'. Thus they may actually have been written before some of the 1683 *Sonnata's*, and what was issued in that year probably represented a deliberately Italianate selection from a remarkable outpouring of works in the trio sonata medium.

What needs stressing in any discussion of these finely wrought pieces is the flexibility of this medium at the time when Purcell started experimenting with it. Those who love trio sonatas will be familiar with them in their more strictly organized late Baroque and Rococo forms, as practised by composers like Telemann, Quantz and Fasch, or in the early Berlin trios of C. P. E. Bach and the works his father Johann Sebastian designed in the same form for organ. In the late seventeenth century, however, the expectations of performers would have been altogether less clear-cut. Although the differentiation was already being made between the *sonata da chiesa* – literally 'church sonata' appropriate for sacred use, with its solemn opening and fugal allegro – and the *sonata da camera*, 'chamber sonata', incorporating dance movements and somewhat lighter in mood, there was still considerable latitude in the interpretation of certain tempo markings and the disposition of the various sections. Purcell's trios tend to look more like the musical equivalent of those Pindaric odes so beloved of his poetic contemporaries than scrupulously defined sequences. In their intervening pauses we might imagine performers taking time to re-tune, or, if it were a music meeting among convivial friends, sipping a glass of Frontiniac, Montalchin or any of the other vintages popular with that deep-drinking age.

Purcell organized his 1683 sonatas according to a series of pairs, a minor key followed by a relative major, and in both this and the 1697 set, whose first two sonatas probably belong to this key pattern as originally planned, unity is imposed by a whole variety of devices within the musical texture itself. The sixth sonata of 1697, for example, takes the form of a chaconne, a stately dance originating in Spain – *chacón* is the root word – which uses a ground bass as an armature upon which to construct a set of variations in the upper parts. This was a favourite building material with great Baroque musical architects like Bach, whose massive exemplar for unaccompanied violin is among his most awe-inspiring achievements, and Handel, whose voluminous output of keyboard music during his early years includes several extended essays in the genre. For Purcell, to whose creative imagination ground bass issued a perennial challenge, the chaconne never lost its allure – he had already composed the splendid G minor essay in the form, for the royal string band, and as late as *The Fairy Queen* in 1692 we find him busy mining fresh possibilities. In this particular trio sonata he flourishes a dazzling array of rhythmic alternations, Italianate echo passages and exuberant semiquaver cascades to create an irresistible momentum.

Elsewhere the binding mechanism might arrive in the form of a canon, as in the sixth 1683 sonata, with the recapitulation of opening themes in the closing movement of the work, a feature of at least two of the earlier set. Above all, especially in the Italianate *canzona* episodes, unity was created by a running together of different themes in invertible counterpoint, balanced against each other with the utmost skill by a series of protean transformations, whether in their note values or in cunning changes to their formal combination. The idiom throughout both sets, however, studiously avoids linking itself too obviously with one particular style. These are sonatas for both professional and amateur musicians, so there is little obvious emphasis on virtuosity, even in the more 'brisk' semiquaver passages of the canzonas. Though Purcell's preface makes a selling point of the Italian manner, features like the deliberate rallentando with the word 'drag' written in the score and the use of festive popular dance rhythms are distinctively English, while the fifth 1697 sonata's dotted adagio opening is markedly French. Each of the two collections is a witness to the composer's extraordinary attentiveness to even the most nugatory detail of musical architecture and to the seriousness of his creative ambition. The irony is that these pieces should have had to wait until our own century to earn the admiration due to them.

The sonata was not the only instrumental form in which Purcell had sought to prove himself during the early 1680s, that major experimental phase in his artistic career. Scholarship remains uncertain as to exactly why, during 1679 and 1680, he should have sat down to compose two groups of fantasias in the viol consort tradition practised earlier in the century by Lawes, Jenkins and Locke. Even before the Restoration the viol as a favoured instrument among sociable amateurs of the kind portrayed in the writings of Roger North was passing out of fashion, yielding ground to the violin, so perhaps these 'fancies' of Purcell's were no more than musical exercises in various aspects of compositional technique, tinged with recollection of his close study of the contrapuntal styles of English and Italian masters from the early 1600s.

Yet these thirteen string fantasias, most of them dating from July and August 1680, are anything but dry academic exercises, and for many to whom the less abstract, more personal and pictorial aspects of his music say nothing in particular, they act as a kind of guarantee that Purcell comprehended the true science underlying his artistic métier. Even if the fantasias inevitably recall the works by Locke or Orlando Gibbons over which he had been studiously poring, their originality establishes itself straight away,

whether in the amazing variety of technical devices – augment-
ation, inversion, double and triple counterpoint, dazzling games
with rhythm and structure – or in the thrillingly unpredictable
character which individualizes each piece.

There is absolutely nothing formulaic or prescriptive in Purcell's
approach to their layout. The four-part G minor fantasia, for
example, contrasts a solemn, learned opening with a middle section
sounding like a theatre curtain tune and a final episode in the
manner of an overture allegro. Nos 7 and 8 in C minor and D
minor, written on the 19th and 22nd June respectively, appear to
grow out of one another, the first marked by astonishing angular
dissonances introducing a sequence of cunningly interlocked episodes, the second a child of its predecessor in the form of a French
overture. Taken together, these and their companions, including
the humorous five-part fantasia 'upon one note', represent one
of the more startling moments in the history of chamber music.

It has been suggested that the one-note fantasia may have been
designed to incorporate an unskilful amateur in a friendly music
meeting. Purcell had strong feelings regarding at least one member
of the viol family, as is related by Sir John Hawkins, who was
friendly with the son of the composer's great bass soloist John
Gostling. 'The Reverend Mr Sub-dean Gostling, a practitioner on
the viol da gamba [was] not more delighted than Purcell was
disgusted, with the tones of that instrument. The composer, to
gratify some little pique, engaged a certain poetaster to write the
following mock eulogium on the viol, which he set in the form of
a round for three voices:

> Of all the instruments that are,
> None with the Viol can compare.
> Mark how the strings their order keep,
> With a whet, whet, whet and a sweep, sweep, sweep.
> But above all this still abounds,
> With a zingle, zingle, zingle and a zit, zan zounds!'

Whatever his distaste for the viola da gamba, Purcell was busy,
during this same period, with yet more compositions for string
ensemble, some perhaps directly related to his function as a court
musician. To around 1680 belongs the much admired G minor

Chacony, in which the energy is largely generated by the work's continuous wavering between its ostensible role as dance music and a loftier excursion into the English fantasia style. Often assigned to these years, though perhaps written later in the decade, is the noble *Overture à 5* for two violins, two violas and bass, reflecting a continental influence in the scoring. Most beautiful of all his individual works outside the sonatas and fantasias is surely the piece entitled in the manuscript score *3 parts upon a Ground*, which may date from as early as 1678. Though on the same score there is a written indication that the music, in D major for three violins and continuo, can be played in F by recorders, the particular string combination proposed was well loved by Restoration musicians, and this pseudo-chaconne sounds very well in the hands of an able trio of versatile 'fideldedies', as Charles II called them. All the contrapuntal skill of the fantasias is channelled into the part-writing as the music swirls and rockets resistlessly towards its grave, authoritative close, marked 'drag' in true old English consort style, to which Purcell's ingenuity brings a novel sophistication.

Even by contemporary standards, Purcell's dedication of the 1683 sonatas to King Charles seems more than usually subservient and self-abasing:

> I had not assum'd the confidence of laying ye following compositions at your sacred feet; but that (as they are the immediate results of your Majesties royall favour, and benignity to me, which have made me what I am) so I am constrain'd to hope I may presume, amongst others of your Majesties ever-obliged and altogether undeserving subjects, that your Majesty will with your accustom'd clemency, vouchsafe to pardon the best endeavours of your Majesties's most humble and obedient subject and servant H. Purcell.

Benjamin Disraeli's celebrated observation made in connection with a later English monarch, that with royalty it was necessary to lay on flattery with a trowel, might have applied with equal justice to Charles II. The image of the sovereign, in this case often so different from actuality, was promoted in the form of state portraits, sculptures and medallions, in the poetry of the court

odes or even in so intellectually sophisticated a work as Dryden's
Absalom and Achitophel, as that of a magnanimous, provident,
visionary Roman Emperor, 'great Caesar', the father of his people,
enjoying a special relationship with the Divine Power.

There may, however, have been more serious reasons behind
Purcell's commending his sonatas to the King, as opposed to
dedicating them to one of the aristocratic dilettanti to whose
children he gave lessons or with whom he was invited to make
music. Shadowed by the hysteria of the Popish Plot and the so-
called Exclusion Crisis, the early 1680s, during which he first made
his mark as a composer, were years when nobody, whatever their
work or the tenor of their life, could avoid scrutiny on the basis
of political allegiance. The lines of 'for' and 'against' were more
strongly drawn than at any time since the beginning of the Civil
War, and the direct result of this ruthless politicization was the
emergence of the party political system by which modern democ-
racies are, for better or worse, nowadays organized.

No one living and working in London during those stormy final
decades of the seventeenth century, so crucial for the formation of
a British political and social culture whose outlines we now take
for granted, could sidestep the challenge of loyalty to one or other
of the conflicting interests. In the closing years of Charles II's
reign these were far less ambiguous than they were to become
during the reigns of his immediate successors James II and William
and Mary. On the one hand stood the loyal defenders of the
restored Stuart monarchy, endowed with its dispensing power over
Parliament and the great offices of state, and supported by the
Church of England whose bishops and deans it appointed. Against
these staunch conservatives, their loyalties rooted in an inheritance
of Civil War royalism, were those for whom a memory of Charles
I's overweening absolutism and threats to the liberty of the subject
vested in Parliament were still vivid, and for whom the Restoration
settlement, with a slippery, foreign-educated king at the head of a
loyal government, offered no real improvement.

The Popish Plot, with its religious scaremongering, saw an
inevitable stiffening of the battle lines. Catholics, who had assumed
a far higher profile in England with the marriages of Charles to
Catherine of Bragança and James to Mary of Modena, aligned

themselves naturally with the court party and its adherents. Nonconformist Protestants, penalized by the draconian acts passed against them through the agency of triumphalist Anglican clergy at the beginning of the reign, and in many cases genuinely nostalgic for 'the good old cause' and a non-monarchical government, supported the Earl of Shaftesbury and the Duke of Monmouth and gave full credence to the wilder flights of Oates's grotesque fancy. The increasing virulence of faction led to both sides, by the early months of 1680, calling each other insulting names, which were to stick side by side for the next two hundred years and one of which is still with us. Those who wanted the King to accept the will of Parliament, and indeed anyone suspected of anti-monarchical or anti-episcopalian sentiment, were called Whigs, from the word 'whiggamore' which the Scots had given to their Covenanting rebels the previous year, while the supporters of a church-and-king establishment were nicknamed Tories, after Catholics who had turned bandits during the Irish revolt of 1641.

Given the nature of his official position as a court functionary and somebody whose professional life brought him into frequent contact with members of the royal family and those closest to them, Purcell could scarcely have sided openly with the Whigs and is far more likely during this period to have demonstrated Tory sympathies. He was in regular contact, what is more, with Catholic musicians such as Draghi and the countertenor John Abell, for whom he had written parts in the court odes, and had also been associated with Matthew Locke, a Papist convert. We can scarcely wonder, therefore, that at a time when either side was morbidly preoccupied with sifting everybody from lords to labourers in order to assess their political soundness, Purcell's own allegiances should have been subjected to a routine examination.

In 1672, fired with anti-Popish zeal, Parliament had passed the infamous Test Act, which required all public office-holders to take oaths acknowledging the King as the supreme head of the Church of England and declaring loyalty to him in that capacity. The immediate result of this, connived at by Shaftesbury and his proto-Whig adherents, was the resignation, from their respective positions as Admiral of the Fleet and influential privy counsellor, of James, Duke of York and his Catholic co-religionist, the ambitious but undeniably able Thomas, Lord Clifford.

Public affirmation of unyielding constancy in Protestant principles – more specifically Anglican articles of belief, centred on the royal authority as ultimate arbiter in ecclesiastical matters – was demanded and proclaimed with ever-growing frequency as the decade progressed. By 1683 Charles's skilful manoeuvres, some of them involving a ruthless sacrifice of those most faithful to him, had defused the xenophobic hysteria of the Popish Plot, so that as Evelyn reported, 'Papists began to hold up their heads higher than ever, and those who had fled, flocked to London from abroad'. Even so, the formality of subjecting court servants and municipal office-holders to strict scrutiny of their Protestantism persisted, and on 4 February 1683 Purcell took holy communion in front of witnesses at the church of St Margaret's, Westminster. The document attesting the ceremony was signed by the vicar Bartholomew Wormell and a churchwarden named Giles Burrowdell, who certified, on 16 April following, in one of the law courts held at Westminster Hall, that 'Mr Henry Pursal ... after divine service and sermon, did in the parish church aforesaid receive the sacrament of the Lord's Supper according to the usage of the Church of England'. Their testimony was backed by two further witnesses, one of whom, Moses Snow, was a fellow musician in the royal household.

Was Purcell suspected of Popery, or was he indeed, as has sometimes been hinted, a crypto-Catholic? Apart from his professional links with foreign musicians and an interest in Italian and French music, there is not a shred of evidence to support the latter possibility. Until a secret cache of Marian antiphons, the odd 'Salve Regina' or a stray 'Ave Maria' come to light, the proof of his firmly grounded Protestantism must rest in the anthems and more intimate devotional works he composed, which, to anyone with the least awareness of seventeenth-century Anglican spirituality, bespeak an intensity and a commitment which would surely not have been present had he inclined towards Rome. Though his wife Frances came from a Catholic family, though an early setting of *Beati Omnes* is, as we have seen, a candidate for a wedding anthem, and though the exact circumstances in which *Jehovah*

Quam Multi Sunt Hostes was written remain obscure, the notion of Purcell as a thoroughgoing cynic, dashing off such superb effusions as *Who Hath Believed Our Report?*, *O All Ye People*, *My Beloved Spake* or *Remember Not, Lord, Our Offences* in total insincerity before rushing away to mass or confession at a Catholic chapel is, to this biographer at least, both laughable and intolerable.

The intriguing alternative is that far from being less of a Protestant, he might have been too much of one. We have already marked the fascination of the metrical psalm settings written for the Charterhouse, which seem to probe towards a deeper, more sombre level of religious meditation than the world of ceremonial rejoicing, its texts sometimes decidedly propagandistic, reflected in the anthems. In this same context a closer look at the works published in Henry Playford's *Harmonia Sacra* collections of 1688 and 1693, which include such masterpieces as *Saul and the Witch at Endor*, *Lord, What Is Man?* and *Awake Ye Dead*, must surely reveal the intellectual sophistication and integrity of Purcell's spiritual outlook. A composition such as *Tell Me, Some Pitying Angel* (entitled *The Blessed Virgin's Expostulation* in the original print) is not specifically Marian in a Catholic sense, though as a dramatic scena it alludes plainly to the world of contemporary Italian oratorio dominated by the figures of Carissimi and Stradella, both of whom had their influence on Purcell. The drama of the work is distinctively Purcellian, rather than the result of a conscious effort to puff wafts of Romish incense into English private devotions. It is significant that in the collection of 1693 where this was first published – a collection dedicated to Henry Aldrich, Dean of Christ Church and a pillar of the Anglican establishment – Playford included music by Carissimi, ostensibly to flatter Aldrich's musical taste but perhaps also to set up a stylistic comparison in which the English would not necessarily be the losers.

A far more convincing explanation than ideas of Purcell as a closet Papist or a late-flowering Puritan is the perfectly simple one that in a time of unrestrained name-calling and political denunciation, it was necessary for those in the public eye, such as a Chapel Royal organist and composer for the violins in the King's Private Musick, to proclaim loyalty openly as faithful servants of the crown and communicant members of the established church.

Thus the dedication of the 1683 trio sonatas may be viewed as a kind of pendant to the sacrament-taking at St Margaret's. Obsequious as all the talk of 'sacred feet', 'undeserving subjects' and 'accustom'd clemency' may appear to us now, it was a perfectly acceptable seventeenth-century mode of pledging service – to a master who, in any case, felt that sort of humbleness was due to him as a matter of course.

Purcell need not have worried that his star was in danger of eclipse at court. In the same summer season of 1683 that the *Sonnatas of III Parts* appeared, he received the commission for another congratulatory ode, this time to mark the wedding of the Duke of York's younger daughter Anne to Prince George of Denmark. The eighteen-year-old princess, noted neither for beauty nor accomplishment, had been talked of at various stages as a prospective bride for the Dauphin of France, the Grand Duke of Tuscany and the Electoral Prince of Hanover, and an attempt on her virtue had been made by the dashing if decidedly mature Lord Mulgrave, who was posted to the English garrison at Tangier for his pains. When a husband was found for her, the choice was based largely on his Lutheran Protestantism and the important consideration that the match would not offend the French King, whose navy was currently backing Denmark in a war with Sweden.

'He had the Danish countenance, blond, of few words, spake French but ill, seemed somewhat heavy, but reported to be valiant, and indeed he had bravely rescued and brought off his brother, the King of Denmark in a battle against the Swedes, when both these Kings were engaged very smartly.' John Evelyn's verdict here was tactful but fair. The Prince made an ideal consort, gave his wife eighteen pregnancies (of which thirteen were miscarriages) lived a blameless life and showed no sort of distinction whatever. King Charles, who famously observed, 'I have tried him drunk and I have tried him sober and can find nothing in him', advised the bridegroom to walk with him, hunt with the Duke of York and 'do justice' on the Princess. Anne's sister Mary, now married to William, Prince of Orange, and doubtless aware that the latest family wedding was designed to set the seal on a commercial treaty between England and Denmark, was suitably realistic in commenting on the union. 'You may believe 'twas no small joy to me to hear she liked him,' she wrote from Holland to a friend, 'and I hope she will do so every day more & more for else I am sure she can't love him & without that 'tis impossible to be happy, which I wish her with all my heart.' Lord Mulgrave's judgment on George was the cruellest of all. Hearing him reported as being asthmatic, he said it was just as well, since at least people noticing him gasping for breath would know he was actually a live human being.

The wedding ceremony took place on 28 July in the Chapel Royal at St James's, with Henry Compton, Bishop of London, presiding and in the presence of the King, the Duke of York, the bride's stepmother Mary of Modena and a throng of courtiers. As part of the festivities, Purcell's ode *From Hardy Climes and Dangerous Toils of War* was presumably performed that same evening. Once again we have no indication of the poem's authorship, and once more the level of invention rarely transcends cliché. (Connoisseurs of official verse will be reminded here of Lord Tennyson's similarly uninspired address, two centuries later, to another Danish consort, Princess Alexandra, arriving to marry Albert Edward, Prince of Wales.) George of Denmark is greeted as a battle-hardened hero, but the anonymous poet slyly hints at a difficulty in finding very much else to say about him:

> As Fame, Great Sir, before you ran
> And told her story ere you came,
> But falter'd as she set it forth,
> For who can reach immortal worth:
> So doubtless back again she flew
> To paint the beauties now you view.

Purcell sets this as a sturdy tenor solo, leading seamlessly into a duet for two sopranos, the whole number rounded off by one of the extended string ritornelli which are the distinguishing pleasure of this elegant little wedding garland, in which his knack of transforming verbal pinchbeck into something of far greater value in musical terms is aptly displayed. The inevitable ground-bass air, without which Purcellians would feel cheated, is given to the tenor in 'The Sparrow and the Gentle Dove', and here the ritornello, as elsewhere in pieces of this kind, is cunningly spun from the thread of the initial accompaniment. Alas, all Purcell's magic art was unavailing in the cause of making the somewhat coarsely articulated prophecy in the closing chorus come true:

> So shall the race from your great loins to come
> Prove future Kings and Queens of Christendom.

Only one of Anne and George's offspring survived infancy, the little Duke of Gloucester, himself the dedicatee of a Purcell ode eleven years later, and even he was doomed to die aged only nine.

As a composer for court ceremonial, Purcell was soon called upon once more to furnish an appropriate piece for a royal occasion, this time the commemoration of the King's delivery from the attempt on his life which was intended as the culminating stroke of the Rye House Plot. Unlike the Popish Plot, which ranks as one of the most elaborate and dangerous hoaxes ever perpetrated in the name of political ambition and religious bigotry, the two conspiracies hatched against the royal family earlier in 1683 were wholly genuine. Their outlines, disclosed in June to the horrified Charles at Windsor by a messenger despatched from London with evidence from the eternally faithful and hardworking Secretary of State Sir Leoline Jenkins, revealed a monstrous design for a *coup d'état* to dismantle the fabric of the government.

One of the plot's two arms aimed at assassinating the King and the Duke of York at Rye House in Essex on their return from Newmarket races. The ringleaders were a disreputable band of former Cromwellian officers, led by an inveterate agitator, a Scottish ex-clergyman named Robert Ferguson. Another, less violent scheme was masterminded by a group of Whig aristocrats including the republican intellectual Algernon Sidney, the louche Lord Grey of Werke, recently involved in a scandalous bid to kidnap an heiress, and the highminded William Lord Russell, eldest son of the Earl of Bedford. They planned to infiltrate the recently created Guards regiments, to take the King prisoner and to raise rebellions in Scotland and the West Country.

The collapse of the double plot was due partly to informers and partly to the sudden flight into Holland of the Earl of Shaftesbury, inevitably embroiled in the conspiracy. The whole scheme was thrown into greater confusion by the King's premature return from Newmarket that spring, owing to a fire which devastated the town – one of a whole series of civic conflagrations (Warwick and Northampton being other notable casualties) sweeping across England during this period, in sinister coincidental mimicry of London's memorable burning in 1666. As the conspirators were rounded up, the Duke of Monmouth, once more the figurehead of Whig scheming, was faced with a choice between giving evidence against his friends and supporters and going into exile. He chose the latter and followed Shaftesbury to Holland, but it was obvious to everyone that sooner or later he would return, to be the darling once again of radical Whigs and disaffected Protestants.

Two of the leading plotters were given high-profile executions. Algernon Sidney went to the scaffold with characteristically philosophic composure, and Russell too met his death in a suitably gentlemanlike fashion, spared the ultimate indignity proposed for him by the vindictive Duke of York, of being beheaded in front of his own house in the Strand. Both men swiftly entered the Whig martyrology, a destiny denied to their unfortunate fellow conspirator Arthur Capel, Earl of Essex, a capable politician who had lost the King's favour by pressing too hard for the Exclusion Bill. After three days as a prisoner in the Tower he had asked for a razor, retired to a latrine and cut his throat:

> Yet it was wondered by some how it was possible he should do it in the manner he was found, for the wound was so deep and wide that being cut through the gullet, wind-pipe and both the jugulars it reached to the very vertebrae of the neck, so that the head held to it by a very little skin as it were . . . an executioner could hardly have done more with an axe.

The effect of the Rye House Plot's discovery was to crush the Whig opposition, rehabilitate the Duke of York, and generate an immense wave of public sympathy for the King, who was plunged into gloom at having to send his wayward but always beloved Monmouth into exile. There was a universal feeling of revulsion at the national crisis which had so narrowly been avoided, and the government lost no opportunity to remind people of the scale of the treason planned. After an official statement outlining the details of the plot had been read to church congregations on Sunday, 2 September, a day of public thanksgiving for the King's deliverance was ordained a week later, and it was presumably around this time that Purcell's ode *Fly, Bold Rebellion* was given its first performance.

Ironically, though the poem (author once again unknown) is of a higher quality than some of the other ode texts and has the distinction of actually being about something – in this case, the preservation of the King's life and the destruction of the plot – Purcell's approach to the business of lifting the words off the ground is notably half-hearted. In the central sections of the work, the bass and tenor solos, 'If then we've found the want of his rays', the trio, 'But Heaven has now dispelled his fears', and the ensuing excursion into political rhetoric, 'Come then, change your notes, disloyal crowd', the music simply responds to the pedestrian character of the verses. The composer's inability to transcend the rhythmic plod of successive lines seems almost un-Purcellian. In the midst of the tenor's

> But Kings, like the sun, sometimes have their clouds
> To make them shine more bright,
> Their greatness exhales the vapour that shrouds
> And seeks to eclipse their light

with its inert repetitions of a not especially animated vocal line, we can almost hear Purcell wondering what on earth to do with his material. Even the alto ground, 'Be welcome then, great Sir', is more routinely attractive than genuinely heart-stopping. This is none of it bad music, but from Henry Purcell we have a right to expect better.

In this respect, the musicians who gathered on 22 November 1683 to celebrate the Feast of St Cecilia were more highly favoured than the King. Who exactly constituted 'the Musical Society' to whom the ode *Welcome to All the Pleasures* was dedicated we do not know, but the names of the four stewards 'for the year ensuing' include Francis Forcer and Nicholas Staggins, Purcell's professional colleagues, together with his former schoolfellow, the lawyer Gilbert Dolben, and the leading civil servant William Bridgeman. Both the latter were enthusiastic Purcellians: Dolben had already secured manuscript copies of certain of the court odes and songs, while Bridgeman was an early amateur performer of the trio sonatas.

Quite when the St Cecilia celebrations began to be held is unclear, but 1683 may well have witnessed the first such 'musick feast'. Ten years later it had become well enough established in the London calendar for Peter Motteux in *The Gentleman's Journal* to write: 'On that day or the next, when it falls on a Sunday, as it did last time, most of the lovers of music, whereof many are persons of the first rank, meet at Stationers' Hall in London, not thro' a principle of superstition, but to propagate that divine science. A splendid entertainment is provided, and before it is always a performance of music by the best voices and hands in town; the words, which are always in the patroness's praise, are set by some of the greatest masters . . . This feast is one of the genteelest in the world.'

In Playford's published edition of the ode, Purcell concludes his dedication to 'the Gentlemen of the Musical Society' with the assertion that 'he is to all Lovers of Music, A real Friend and Servant'. *Welcome to All the Pleasures* amply bears this out. The poem, by Christopher Fishburn, himself a composer of songs, is more than adequate to the occasion's demands, and Purcell's musical response is characteristically warm and brilliant. The invertible counterpoint of the introductory string sinfonia acts as a sort of professional *carte de visite*, but his first hearers, at Stationers' Hall or elsewhere, must have been equally struck by the stalking beauty of the alto ground 'Here the deities approve' and by the skilful disposition of the final chorus 'In a consort of voices', in which, over an insistent tonic chord, the four vocal parts fade away in succession on the words 'Iô Cecilia' (on the 'Farewell Symphony' principle) leaving the basses very quietly to finish off the piece.

Two other works are often attached to these early St Cecilia celebrations, both of them, however, on a somewhat smaller scale. *Laudate Ceciliam*, described by Purcell as 'a Latine song . . . made in the year 1683', has a far more self-consciously religious slant to its text, with references to the 'Ecclesia sanctorum' and 'gloria Domus Dei', as well as allusions to the Holy Martyrs and the Bride of Christ. So could it have formed part of a morning service before the 'splendid entertainment', or was it given, as some have implied, at a comparable festivity in one of the two universities of Oxford and Cambridge? In either context, Purcell's employment of 'white' note-heads in writing out his score was just one of many features of this piece designed to accentuate its Italian character, powerfully influenced by the numinous genius of Giacomo Carissimi, to whose work so many younger composers in late seventeenth century Europe turned for inspiration.

Another ode, *Raise, Raise the Voice*, to anonymous English words, not necessarily connected with St Cecilia, is really not much larger than a brief cantata, but Purcell's deftness in expanding the textures by giving independent parts to the violins as accompaniment to a trio of soloists gives vibrant life to this elegant little work, which manages to incorporate a most engaging ground bass number, 'Mark how readily each pliant string'. Here the soprano solo transmutes into a chorus, followed by an extended string ritornello, before the ode ends with an unpretentious choral coda.

The winter of 1683 and early 1684 was one of those harsh seasons of extreme cold which caused many during the late seventeenth century to believe that the world was in a sort of old age, developing the telluric equivalent of grey hair, and that the Judgment Day was not far off. Echoes of this are to be heard in some of the poems chosen by composers for musical setting at this time, such as Dryden's 'Song for St Cecilia's Day', 'From Harmony, from Heavn'ly Harmony', in the climactic paradoxes of its closing section:

> So when the last and dreadful hour
> This crumbling Pageant shall devour,
> The trumpet shall be heard on high,
> The Dead shall live, the Living die
> And Musick shall untune the Sky,

or the hair-raisingly apocalyptic Cowley ode 'Awake and with attention hear', which Purcell set in 1688.

Gloomy forebodings as to the possible fate of the planet as the century's close approached would have been deepened by the frosty January which overtook London in 1684. The river Thames iced over so hard that whole streets of temporary shops were set up on the frozen surface, and it became possible to drive coaches from one bank to the other. At the famous Frost Fair a printing press was established, where customers might purchase little certificates with their names printed, accompanied by the words 'Printed on the river of Thames being frozen' with the exact date. From this one enterprise the printer apparently made the not inconsiderable sum of £5 a day. Besides this, there were 'sleds, sliding with skates, a bull-baiting, horse and coach-races, puppet-plays and interludes, cooks, tippling, and other lewd places, so that it seemed to be a bacchanalian triumph or carnival on the water, whilst it was a severe judgment on the land'. Fires made with Newcastle 'sea-coal' created a thick smog cloud over the city, and so many frozen pipes and conduits made it impossible for businesses depending on a regular water supply to sustain the normal rhythms of work.

One of those whose trade had suffered during the cold weather was the younger John Playford, a partner with his brother Henry in their father's music publishing firm. Though the son's name appears on the title page of *Choyce Ayres and Songs to Sing to the Theorbo-Lute or Bass-viol*, it was Playford senior who wrote the preface. Introducing the collection, which was issued in the new year, he pleaded with 'all lovers and understanders of musick' that 'this fifth book of new songs and ayres had come sooner (by three months) to your hands, but the last dreadful frost put an embargo upon the press for more than ten weeks', but admitted that he had been somewhat reluctant to publish the book anyway. His motive in finally doing so, he claimed, was 'to prevent my friends and country men from being cheated with such false wares as is daily published by ignorant and mercenary persons who put musical notes over their songs, but neither minding time nor right places turn harmony into discord'. He was getting old, too old, he declared, to be able to supervise the careful printing of the various songs, which he now entrusted to the younger John and to Richard Carr, son of the book's printer, 'my self engaging to be assisting to them in overseeing the press for the future, that what songs they make public be good and true musick, both for the credit of the authors and to the content and satisfaction of the buyers'.

These satisfied buyers, in purchasing this latest set of *Choyce Ayres and Songs*, could sample seven of Purcell's songs, though they would have found him just as well represented in two of the earlier volumes, testifying to his growing reputation as a composer who could rise to the challenge of any sort of text, lofty or light-hearted. His achievements in the form throughout the early 1680s amply justify his claim to be considered the greatest writer of 'single songs' in the two hundred years before the ascendancy of Franz Schubert in this form. No other master, throughout the seventeenth and eighteenth centuries, could boast his catholicity of style or expressive range within the genre, and none in that time so avidly exploited its microcosmic possibilities, harnessing brevity and seeming slenderness of resource to encompass states of being in astounding diversity.

To these crucial years belong such negligently charming trifles as 'Amintor, heedless of his flock', with its erotic double edge, or the agreeable little 'He himself courts his own ruin', a sardonic meditation on what women really want from men. Pieces of more substantial architecture show Purcell continuing his experiments with recitative in the creation of small, cantata-like structures. Among these latter is another of his various settings of the ever-popular Abraham Cowley, 'No, to what purpose should I speak', in which the increasing emotional pitch of the poem, a monologue by a hopeless lover weighing up his chances, is matched by the music's shift from a declamatory opening to a sombre arioso, followed by a more dramatic episode which ends with a mocking chorus:

> Then she herself, the mighty she,
> Shall grace my fun'rals with this truth;
> 'Twas only Love destroy'd the gentle youth.

Still freer in its treatment of the text is 'Amidst the shades and cool refreshing streams', where the singer enacts the fluttering and warbling of the birds trying to cheer 'poor Damon' and the predominant A minor implies that their efforts are quite in vain.

Purcell and his admirers were evidently fond of this gloomier

mood as a background to solo songs, the more so perhaps because of the chance it offered for the kind of tragic female monologue currently so popular on the Continent with French and Italian cantata composers. 'Beneath a dark and melancholy grove', dating from 1681, affords a typical example, based as it is on a lament by the Greek poetess Sappho, mourning the loss of her lover, 'thou charming dear, thou better soul of mine', a young girl who, she claims, was as good a poet and musician as herself. The anonymous translater has imagined Sappho and her inamorata as accomplished young Restoration ladies – one line tells us that 'my harpsichord and lute have long been mute' – but Purcell's lovely, ardent setting, snatching at every cue for musical illustration, has a timeless eloquence which makes this one of his most impressive early songs.

The best-known of his dramatic pieces from this repertoire requires us to imagine the singer as being gripped by total insanity. 'From silent shades', subtitled 'Bess of Bedlam', is not only interesting for its theatricality, at a time when Purcell was only marginally involved with the stage, but also for its subject. Madness was invariably fascinating to the men and women of the seventeenth century, partly because it was so little understood, and also because it seemed to some to present a glimpse of another world, exotic by virtue of its disdain for that rationality to which the contemporary ethos increasingly clung. Dryden's famous lines:

> Great wits are sure to madness near allied
> And thin partitions do their bounds divide

may have achieved cliché status since they were written, but their implication for Purcell's age was serious enough. 'From silent shades', the ranting of a love-crazed woman, is remarkable enough as a mad scene to rival anything by Donizetti or Bellini, but its authenticity is the stronger for the way in which the music replicates our unease in reacting both to the imagined situation's comic potential and to its genuine pathos.

To his continuing exploration of the song medium Purcell added another type of composition, in which his teacher, friend and competitor John Blow was, as so often, the model. This was the so-called 'symphony song', in which voices and continuo were enriched with ritornelli for violins or a pair of recorders. These works seem to have been expensive to publish and most of Purcell's appear in manuscript only, but he obviously enjoyed composing them, since eight were written between 1681 and 1686, all markedly different in character, though their poetry in many cases is touched with a strong feeling for country life and the joys of spring. The most complex and skilful in organization is probably the last, 'If ever I more riches did desire', using a paraphrase by Cowley of some celebrated lines by the Roman dramatist Seneca lauding the joys of a humble retirement as 'an old plebeian' living 'wrapt in the arms of quiet'. Purcell cleverly sidles past the pitfalls of overmuch pomposity and stiffness in the poem's sentiments by alternating the disposition of his musical forces, a quartet of two sopranos, tenor and bass with a pair of violins and continuo, creating in the process one of his most rewarding small-scale works.

If, as is quite possible, some of the symphony songs were intended for court performance, did Cowley's poem answer some new impulse in the bosom of the aged Charles II? The King had begun building his own rural retreat, a palace near Winchester designed to become the English Versailles. The architect was Sir Christopher Wren, and though the work never got much beyond the drawing board, we can speculate tantalizingly on the magnificence of the project. It was for Charles's return in September, 1684, from a progress which included a visit to the intended Winchester palace site that Purcell composed the welcome song *From Those Serene and Rapturous Joys*, to words by Thomas Flatman, a miniature painter, lawyer and Fellow of the Royal Society with a genuine gift for verse, whose fondness for music had earlier been expressed in a poem on Pelham Humfrey's death and a lively eulogy of the Italian song-writer Pietro Reggio.

There is a cheerful urbanity about Purcell's music which makes this one of his most engaging early essays in the form. Regardless of the inequality in status between king and composer, the tone here is one of civilized condescension, one gentleman welcoming another to his native element while conceding that the country has its pleasures. The opening symphony is particularly persuasive in this respect, as is the discursive alto solo which follows it, not to speak of John Gostling's bass air 'Welcome as soft, refreshing showers' and an exceptionally fine tenor ground, 'Welcome, more welcome does he come', somewhat blasphemously invoking Christ's raising of Lazarus. Throughout, the chorus, though the writing in some of its interventions seems here and there a little crude, is closely integrated with the solo items, and the string ritornelli grow out of these various numbers with the rich abundance of those swags of fruit and flowers carved at this very same period by the enchanted hand of Grinling Gibbons.

Given the financial embarrassments of the crown earlier in the reign, the notion of building an entirely new palace at Winchester on the grandest scale may seem quixotic, indeed irresponsible, but the reality was that the royal resources were in considerably better shape during 1684–5 than they had been for some time. There was no danger of an expensive foreign war, the economy was in good heart, the collection of taxes had been streamlined and the national debt dramatically reduced by half a million pounds. Hand in hand with these improvements went more efficient management of the royal household, and the 'trickle-down effect', to use a phrase beloved by modern free-marketeers, was felt among the musicians of the Chapel Royal and the Private Musick, who began for the first time to enjoy prompt payment of their salaries.

In the Chapel itself Purcell was as busy as ever with composing new anthems. In recent years he had concentrated almost exclusively on developing the 'symphony' form, and the period from 1681 onwards saw the production of several outstanding examples from his pen. Of course the genre dictated its own clichés, and a comparison of several anthem profiles from this time, whether by Purcell or other composers, establishes some of the more obvious, from the duple-time introduction to the opening symphony, followed almost invariably by a faster passage in a buoyant 3/4, to sequences of repetition and refrain and florid, declamatory solo sections calculated to display individual talents. Yet none of Purcell's anthems from this time suggest anything like a doodling or formulaic approach, and in an acceptable modern performance it is impossible for us to accuse him of mere attitudinizing.

Everywhere throughout these expansively designed works we feel him seeking to realize that ideal synthesis in which music and text achieve interdependence, so that there is never any sense of us knowing, from the outset, what profile the piece will adopt. This organic inspiration dominates *Why do the heathen so furiously rage together*, for example, in which the various theatrical elements, the trio representing 'the kings of the earth', the laughter of God embodied by the bass soloist, or the same singer's meditative exchange with a pair of tenors admonishing 'be wise now therefore', hang together by virtue of the composer's grip on the restless, unsettled character of the text.

The same principle applies *par excellence* in the most famous of all Purcell's anthems, composed as it was during this period, *Rejoice in the Lord Alway*, whose effectiveness is based on the insistent idea of rejoicing which the music, partly through repetition, drives home from its bell-like opening onwards. I cannot help wishing that organists and choirmasters might now be a trifle more imaginative in their choice of Purcellian repertoire and put *Rejoice in the Lord*, beautiful as it is, briefly to one side in favour of other symphony anthems from 1681–5. How about, for instance, the superb, blood-stirringly memorable *Awake, awake, put on thy strength*, one of his most original sacred works? The imaginative impetus was probably given, as in other cases throughout his career, by John Blow, certain features of whose own symphony anthems Purcell here adopted, including the use of a fugal fast section at the beginning instead of the regulation dotted minuet. Shades of contrast are cleverly deployed in the trio 'Therefore the redeemed of the Lord', poignant and pensive after the exhilarating fanfare-like 'awake, awake's of the opening sections, but the real surprise of the piece is the elaboration, out of the fugue material of the symphony's reprise, of a ground bass over which the three singers eventually break into an Alleluia.

In nearly every symphony anthem of the fifteen or so which have been dated to this period, Purcell provided a flamboyant exhibition of John Gostling's phenomenal talent. Across the Purcellian cosmos the bass voice reverberates in echoes of divine power, wisdom, authority and unshakable truth. At least one among these works is nevertheless rooted in circumstances a little less abstract. King Charles, a great admirer of Gostling, decided to take him along on a boating trip down the Thames in a newly built yacht he had christened the *Fubbs*, after the nickname he gave his roly-poly mistress the Duchess of Portsmouth. Together with the Duke of York and others, they got as far as the North Foreland when a storm arose, and the two royal brothers (James, it may be recalled, had once been Lord High Admiral) had to 'hand the sails and work like common seamen'. Though they managed to come safely to shore, 'the distress they were in made an impression on the mind of Mr Gostling which was never effaced'. Once back in London, he besought Purcell to write an anthem on psalm texts associated with 'the wonders and terrors of the deep', and the result, *They that go down to the sea in ships*, was the most formidable display piece ever composed for this stellar performer.

To many it must have seemed as if the realm was now entering upon a halcyon season of High Tory calm, in which all opposition to the King's will had been effectively neutralized or suppressed. Even in places as far afield as New Jersey or the Bahamas the colonists, like borough corporations in England, had been compelled to accept new charters ensuring direct submission of the local government to royal authority. Charles himself, though heavily involved in the management of all public affairs, could enjoy a greater serenity in his private life among the extended family of mistresses and bastards at Whitehall, St James's, Windsor and Newmarket, surrounded by courtiers who assuaged his tendency to boredom. It came as a shock to the entire nation, therefore, when on 2 February 1685 he was laid low with the symptoms of a glandular kidney disease which, after four days of bleedings and poultices and 'the famous Jesuits' powder', carried him off at the comparatively youthful age of fifty-four.

His deathbed, perhaps the most publicized of any monarch between Elizabeth I and Queen Victoria, quickly became surrounded with an accretion of wish-fulfilling legend. Most significant of many telling details, since it became known almost immediately, was the King's reception, on the last night of his life, into the Roman Catholic church. The bringing to him of the last rites by John Hudlestone, a priest whom he had encountered during his famous escape after the Battle of Worcester in 1651, has been much discussed, and even at the time Catholics were eager to claim Charles as a secret adherent of the faith, carrying out a long premeditated plan. More sober and dispassionate historical assessments suggest that it was boredom rather than subversive irreverence which made him prefer his Chapel Royal services to be enlivened with sprightly symphonies played by neat-handed fiddlers or with vocal acrobatics from John Gostling. The King's spirituality was a good deal less deep-rooted than some of his other instincts, but the deathbed conversion was undoubtedly responsible for the somewhat hugger-mugger nature of the royal funeral, which took place in Westminster Abbey with very little pomp or publicity and apparently without the presence of the choir or the organists.

Baulked of a chance to commemorate his sovereign in a manner appropriate to that regal dignity on which Charles had always piqued himself, Purcell was nevertheless moved to compose a more intimate elegy for the man in whose service he had made his mark among English musicians, and with whom several of his most elaborate early works had been directly associated. The circumstances surrounding the mourning ode *If Pray'rs and Tears* are obscure. It was first published by Henry Playford three years after the composer's death, in the famous collection of his vocal music entitled *Orpheus Britannicus*, with the additional superscription 'Sighs for Our Late Sovereign King Charles'. Nothing is known as to a specific commission, and the author of the text remains anonymous. From the decidedly Anglican religious slant of the poem, we can safely assume that it was not written at the command of the new king, James II, whose openly avowed Catholicism now assumed a dangerously proselytizing zeal which soon proved his undoing. It may have been designed for performance at a concert or private music meeting of loyal Tory magnates, of the kind with whom Purcell was accustomed to play chamber music.

The expressive fervour of the unknown poet is nowhere in doubt. Though the irregularity of the lines, following the approved Pindaric model, was obviously intended to facilitate a flexible musical setting, their fragmentation effectively mirrors a universal grief.

> No sort of people could you meet
> But did devoutly bow,

And as devoutly pray'd;
   And yet no pharisaick hypocrites,
In corners with well-guided zeal
   Their orisons were made.

The tone of verses like these seems to hint that the author himself was a clergyman, and this implication is strengthened by the almost apocalyptic nature of the rest of the poem. Beginning with a vision of the Church of England defended only by the shields of prayer and tears, the writer invokes a doom-laden prospect of Charles's death opening up the possibility of religious conflict.

Albion is now become a holy land,
And wages holy war to stay the threat'ning hand.

Memories of ancient battles won solely by the force of prayer are summoned up, but for modern England to resort to such spiritual weaponry is shown to be in vain.

Alas! we'ld conquer too,
   But for our former crimes,
Treasons, rebellions, perjuries,
   With all the iniquities of the times . . .

With a final, sinisterly oblique allusion to 'the powers that strike the kingdom dead' and a parallel of the late sovereign with the righteous Josiah in the Old Testament, the ode accomplishes its bleak close.

What Purcell made of this portrayal of an imminent Protestant Armageddon can only be guessed at via the music itself, some of the most arid and sparely conceived he ever wrote. French adornment and Italian fancy work are evidently out of the question, and there is absolutely no appeal to virtuosity on the part of the singer. Still more striking is the almost complete absence of that element of musical word-painting which is such an obsessive trademark elsewhere in his work. *If Pray'rs and Tears* is emphatically not what we want our Purcell to be, and its lack of what the Germans call a 'grateful' element in the workmanship has condemned it to being one of his least frequently performed pieces.

There is, all the same, an inherent audacity in the ruthlessness with which it sustains a single vast declamatory paragraph. Once again, as in the case of the elegy for Matthew Locke, 'What hope for us remains', this is technically recitative, moving with the syntax and sentence structures of the text. But the seemingly aleatoric quality of the vocal line (its shifts from note to note persistently unpredictable), embodies, more than in the earlier work, a sense of grief and terror breaking down the order imposed by art. All that divides us from anarchy, the music seems to say, is the composer's gaunt hand guiding us from point to point across the score like a sighted man leading the blind. If it is to be performed at all effectively, this remarkable essay in the reductive and the scaled-down requires a degree of passion in the singer which will give authenticity to its world of sudden, overwhelming emptiness, an emptiness significantly unredeemed by any Christian promise in the text of rebirth and continuity.

Others besides Purcell and his unnamed poet had felt the same finality. Evelyn, in one of his most memorable paragraphs, written some days after the King's death, summed this up:

I can never forget the inexpressible luxury and profaneness, gaming, and all dissoluteness, and as it were total forgetfulness of God (it being Sunday evening) which this day se'nnight I was witness of, the King sitting and toying with his concubines, Portsmouth, Cleveland and Mazarine &c., a French boy singing love-songs in that glorious gallery, whilst about twenty of the great courtiers and other dissolute persons were at Basset round a large table, a bank of at least 2000 in gold before them; upon which two gentlemen who were with me made reflections, with astonishment. Six days after, was all in the dust.

4

Fools and Fanaticks

The coronation of the new king, James II, and his queen, Mary Beatrice, took place on St George's Day, 23 April 1685. For the royal couple it was a formality, since, as devout Catholics, they were both bound to lend more significance to the secret ceremony of anointing and crowning which had been conducted the previous night at the hands of the King's confessor Padre Mansueti in St James's Palace. For Protestant Londoners, on the other hand, it represented one of the most gorgeous and elaborately organized royal occasions in recent memory, far statelier and more magnificent even than the service which set the crown on Charles II's head in 1661. A special set of crown jewels was made for Mary Beatrice, and these, together with her purple velvet train and pearl-embroidered brocade robes, were reckoned to cost over £100,000. What with this and the magnificent banquet served in Westminster Hall, consisting of 1,445 different dishes, the vast crowds thronging the streets and the general popularity of the royal couple at this initial stage of what was soon to prove a thoroughly mismanaged and disastrous reign, the whole event could safely be judged a triumph. Music, Purcell's music especially, contributed significantly to its success.

Perhaps not surprisingly, it was Mary, rather than the tactless, high-handed James, who managed the more convincing show of devotion during the complicated ritual. With her typically Italian instinct for survival she knew how to please the Anglican clergy surrounding her in Westminster Abbey, and 'answered *Amen* to every prayer with much humility'. According to her brother the Duke of Modena's informant, 'she showed herself perfectly instructed in what she had to do, and acted throughout with great grace and composure'. James, on the contrary, failed to answer any of the responses and looked about with notable unconcern while kneeling beside her at the altar. Evidently he suffered no qualms at taking an oath he had not the slightest intention of keeping to defend the Church of England. Despite the various extremely ostentatious signs of Papist fervour the King had shown since his accession (mass had been celebrated in Whitehall Palace and a small community of English Benedictines established at St James's) the service followed the course prescribed for the crowning of a Protestant sovereign.

We know exactly what the coronation and many of its participants looked like to the crowds, thanks to a handsome set of plates issued in 1687 by Francis Sandford, present on the occasion in his official capacity as Lancaster Herald. All the royal musicians were mustered to walk in procession, where they came immediately behind the flower-women who, following the beadles clearing the way ahead with their staves, strewed the path of the richly clad cortège with nosegays and sweet herbs. Four side-drummers (one was named Devereux Clothier, another Tertullian Lewis) 'beat a march', then came the sixteen royal trumpeters, including Matthew Shore, for whose son John some of Purcell's most characteristic trumpet parts were to be written. There followed the choirs of Westminster Abbey and the Chapel Royal, divided by a trio of instrumentalists, two playing slide or 'flat' trumpets and one performing on the cornet, by then distinctly outmoded but presumably intended to sustain the correct pitch for the choristers as they moved along.

Clad in surplices and mantles came the Gentlemen of the Chapel Royal, among them John Gostling and John Blow: the 'Dr. in music and Master of the Children of the Chapel and Organist' wore a special cloak made of five yards of fine scarlet cloth. Present too was the inevitable Nicholas Staggins, Master of the King's Music, a totally undistinguished figure whose indestructibility as a talentless official *apparatchik* makes him a late seventeenth-century equivalent of the egregious Tikhon Khrennikov, for so long the state-approved panjandrum of musical activity in Soviet Russia.

Somewhat ahead of Staggins in the procession walked the 'Organist of Westminster', Henry Purcell. Singing bass in the ambulant choir of nearly fifty voices, Purcell took part in the performance of William Child's anthem *O Lord, Grant the King a Long Life*, apparently not among the pieces composed expressly for the occasion. The music covered part of the procession's course along a route lined with blue broadcloth 'which cloth was strewn with nine baskets full of sweet herbs and flowers, by Mary Dowle, Strewer-of-Herbs-in-Ordinary to His Majesty', and guarded by the various horse and foot guard regiments whose continuing presence as a standing army during James's reign was to become so obnoxious to his subjects. Once inside the Abbey, the choir broke into the first of two anthems Purcell had written specially to frame the entire coronation service.

I Was Glad When They Said unto Me, using the well-known text from Psalm 122 which Purcell had already set with string symphonies some three years earlier, is a breezily exuberant piece, a full anthem with a five-part opening making the best use possible of that 'step tripla' rhythm formerly so beloved of the foot-tapping Charles II and now employed to underline the delight of the psalmist as he enters the temple and 'the tribes of the Lord' follow in carefully separated choral entries. There is an appropriately meditative interlude, to the words 'O pray for the peace of Jerusalem', before a surprisingly learned Gloria, with the 'world without end' section treated to a sequence of inversions, augmentations and changes of tempo – the composer signing himself in, as it were, with a flourish.

At the entrance of the Queen, the scholars of Purcell's old school, Westminster, burst into their traditional 'Vivat's, and once the royal couple were seated on their respective chairs of state (the actual enthronement was a separate part of the ceremony) Blow's *Let Thy Hand Be Strengthened* was performed. At the anointing, the very heart of the ritual, the choir sang William Turner's setting of *Come Holy Ghost, Our Souls Inspire*, the English version of the *Veni Creator Spiritus*, and this was followed by an anthem from Charles II's coronation service, Henry Lawes's *Zadok the Priest*. Before the investiture came another piece by Blow, *Behold O Lord Our Defender*, and Turner's *Deus in Virtute* was then followed by a Te Deum setting from the not especially inspired pen of the aged William Child, organist of St George's Chapel,

Windsor, whose life spanned almost the entire century – he was born in 1606 and died at the age of ninety-one, outliving Purcell by two years.

For his part, Blow had excelled himself in the music he furnished for the service's various high points, and never more so than in the awesomely proportioned *God Spake Sometime in Visions*, in which the sense of his friendly rivalry with Purcell can clearly be felt. Looking at the coronation's overall layout, we may ask to what extent its musical elements were consciously planned as a sequence. In the case of another musically distinguished coronation service, that of George II in 1727, it is perhaps easier to apprehend this sort of relationship, since four of its anthems were provided by George Frideric Handel for specific moments in the ceremony. What seems to have happened in the 1685 crowning was that somebody – Blow himself perhaps, in consultation with court and religious authorities – evidently paid attention both to the character and appropriateness of the individual items, and to the feeling of continuity and climax needed to give maximum impact to the occasion.

Thus the position of Purcell's *My Heart Is Inditing a Good Matter* at the close of the service, following Queen Mary Beatrice's crowning, was perfectly judged in relation to the magnificence of Blow's anthem which had preceded it. The text is drawn from Psalm 45, 'To the chief Musician upon Shoshannim, for the sons of Korah, Maschil, A song of loves', a ravishingly beautiful poem in its King James Bible translation, which it is tempting to imagine David writing to one of his various consorts – haughty Merab, gentler, more sympathetic Michal, or perhaps even in celebration of the adulterous Bathsheba. Purcell's is one of two monumental English settings, the other being by Handel, and between them the composers divide the honours of capturing the psalm's ideally calculated blend of grandeur and sensuousness.

For the coronation the entire string band of the Chapel Royal was mustered, and Purcell was thus able to furnish an anthem along the most opulent lines. A superb French overture, airy and elegant yet somehow beautifully insidious in the way whereby its opening sidles obliquely towards the bobbish triple-time movement which follows, heralds the choral entries, which unite with crucial harmonic effectiveness on the words, 'I speak of the things which I have made unto the King'. In the ensuing section, describing the Queen 'all glorious within', the choir replicates the richness of her 'clothing . . . of wrought gold' by dividing into eight parts and throwing the words to and fro in dotted melismata like dazzling ripples in a royal mantle. A sextet of soloists handles the antiphonal 'She shall be brought unto the King', its tranquil opening branching out into playful contrasts of texture and rhythm before swelling towards an infectiously joyful climax involving full choral and instrumental forces.

Somewhat unexpectedly, Purcell now causes the entire overture to be repeated, perhaps because the shift of mood in the subsequent 'Hearken, O daughter, and consider' is so emphatically pronounced. The minor key induces a pensive intimacy, as once again the composer deploys his alternating solo groups, combining them at last in the opulent harmonies of 'whom thou mayest make princes in all lands'. The final movement, 'Praise the Lord, O Jerusalem', has an architectural massiveness in its opening chords, stacked high in twelve-part blocks, and, as in *I Was Glad*, Purcell goes on to dazzle his hearers with a last brilliant flourish of counterpoint as a prelude to rolling 'Alleluia's.

The reign thus gorgeously proclaimed in music ought to have been a period of consolidation and binding together for a nation which, at certain stages during the previous seven or eight years, must have felt itself poised on the brink of anarchy. A more visionary and intelligent monarch than James would have tried to reconcile the disparate forces in politics, religion and local government by encouraging a readiness to work together for the good of the nation and through a determined public display of patriotism in the face of the eternal English paranoia regarding the dark designs of foreigners on the spiritual, moral and economic integrity of the realm. Though he had some virtues – he was hardworking, relatively sober, only had one mistress and was not without courage and loyalty to friends – the new king fatally lacked his brother's charm and sense of humour, was far too readily convinced of his own invincible rightness of judgment, and was implacably vindictive in paying off old scores against those who had dared in the past to question his fitness for the role he was now called upon to play.

One of these was the darling figurehead of the Protestant radicals, James, Duke of Monmouth, whose return from exile to lead a rebellion against his uncle was almost a foregone conclusion. On 11 June 1685 Monmouth landed at Lyme Regis and was proclaimed King of England in the town's market place, denouncing James as 'usurper, murderer, traitor and tyrant'. The first three epithets were wholly unjustified and even the last was as yet inappropriate, but the disaffected elements in the West Country, where nonconformist Protestantism had seized a firm hold in large areas during the previous thirty years, were ready to believe anything against a Catholic king, and volunteers flocked to join the still glamorous royal bastard. At Taunton his proclamation was reiterated and he 'touched for the King's Evil', the laying on of royal hands traditionally supposed to heal sufferers from scrofula. A party of schoolgirls led by their headmistress came to do homage, and prayers were said for 'His Majesty'.

The rebellion ultimately failed because Monmouth had no adequate military organization or definite plan of campaign. After failing to secure the key cities of Bath and Bristol and having allowed his rag-tag and bobtail army of ill-accoutred peasantry to desecrate the cathedrals at Wells and Salisbury, he was finally forced to turn and fight at Sedgemoor on the marshy Somerset Levels, where his troops were swiftly routed and he himself forced to flee, only to be captured while hiding in a ditch at Ringwood in Hampshire. There was no question of mercy from the King, and Monmouth was sent to the Tower. His execution was a wretchedly botched business, in which the headsman, having initially lost his nerve, took six strokes of the axe to complete his task.

While Lord Chief Justice Jeffreys embarked on his notorious 'Bloody Assize', hanging the poorer rebels or sentencing them to transportation to the West Indies, while accepting bribes from prisoners rich enough to buy their acquittal, the nation in general was inclined to view the failure of Monmouth's rebellion as a merciful providence. 'For my own part', says Evelyn, reflecting a widely held view, 'I looked upon this deliverance as most signal. Such an inundation of fanatics and men of impious principles must needs have caused universal disorder, cruelty, unjustice, rapine, sacrilege and confusion, an unavoidable civil war and misery without end.' Evidently the Queen's brother Francesco, Duke of Modena, felt the same, since he promptly commissioned his *sotto-maestro di cappella*, the distinguished Giovanni Battista Vitali (whose instrumental works had provided inspiration for Purcell's trio sonatas), to write an oratorio *L'Ambitione Debellata ovvero la Caduta di Monmouth*, in which the drama's allegorical participants, Faith, Ambition, Treachery and Innocence, were clearly identified in the libretto as Mary, Monmouth, his fellow rebel the Duke of Argyll, and King James. The central conflict is between Mary, as the Catholic champion, and Monmouth as a subversive warmonger. The latter is finally reduced to penitent humbleness while the King and Queen celebrate their victory in a duet.

Though no similar musical tribute was demanded from Purcell, the text of the birthday ode *Why Are All the Muses Mute?* made obvious references to the suppression of the revolt, doubtless still fresh in the minds of those who heard the first performance, probably on the evening of 15 October, when Evelyn, who was present, noted: 'Being the King's birthday, there was a solemn ball at Court, and before it music of instruments and voices. At the music I happened by accident to stand the very next to the Queen and the King, who talked with me about the music.' The writer of the text, again anonymous, not only portrayed 'accurs'd rebellion' as 'back'd by all the Powers of Hell, Pride, Ambition, Rage and Zeal', but quite excelled himself in poetic sycophancy, beside which the elaborate compliments paid to Charles II in the earlier odes seem positively understated.

Why Are All the Muses Mute? was almost more of a tribute than James deserved in the ornate variety of musical invention lavished upon it by the composer. The work opens with a surprise: where on earth is the overture? Only when the solo tenor, asking the initial question, has aroused the chorus to proclaim, 'Awake, 'tis Caesar does inspire, And animates the vocal choir', do the strings launch into the sort of finely proportioned sinfonia which we might have expected at the opening.

The balance between soloists, combined voices and choral interjections is expertly maintained, and for the first time we catch the signatures and trademarks of the mature Purcell as a writer of court odes. Who else could have spun the thread of the counter-tenor's 'Britain, now thou art great' above its ground bass or created the harmonically playful ritornello with which it concludes? What other hand than Purcell's would have furnished the bass soloist – doubtless the phenomenal Gostling – with the deep-plummeting arioso 'Accurs'd rebellion rear'd his head' or so wittily measured the overlapping lines of the duet 'In the equal balance laid'? As for the final number, this beyond anything else in the work shows us a master arrived at the height of his powers. Solemnity, even wistfulness take over in the tenor solo 'O how blest is the isle to which Caesar is given', but instead of festive exuberance, the chorus answers in a similar vein of softened reflection, almost a lament, so that the last words,

> His fame and the world together shall die,
> Shall vanish together away

do just that, sinking like a flame, to leave us marvelling at the fecundity of the invention which kindled it.

Purcell's position as part of the court musical establishment was now entirely secure, and this may explain the relative swiftness with which, following the coronation, the Secret Service, always entrusted with this sort of payment, made out a warrant to the composer 'for so much money by him disbursed and craved for providing and setting up an organ in the Abbey Church of Westminster for the Solemnity of the Coronation, and for removing the same, and other services performed in His said Majesty's Chapel since the 25th March 1685 according to a bill signed by the Bishop of London'. On 31 August members of the Private Music were confirmed in their places, including the two fine countertenors John Abell and William Turner (the latter a soloist in *Why Are All the Muses Mute?*). An Italian flautist, named as 'Monsieur Mario', perhaps a Modenese in Mary's entourage, was added to the list, and the French oboist and fiddler Jacques Paisible, 'James Peaseable', made his appearance, having first figured among the 'French violins and hoboyes' who had taken part in the court masque *Calisto* in 1675. John Blow is labelled in the roster as 'Composer' and Henry Purcell features simply as

'Harpsicall' – the customary mutation, during these years, of the more usual 'harpsichord'.

His duties as a keyboard player at court can scarcely have been onerous enough to keep him from his friends, or from the provision of the sort of music which Londoners in this most convivial of times liked to sing and play for pleasure. It would be agreeable to come across a mention or two of the composer at his musical recreation, but such visions are alas almost non-existent among Purcellian life records. Only Roger North gives us the briefest of glimpses. Among various writings, biographical, musical and architectural, is an account of his elder brother, Francis, Lord Guildford, whose career at the bar earned him the successive offices of Solicitor-General, Attorney-General, Chief Justice of the Common Pleas and finally Lord Keeper of the Great Seal. Unlike many senior legal figures under Charles II, the Lord Keeper – at least according to the loyal and admiring Roger – was a man of principle, whose severely limited leisure was given over to connoisseurship, music and an interest in science of the kind which engrossed many of his educated contemporaries, King Charles included, and which had resulted in the consolidation, early in the reign, of the Royal Society. John Evelyn, a fellow member of the Society, described him as 'a most knowing, learned, ingenious gent, & besides an excellent person, of an ingenuous sweete disposition, very skillful in Musick, Painting, the new Philosophie & politer studies'.

Lord Keeper North, who married Frances Pope, daughter of the Earl of Down, had formerly lived in the legal heartland of Chancery Lane, but the pair of them moved, on his elevation, to Great Queen Street, at the north-eastern edge of Covent Garden. The street had originally been developed along the line of a private roadway used exclusively by James I to drive through the fields in his coach towards his favourite country retreat at Theobalds in Essex. His queen, Anne of Denmark, had been petitioned to give her title to the new thoroughfare and by the 1630s, in 'the new fair buildings called Queene's Street, leading into Drury Lane', prominent courtiers such as Sir Kenelm Digby and the Marquess of Clanricarde were buying up plots on which to build houses, possibly to designs by Inigo Jones's pupil John

Webb. The street's northern side is all that now remains of this early development, and many of its buildings date in any case from the first decades of the eighteenth century, by which time the neighbourhood's smartness had fallen away. It is intriguing, nevertheless, to view Great Queen Street as part of a Purcellian tour through London, since it was almost certainly here that Henry visited the music-loving Lord Keeper to bear him company in performing trio sonatas.

The Norths, as noted earlier, had a family passion for music, and Francis, having learned the bass viol as a boy, apparently found it invaluable as a pastime with which to temper his hard study of the law as a fledgling Middle Temple student. Described by his brother as 'musitian in perfection', he 'turned composer, and from raw beginnings advanced so far as to complete divers consorts of two and three parts, which at his grandfather's house were perform'd with masters in company'. Even as Chief Justice he had found time to set one of the Italian poet Giovanni Battista Guarini's *canzone* to music, and the two brothers relished the pleasure of singing duets together. 'There was seldome a night of his life', writes Roger, 'but if wee were by our selves, this was the enterteinement, and it was my buissness as well as his to pick up duo's, as wee did with all imaginable industry, as well in wrighting as in print ... And what shewed us to be true lovers was [that] any vulgar musick served our turnes; nothing came amiss for variety.' Though he never cared for the new French style of the royal band of fiddlers, 'that theatricall sort of musick', yet 'was he a Mecenas to the musik masters who had the good luck to be living'.

One of these was Henry Purcell, whom the Lord Keeper clearly respected, since, as Roger implies, it was not generally his way to encourage 'a set of masters to consort it with him'. Nevertheless North goes on to tell us that he kept up his bass viol 'after buissness took up most of his time, and he had little to spare', even if he was not especially keen on simply playing a consort bass part. 'But yet, even when he had the Great Seal, he caused the devine Purcell to bring his Itallian manner'd compositions; and with him on his harpsicord, my self and another violin, wee performed them more than once, of which Mr Purcell was not a litle proud, nor was it a common thing for one of his dignity to be so enterteined.'

Musicians during the Restoration were often merely a superior sort of servant and required to know their place, especially in a society so conscious of rank, title and family. North's words make it plain that however 'devine' Purcell might have seemed, his profound sense of the honour accorded him by the Norths of Kirtling and Rougham was only to be expected. The kind of familiarity and classlessness later accorded to musical genius by princes and aristocrats of the Romantic era was decidedly not to be taken for granted in the closing decades of the seventeenth century.

And what were these 'Itallian manner'd compositions' which Purcell played with the North brothers? None other, surely, than the *Sonnatas of III Parts*, published in 1683. Francis North had received the Lord Keeper's office the previous year and was to die not long afterwards, in 1685, so since Roger specifically identifies the meetings in question as taking place 'even when he had the Great Seal', they must have occurred as a much-needed interlude of pleasure in this brief but ultimately fatal epoch of the great lawyer's life, when overwork, constant harassment from political opponents and the intolerable pressures of his official position became 'more than enough to oppress the soul of an honest cordial man'. Reading Roger's poignant account of his brother's last illness, so stoically born, it comes as some consolation to think of Purcell's radiantly inventive essays in the sonata form lighting up the grimmer moments of a man whom many of us, from Evelyn's description of him, would have been enchanted to meet.

In his capacity as an amateur architect, Roger North had designed the fine gateway to the Middle Temple from Fleet Street, with its tuck-pointed brick facing, stone pilasters with Doric capitals and stately triangular pediment. Characteristically he had found room to include, at one side of its entrance arch, space for a music shop for the bookseller and publisher John Carr, to replace an earlier building on which Carr had taken a lease in 1675. The premises are still in existence, though long since converted to other uses, and here again we are entitled to imagine Purcell's presence, since Carr issued several of his songs and sold most of the Playford family's publications, featuring so many of the composer's works.

One of these musical compilations, published in 1685, was *The Theater of Musick: or, A Choice Collection of the Newest and Best Songs Sung at the Court and Public Theaters.* 'The words', according to the title page, were 'composed by the most ingenious wits of the age and set to Music by the greatest masters in the science'. Advertised as 'The First Book', it was dedicated, not to a great nobleman or to some accomplished daughter of the peerage, but to John Blow and Henry Purcell, acknowledging their help 'in perusing several of the songs of this book before they went to the press, whose authors we could not so well apply our selves to, and adding thorow-basses to such as wanted them'. Composers were invited to leave copies of their latest songs with Playford and Carr, so as to 'prevent such as daily abuse you by publishing your songs lame and imperfect, and singing them about the streets like ordinary ballads'.

Quickly followed up by a reprint unscrupulously advertised as 'The Second Book', this first volume contained nine of Purcell's vocal compositions, including a specially written 'Pastoral Coronation' entitled 'While Thirsis, wrapp'd in downy sleep', and the lovely 'If grief has any pow'r to kill', its plangent vocal line appealing to singers with a versatile range. Another was his setting of Thomas D'Urfey's half-blasphemous 'Musing on Cares of Human Fate', in which a shepherd is encouraged by Love to shun Virtue and Fame in pursuit of a mistress.

> Swift as a thought, the am'rous swain
>   To Sylvia's cottage flies,
> In soft expressions told her plain
>   The way to heavenly joys.
> She, who with piety was stor'd,
>   Delays no longer crav'd;
> Charm'd by the god whom they ador'd
> She smil'd and took him at his word
>   And thus they both were sav'd.

Harmless eroticism of this kind was part of the small coin of Restoration musical conviviality, as indeed was the far more obvious bawdy inherent in another species of vocal writing in which Purcell was now only too pleased to show himself an accomplished master. In the same year that the Playfords published *The Theater of Music*, they issued the second instalment of a collection first sold nearly twenty years earlier under the title *Catch that Catch Can*, though John Playford claimed, in his preface to the new work, that it was actually the latest part of another anthology called *The Musical Companion*. The present publication consisted of 'divers new catches, songs and glees', which Playford had originally gathered together simply in order to enjoy them with his friends as part of that recreational music-making which, as in the case of the North brothers, made a frequent feature of English seventeenth-century social life.

'Bearing a part', an ability to sing at sight from music books ranged around the table, had been one of those graces taken for granted in musically inclined Elizabethans and Jacobeans, though it is maybe a little too romantically Merrie England–ish to think of a whole nation in doublets and farthingales trilling 'Sweet Suffolk Owl', 'The Silver Swan' or 'Thule, the Period of Cosmography' as a matter of course after a hearty supper. At its most basic, this skill in holding the line of a part-song could be demonstrated by the singing of catches, little canons, generally humorous in mood, their texts sometimes topical, now and then designed to reproduce familiar sounds and situations from daily life, and often outrageously bawdy and scatological.

Some derived the word 'catch' from the Italian *caccia* or the French *chasse*, both meaning 'hunt' and implying that the various parts could chase one another through an infinite sequence. Others supposed it to refer to the catch or double meaning in the words themselves. Essentially such pieces involved three or four melodic sections, each threatening resolution as the next voice chimed in. The form had already gained popularity by the end of Elizabeth I's reign: in Shakespeare's *Twelfth Night*, first performed in 1601, the drunken revellers Sir Toby Belch, Sir Andrew Aguecheek and Feste the clown launch into 'Hold thy peace', only to be interrupted by Maria, who warns them too late of Malvolio's wrathful approach. 'I am a dog at a catch' claims the ludicrously pathetic Aguecheek.

By 1652, seven years before Purcell was born, John Playford had published the first extensive collection, called, like its successors, *Catch that Catch Can*, after a popular children's game. The editor was John Hilton, whose own compositions featured beside those of other musicians in an assembly of twelve dozen such pieces. 'My wishes are', he declares in a jokey preface, 'that they who are true Catchers indeed, may catch them for their delight; and may they that desire to learne, catch them for their Instruction: But let those that catch at them with detraction, (as that is a catching disease) catch only the fruits of their owne Envy.' To the English of the 1650s, settling down to the sobrieties of institutionalized Puritanism, the appearance of this first *Catch that Catch Can* volume may have seemed a little surprising, but as Hilton pointed out, catch-singing was 'full of harmless Recreation'. As so often in Cromwellian society, the ethos here seems to have been based on an ideal tension between public demeanour and private enjoyment. It says something about the ambivalence of contemporary attitudes that no difficulty was made over the inclusion of a catch such as William Lawes's blatantly lewd 'I'le tell you of a matter', about 'a man that provok'd his maid to break the Commandement', or over any of the other off-colour material gathered by Hilton and Playford.

Under the Restoration, the catch found its perfect constituency among the boozers and topers of a society apparently desperate to compensate for those pleasures it had notionally forgone during the previous decades of war and republicanism. While the texts elaborated on the various possibilities for double entendre or outright obscenity, or else explored areas of political satire and genre painting of the sort we find in the realistic backgrounds of contemporary comedy, the music was equally responsive to the form's elasticities and to its dominant characteristics of witty anecdote and microcosmic descriptiveness.

The *Catch that Catch Can* issue of 1685 included seventeen catches attributed to Purcell, four of them almost certainly spurious, though the fact that they bear his name implies he was already gaining the reputation he was to enjoy among his contemporaries as the age's most accomplished catch-maker. There are two loyal effusions – one to 'our sov'raign Charles, our Faith's Defender' invites God to 'protect Queen Cath'rine, England's nursing mother', the other making a clever play on the Duke of York's refusal to take the Test:

Then to His Highness, see, see, there wine is
That has passed the test, above the rest.

There are drinking songs such as 'Let the grave folks go preach', whose harmonic and rhythmic sophistications offer a comic antithesis to its picture of fuddled carousers, and political pieces like 'Now England's great Council', apparently written when Purcell was only seventeen, and 'Since the Duke Is Return'd', which he probably composed to celebrate the appointment of the Tory Lord Mayor of London, Sir William Pritchard, in 1682. One catch, 'Upon woman's love', skilfully fuses drink and sex, the favoured themes of the genre, an idea more explicitly taken up in 'To thee, to thee and to a maid', while 'Young John the gardiner' is relentlessly coarse in its pursuit of the horticultural metaphor.

Some fifty more catches were to appear under Purcell's name, but in 1686, the year which followed Playford's collection, he was invited to assume a somewhat graver role as the professional assessor of a new organ by the German, Bernhard Schmidt, 'Father Smith', installed in the church of St Katherine Cree, one of several which had survived the 1666 fire relatively unscathed. The vestry minutes note an order 'that Mr Joseph Cox do procure Mr Purcell, Mr Barkwell and Mr Moses, masters in music, and Mr White, organ-master, or such other competent judges in music as may be prevailed with to be at our church on Thursday next, the 30th of this instant September, at two of the clock in the afternoon to give their judgments upon the organ'. Those who in fact turned up at the appointed time were Purcell, Blow, John Mosse, the 'Mr Moses' referred to, who had taken Jenkins's place in the King's Private Musick, and a 'Mr Fforcell', who was perhaps Francis Forcer, the house composer of Dorset Garden Theatre. Purcell sat down to try out the organ, 'and after he had done playing they all reported to the Vestry that in their judgements the organ was a good organ, and was performed and completed according to contract'. The four candidates for the post of organist were then invited to demonstrate their respective skills, and from the wording of the document it seems that Purcell, Blow and the others were so placed to listen that each performer was unseen. 'The third person that played (which fell out to be Mr Snow) did in their judgements play the best and most skilfully of all.' Swayed by this opinion, the assembled vestrymen gave the nod by three votes to Purcell's friend and colleague Moses Snow, who had witnessed him taking holy communion some years earlier, and 'the said Mr Snowe being afterwards made acquainted with the said choice, gratefully accepted of the said place'. He appears to have received two quarters' salary in advance, and the musicians' committee was given its expenses for coach hire on top of hospitality at a nearby tavern.

It has been argued that the following day, 1 October, heard the earliest performance of Purcell's new court ode, *Ye Tuneful Muses, Raise Your Heads*, designed as a welcome song to King James and Queen Mary Beatrice on their return from Windsor. This seems unlikely, since the composer would hardly have spent what was probably the best part of a day in auditioning church organists when an elaborate new work was scheduled for presentation to royalty the next evening. The piece is, however, a welcome rather than a birthday ode – there are allusions to 'this point of time . . . bringing Caesar' and to 'his so much wish'd return' – so perhaps we should assume a première at some stage in early October, rather than on the King's birthday, the 14th of the month, when Narcissus Luttrell mentions 'ringing of bells, bonefires and a ball at Court'.

On this occasion the anonymous versifier was a little more forthcoming than some of his earlier counterparts where opportunity for contrast was involved, though every chance is seized for larding James and Mary Beatrice with flattery. Protestant extremism is duly damned as 'fanatical fury and sanctified spite', and the Italian Queen is termed

> That brighter jewel than a crown
> In whom does triumph each commanding grace,
> An angel mien and matchless face!

The celebration of the pair as 'happy in a mutual love' must have raised a few sardonic smiles. In August James had recalled his mistress Catherine Sedley, Countess of Dorchester, from banishment in Ireland, upon which Mary, invoking conjugal rights and Catholic scruples, had forced him to dismiss this undeniably entertaining creature. Though the King solemnly promised not to visit Catherine on her return, he made frequent calls at her lodgings in St James's Square, the fashionable new development begun in the 1670s by Henry Jermyn, Lord St Albans, south of the street which bears his name.

Purcell's ode is not one of his most consistently inspired. To certain of the numbers there clings a faint suggestion of doodling insipidity, and the invention elsewhere seems somewhat forced as a result. His concept of the medium had now assumed clearly determined outlines, which were to persist, in one form or another, to the close of his career as composer of these yearly panegyrics. The pleasure of the best of the odes lies to some extent in their formal predictability: we know that there will be an opening instrumental symphony, that at least one of the airs will spin an ornate vocal web across the framework of a ground, that tremendous ariosos for basses like Gostling and Bowman will execute handsprings and cartwheels over a spread of two octaves, and that the composer's unquenchable sense of fun will declare itself somewhere along the score. None of this reduces the music's impact. Purcell is a polyglot, discoursing in distinctive idioms, and we listen with delight to his subtle expounding of this courtier's vein, surely enjoyed with more than half an ear by those to whom it was first addressed.

Humour in this piece breaks through in its third section, where the bass line underpinning the tenor soloist and chorus consists of the popular song 'Hey boys, up go we', a Tory satire on Whig pretensions, whose appearance here, and in the violin line as well, must have delighted James. Neither can the composer resist the hint given in the following number by the lines:

> Tune all your strings to celebrate
> His so much wish'd return.

What the seventeenth-century poet Edmund Benlowes so memorably described as 'the grumbling cat-lines' are heard to splendid effect at this point, when the fiddlers scrape ferociously across their open strings. William Turner's countertenor was offered another seductive display in the address to the Queen, 'With him he brings the partner of his throne', where the ground's agreeable saunter is diverted by a sudden modulation up a fifth, but the courtly audience must have been even more enchanted with the trio for two altos, bass and recorders 'To music's softer but yet kind'.

By the end of 1686 King James and Queen Mary Beatrice had made the most public demonstration so far of their faith by establishing a Roman Catholic Chapel Royal in great magnificence at Whitehall. There were to be six preachers and two chaplains with 'assistants', a brace of organists and seven boy choristers with a master. The list of musicians gives the lie to the idea that Mary of Modena had no interest in music. It was surely through her influence that the Roman composer Innocenzo Fede, formerly *maestro di cappella* to Christina of Sweden, had arrived to supervise the choir and instrumentalists. Two further Italian musicians named Grandi and Sansoni immediately follow him in the official roster, at handsome salaries of £110 and £100. We know also that several of the English singers had travelled in Italy. John Abell, a high countertenor, had been praised by Evelyn some years earlier. 'I never heard a more excellent voice; one would have sworn it had been a woman's, it was so high and so well and skilfully managed.' Thomas Pordage, in holy orders, was also much admired by the diarist, who commended his singing 'after the Venetian recitative, as masterly as could be, and with an excellent voice both treble and bass'. An international flavour to the new chapel's services was intensified by the presence of the Moravian composer and gamba player Gottfried Finger, who quickly adapted to the busy London musical scene, writing incidental music for plays by dramatists such as Congreve and Farquhar and producing an extensive sonata literature for various instruments.*

John Evelyn was one of many curious visitors who inspected the Catholic chapel almost immediately after its opening on Christmas

---

*He was later one of the contenders in a competition to set Congreve's masque *The Judgment of Paris*. Other entrants included John Eccles and John Weldon, but the winner was Purcell's brother Daniel. Finger is said to have destroyed his score and quitted England in disgust.

Day, 1686. Acknowledging the splendour of the architecture and ornament, including Grinling Gibbons's four statues of saints and the vault frescoes by the Tuscan painter Antonio Verrio, showing 'the Assumption of the Blessed Virgin, according to their tradition', he was understandably appalled by the priest-crammed opulence of the ceremonial:

> The Bishop in his mitre and rich copes ... who sat in a chair with arms pontifically, was adored and censed by three Jesuits in their copes; then he went to the altar and made divers cringes, then censing the images and glorious tabernacle ... with a world of mysterious ceremony, the music playing, with singing. I could not have believed I should ever have seen such things in the King of England's palace, after it had pleased God to enlighten this nation ...

It is difficult to resist the impression that a deliberate attempt was being made by James and Mary to allure potential converts through the sensuous exoticism of an alien liturgy carried out at the fullest possible pitch of ritual pomp. To thicken the brew more enticingly, the Queen had secured the temporary service of one of her brother's star singers, the castrato Giovanni Francesco Grossi, known by his nickname Siface, derived from the role of King Syphax of Numidia with which he had made his reputation in Francesco Cavalli's opera *Scipione Africano*. A former member of the papal choir and a leading performer in the oratorios given at the Roman church of San Marcello, belonging to the Servite order, he had moved to the Modenese court in 1679. There he had taken part with increased *réclame* in the brilliant sequence of oratorios mounted by Duke Francesco and his music director Giovanni Battista Vitali, and also sung in opera performances in Florence, Naples and Venice.

Castrati, rapidly claiming primacy in male roles on the Italian operatic stage (in the Papal States they took women's parts as well), were not altogether new to London ears, but Siface was the first of any real quality to make an impression in England. Evelyn went back to the Catholic chapel at the end of January 1687 to hear 'the famous eunuch Cifaccio' sing, and though he enjoyed the music, commented sourly on the occasion as a whole, 'much

141

crowding – little devotion'. In April his old friend Samuel Pepys, who had confided years earlier to his diary 'Music and women I must give way to, whatever my business is,' invited Evelyn and others to a special recital at his house, where Siface, displaying the classic male prima-donna airs and sulks of the eunuch as megastar, had been induced to sing as a particular favour. 'His holding out and delicateness in extending and loosing a note with incomparable softness and sweetness, was admirable; for the rest I found him a mere wanton, effeminate child, very coy, and proudly conceited, to my apprehension.'

This arrogance had been noted elsewhere in Europe. The Modenese agent in Paris called Siface 'un gran fantastico', and while still at Rome he had disdained to sing for the French Ambassador, claiming he wanted 'doubloons, not sorbets' and that the latter was all musicians ever got at the embassy. His skill was universally cried up, however, and Evelyn adds that 'he touched the harpsichord to his voice rarely well'. Complaining that the English climate was bad for his voice, he left London on 19 June 1687. Among Purcell's miscellaneous keyboard pieces is a little minuet in D minor entitled *Sefauchi's Farewell*, whose exact context has never been established. Was it linked with one of the castrato's operatic airs, or perhaps played as part of a music meeting at which he gave his last London performance? And was its faintly wistful cast entirely without a touch of tongue in cheek? Siface went home to further Italian triumphs, but his career was fatally cut short as the result of an absurd love affair with a noblewoman, whose family had him murdered on the road from Ferrara to Bologna in 1697.

The foundation of the King's popish chapel inevitably diverted resources from an already reduced establishment at the Chapel Royal. James was certainly more assiduous than his late brother in honouring promises and keeping accounts – he had inherited, through his mother Henrietta Maria, the famously infallible Bourbon power of memory – and to all intents and purposes the various court musicians, Purcell among them, could consider themselves on a somewhat better footing than they had been in the previous reign. The significant matter of riding allowances whenever they were summoned to follow the royal family out of London was taken care of in a note from the King to the Lord Chamberlain, the stolidly loyal Thomas Bruce, Earl of Aylesbury, that they were to be awarded three shillings a day. Purcell kept all his appointments, including that of tuner and repairer of instruments, but interestingly does not appear as an official composer in the Private Musick.

Nevertheless, without the King's presence the Chapel Royal assumed a somewhat anomalous position, lying cheek by jowl, as it were, beside its new and favoured Catholic rival in the sprawling palace complex of Whitehall. A wryly amusing letter from James's daughter Anne to her sister Mary describes the odd sensations she felt in occupying the place which ought to have been taken by her father at divine service and receiving the same reverence due to him in her capacity as token Protestant member of the royal family. The princess had no great musical ear and frankly there was little incentive for Purcell, Blow or any of the other Chapel Royal musicians to produce anthems with anything like the same enthusiasm with which they had striven to delight Charles II. He at least had had the grace to make fairly regular appearances at Sunday services, whatever his genuine religious affiliations or lack of them. That James's public espousal of Catholicism had been a blow to the Chapel's overall morale is perhaps indicated in a note from Aylesbury to Nicholas Staggins on 21 October 1687: 'Whereas you have neglected to give order to the violins to attend at the Chapel at Whitehall where Her Royal Highness the Princess Anne of Denmark is present, these are therefore to give notice to them that they give their attendance there upon Sunday next, and so to continue to do so as formerly they did.'

It would be quite wrong, however, to assume that Purcell's comparatively few anthems written for the Chapel Royal and other choirs during this period showed any professional half-heartedness or waning interest. On the contrary, he seems to have used the occasional opportunity to compose a new sacred work as a means of developing the more Italianate aspects of his personal style. The expansively conceived *Behold, I Bring You Glad Tidings*, written for Christmas in 1687 and his only piece associated with that festival, starts with a string symphony whose fast section is not unlike something from one of his trio sonatas, then moves

143

to a recitative in which the bass (unusually, though Gostling's holy orders may have fitted him for the task) takes the angel's part. Here as elsewhere, the violins, dilatory as their attendance on Princess Anne at Whitehall may have been, are fully engaged in the proceedings, as opposed to certain of the earlier symphony anthems, where their role appears more independent and episodic. What is more, the dramatic impact of the Gospel story of the annunciation to the shepherds is brought vividly home to us through the choral–solo interchange. The total effect is that of some splendid Italian Baroque altarpiece by Guercino or Gentileschi, with the same sense of colour and luminosity.

Just as powerful, to the point at which we might be tempted to feel that Purcell was consciously trying to rival the Papist theatricality and sensual heat of the King's new chapel that had so embarrassed old Evelyn, are the anthems without symphonies, accompanied only by continuo on organ and theorbo. Quite the most outstanding are *Thy Way, O God, Is Holy*, dating from 1687, and *Blessed Is He that Considereth the Poor*, composed the following year, both of them gaining deserved popularity among cathedral choirs in the years following Purcell's death. The first is a bold, passionate display of his absolute mastery of form and resource. The lofty rhetoric of Psalm 77 – 'The voice of thy thunder was heard round about; the lightning shone upon the ground' – is given to two voices only, a tenor and a bass, who sustain the excitement through what is made to sound like a sequence of inspired improvisations on the cosmic drama implicit in the text, framed by carefully placed repeats of the initial duet. More pensive in mood, *Blessed Is He that Considereth the Poor* makes equally startling use of soloists, this time without the choral conclusion which wraps up the earlier anthem. Instead, after a dazzling sequence of harmonic games played with the two tenors and bass, the three are appointed by the composer to personate the Holy Trinity in one of the most elaborate settings of the Gloria he ever wrote.

Such exposed and demanding use of solo voices in these anthems may be the result of the Chapel personnel looking elsewhere for employment and neglecting their duties. As far as Purcell was concerned, money seems to have remained a problem despite the relatively increased efficiency of the new payment system in the royal household. We know that he added to his regular income by taking pupils, but not all these music students were accompanied with the security of prompt payment from parents and guardians. In November 1686 he had been compelled to write to the Dean of Exeter, who seems to have been responsible for a pupil named Hodge, put to board with the Purcells, asking for settlement of overdue fees:

> Sir, I have wrote several times to Mr Webber concerning what was due to me on Hodg's account and recd no answer, which has occassion'd this presumption in giving you the trouble of a few Lines relating to the matter. It is ever since the beginning of June last that Money has been due: the sum is £27, viz. £20 for half a years teaching & boarding the other a Bill of £7 for nessecarys wch I laid out for him, The Bill Mr Webber has; Compassion Moves me to acquaint you of a great many debts Mr Hodg contracted whilst in London to some who are so poor 'twere an act of Charity as well as Justice to pay 'em. I hope you will be so kind to take it into your consideration and also to pardon this boldness from Sir
> Your most obliged humble ser't Henry Purcell.

This is almost the only holograph letter of the composer's to have survived, offering a fine demonstration of his elegant hand-writing, legible and confident like that of his manuscript scores. The epistolary style is that of a reasonably well-educated man. Even if the punctuation looks decidedly slippery and the spelling is no better or worse than usual in an age of notoriously irregular orthography, phrases such as 'Compassion moves me to acquaint you' and ''twere an act of Charity as well as Justice' are what Purcell's contemporaries would not scruple to term 'gentleman-like' or 'well-bred', and the overall tone scarcely suggests undue obsequiousness on the part of somebody whose profession was rated at a fairly low level in the social register.

By June 1687 Purcell's payments as organ tuner were falling behind, doubtless because, due to some oversight, the post had not been officially reconfirmed for the new reign. A note in the Treasury accounts mentions that 'the organ is so out of repaire that to cleanse, tune and put in good order will cost £40 and then to keep it so will cost £20 per an. at the least'. Purcell must have felt well entitled to petition the crown for his recent outlay of £20 10s on tuning, and, more important, to ask for a proper yearly salary of £56. The plea at any rate was accepted by the 'Treasurer of the Chamber' Edward Griffin, who summarized his requests, noting the 'absolute necessity' for someone to do the job and that he 'hath hitherto supplied the same without any consideration', though whether they were granted is not yet clear.

As if financial worries were not enough, the Purcell family was oppressed by a deeper sadness. Frances had by now been three times a mother, first of a son named Henry, who had lived for barely a week during July 1681, then of little John Baptista, buried in Westminster Abbey cloisters the following year, and afterwards of Thomas, named after his great-uncle. The boy may have survived somewhat longer than his brothers before he too was laid to rest in the Abbey in August 1686. A year later a fourth child was baptized Henry, on 9 June 1687, but if the Purcells cherished any hopes of him proving tougher than his infant siblings, these were dashed by his sudden death that September.

Severe infant mortality was one of the enduring misfortunes suffered by families in Purcell's time. Obstetrics and midwifery remained beset by a whole gallimaufry of superstitions and folk customs, let alone by the confused state of medical knowledge in an age which was beginning to adopt a more scientific approach to understanding the workings of the body and the operation of credible treatments and therapies in the handling of various illnesses. Written testimonies, whether in poems like John Milton's 'On the Death of a Fair Infant Dying of a Cough' or in Evelyn's heart-wrenching and almost implausible description of his prodigious little son Richard, who died at the age of five 'after six fits of a quartan ague', constitute a leitmotiv of sorrow and horrified incomprehension spanning the entire century. No household was safe from these dramas of loss through ignorance, dirt and disease. Even royalty, with its elaborate preparations for lying in and solemn supervision of labour by the great officers of state, was not spared. Charles II's queen, Catherine of Bragança, had stirred up vague slurs on her supposed barrenness via a dismal sequence of miscarriages, stillbirths and cot deaths, while James II's daughters Mary and Anne were each similarly condemned in successive attempts to fulfil public expectation of a legitimate Protestant heir to the Stuart line. The modern resources of counselling and psychotherapy were unavailable, religion supplying instead its bleak comforts of Christian resignation to God's will and the promise of happiness beyond the grave. Most couples simply gritted their teeth and tried again. Something at least of this bitter experience must have found its way into Purcell's unique distillation through music of what the Latin poet called 'lacrymae rerum', the sorrowfulness of things, in works such as the two settings of the funeral sentences or the starkly majestic closing chorus of *Dido and Aeneas*, 'With drooping wings'.

There was work to be done and a living to earn, whatever the gloomy shadows over the Purcell household. October 1687 brought the royal birthday and the obligation of another congratulatory ode, but the composer's loyalties were unlikely to have remained as constant towards King James as they unquestionably had been to Charles II. The new monarch's overmastering zeal for his faith was combined with an evident belief that whatever he did must inevitably be justified by virtue of his regal status. Together with a staggeringly consistent failure to grasp the national mood in respect of Catholicism as a reflection of foreign plots against the independence of the realm, these certainties encouraged him in a series of disastrous attempts to bolster his royal prerogative and enforce a Papist ascendancy in crucial areas of English public life. The good impression he had made initially, underwritten as it had first seemed to be by his strength of purpose in successfully crushing Monmouth's rebellion, was forgotten under the disastrous impact of his tactlessness and downright bullying in the attempt to realize his vision of an England redeemed for Holy Church.

While a wave of high-profile conversions swept through the aristocracy, and while the civil service, the judiciary, the court and the armed services were systematically packed with Papists in a 'one of us' fashion foreshadowing government quangos in our own day, James secured Parliament's consent to his permission, granted to favoured Catholic careerists, that they should dispense with the requirements of the Test Act. No fewer than five monastic houses were opened in London, Jesuit schools were established throughout the kingdom, a nuncio, Count D'Adda, was received from the Pope, and, ominously as it turned out, the royal eye, so clouded with piety, fell upon the two universities of Oxford and Cambridge, where vacant college headships and fellowships could now be supplied with 'Romish' candidates, regardless of their genuine suitability for the posts in question.

The irony of the steadily worsening tension throughout 1686 between James and the majority of his subjects lay in the embarrassment and real apprehension shown by Catholics themselves at the monarch's blundering high-handedness. Even the Pope, reluctantly receiving an English embassy led by Lord Castlemaine (whose chief distinction was that of having been cuckolded by Charles II), became nervously aware of the potential for disaster. Closer to home, both the Tuscan Ambassador and the Holy Roman Emperor's chargé d'affaires trembled at the sheer aggressiveness of the royal onslaught on the nation's Protestant infrastructure, while many of the old recusant families, knowing what persecution and penal laws really meant, were in dread of a violent backlash. Apart from anything else, these cradle-Catholics were often fervently patriotic and shared the national odium for foreign infiltrators and meddling from across the Channel.

By the autumn of the following year, the King, hardened by his *éminence grise* Father Petre and his chief minister Lord Sunderland, had quite outdone himself in political rashness. Visiting Bristol, he took measures to replace the entire corporation, including the mayor, with dissenters, whose interest he used as a cover for his promotion of a projected Declaration of Indulgence, removing penal restrictions from all non-Anglicans. He had the Vice-Chancellor of Cambridge University ousted for refusing to confer a degree on a Benedictine monk, and ordered mass to be sung in his presence at Bath Abbey, with a Jesuit preacher delivering a hell-fire sermon against heretics. Trying to face down the contumacious fellows of Magdalen College, Oxford, with a show of regal menaces, he was met with courageous resistance from the dons and their president Dr Hough, which impressed even Father Leyburne, the Vicar Apostolic, who warned in vain against trying

1. Portrait sketch of Henry Purcell by the German painter John Closterman (1656–1713).

2. King Charles II, attributed to T. Hawker, a classic image from the close of his reign, mixing cynicism with extravagance.

The Royal BANQUETING-HOUSE in Whitehal.

3. The busy and varied life of late seventeenth century Whitehall, dominated by Inigo Jones's Banqueting House.

4. The coronation of King James II in 1685. Note the musicans in the right hand gallery and the Church of England bishops gathered below.

5. Mary II, a coronation portrait by Willem Wissing of the reluctant queen celebrated in Purcell's odes.

6. John Dryden, *chief poet of the Restoration and Purcell's theatrical collaborator during the 1690s.*

7. Thomas Shadwell, *poet laureate under William and Mary, for whose play* The Libertine *Purcell wrote some of his most powerful incidental music.*

8. Thomas Betterton, *star actor, impresario and adaptor of the highly successful* Dioclesian.

9. John Blow, *Purcell's mentor, friend and musical model, a recently discovered portrait by John Riley.*

10. *Dorset Garden Theatre, where some of Purcell's more ambitious stage works were premiered.*

11. *Gorges House in rural Chelsea, scene of the first performance of* Dido and Aeneas *by Josias Priest's girl pupils.*

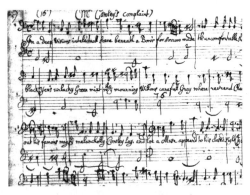

12. ABOVE *In a deep vision's intellectual scene, Purcell's manuscript setting of a poem by the popular Abraham Cowley.*

13. RIGHT *Purcell's song* O Solitude *as it first appeared, an ingenious setting of a poem by Katherine Philips.*

to turn the foundation into a Catholic seminary. In London parish churches meanwhile, preachers routinely ignored the ban on topical anti-Popish sermons, and issued a series of grim warnings to their congregations, based on scriptural texts whose messages of impending doom for beleaguered Protestantism, particularly in the light of Louis XIV's harrying of the French Huguenots, it was impossible to neglect.

Purcell's birthday ode *Sound the Trumpet, Beat the Drum* needs to be assessed within the context of this increasing alienation between a sovereign whose characteristics a contemporary, Madame de Sévigné, briskly summed up as 'great courage and a vulgar intellect', and his subjects, most of whom had been quite prepared to welcome him to the throne two years previously, whatever his faith. In 1686 there had been 'bonefires' and a review of troops. On the present anniversary, James, wary, despite his thick skin, of what the mob might do with a few burning brands and an adjacent Catholic chapel, had given orders against such celebrations, and the performance of Purcell's music at Whitehall would have taken place among a gathering of safely well-affected courtiers, the Queen's Italian attendants and a goodly sprinkling of priests.

The text is arguably the worst he ever set in this genre, so stale indeed that we have the impression that the poet, concealed for the time being under anonymity, was genuinely hard-pressed to work up any sort of enthusiasm for the unpopular monarch and his not especially well-loved consort.

Faced with couplets such as

> Crown the year and crown the day
> While distant shores their tribute pay,
> While never-failing Thames shall glide
> With treasures and pleasures renew'd by each tide,
> To Caesar all hail, unequall'd in arms,
> To Urania all hail, unequall'd in charms

Purcell might be forgiven for supplying music of decidedly uneven inspiration. The overall character of the work lacks unity or conviction, making it the least distinguished of his courtly celebrations.

Neither trumpet nor drum appear in the original score (though one later contemporary source manages to include them) and the martial mood is induced instead by imitation of rub-a-dubs and clarion calls among the string band and in the vocal lines of the opening number. There is a fine ground-supported duet for two altos, an amazing bass arioso for the Chapel Royal singer John Bowman, whose range evidently rivalled Gostling's, and the work is cut across by the inclusion of the robustly attractive D major Chaconne more familiar to us from its appearance at the end of Act IV of *King Arthur*, written four years later. The suggestion that this might actually have been danced by the courtiers in the royal presence is by no means far-fetched, but it is just as likely that Purcell felt the need to eke out a rather thin text with an additional item. In a final analysis, the Chaconne's inclusion merely enhances the impression that we are listening to a string of enjoyable fragments, as opposed to a piece in which the composer has paid proper attention to balance and momentum.

None of the odes was published during Purcell's lifetime, though keyboard adaptations and individual numbers found their way into musical collections issued in the succeeding decade. His links with the world of printers and booksellers seem always to have been positive: they needed his expertise as much as he relied on them for a wider diffusion of his works, even in an age which leaned so heavily on the distribution of music through manuscript copies. Thus his sense of loss when John Playford the elder died in 1686 was surely quite genuine, deepened as it must have been for so many of his composer contemporaries by the recollection of the great music seller's missionary enthusiasm in promoting the art among amateurs in all its branches.

During 1687 Playford's son Henry published *A Pastoral Elegy on the Death of Mr John Playford*, 'the words by Mr Tate. Set by Mr Henry Purcell'. This has been thought to refer to Henry's brother John Playford the younger, but it now seems likely that the death commemorated so movingly was that of their father. Nahum Tate's verse is decorous and smooth-flowing, and the elegiac structure, with its alternations of rhyme and line length, shows his customary alertness to the needs of musical setting, a sensitivity soon to be displayed to the best possible advantage in

Dido and Aeneas. The 'gentle shepherds' are bidden to lament 'pious Theron's death'.

> Could innocence or piety
> Expiring life maintain,
> Or Art prevail on Destiny,
> Theron still had grac'd the plain.

His fame is assured, and the mourners are exhorted to be

> Prepar'd like him, by harmony and love,
> To join at first approach the sacred choir above.

Nothing could more powerfully underline Purcell's responsiveness to the quality and intention of his texts than the contrast offered between the eloquence of this beautiful little piece and the stilted attitudinizing of *Sound the Trumpet, Beat the Drum*. The structure is created by deftly offsetting a sense of untrammelled grief against the salving rationality and order of music whose insistent rhythmic patterns work towards a redemptive climax, in which the high voice (recent recorded interpretations feature either a soprano or a tenor) is joined by a bass, to embody the culminating harmonies of heavenly song. From another aspect the elegy (often known by its opening words as *Gentle Shepherds, You that Know*) can be viewed as a small Italian cantata, in which passages of free-flowing recitative are alternated with ground-bass sections founded on a tolling bell, a device Purcell had famously used in a more festive context for *Rejoice in the Lord Alway*. Yet its affiliation with the earlier style of Matthew Locke (the 1677 elegy was surely not forgotten) implies a respect for the English musical tradition Playford himself had done so much to foster.

Henry Playford may not have been such a shrewd businessman as his father, who, whatever his ideals, kept a sharp eye on fluctuations of popular taste and gaps in the market, but during the last twenty years of the seventeenth century he enthusiastically sustained the firm's readiness to publish new music by London composers. When however, on 7 November 1687, he advertised *Harmonia Sacra or Divine Hymns and Dialogues*, the initiative may not have been prompted by purely musical considerations. The book was given its imprimatur on the same day at Lambeth

Palace by William Needham, chaplain to the Archbishop of Canterbury William Sancroft, and when it actually appeared the following year, the epistle dedicatory was addressed to Thomas Ken, Bishop of Bath and Wells. The names of both prelates were soon to achieve national significance as being among those of the seven bishops who were imprisoned in the Tower of London rather than authorize their clergy to read King James's Declaration of Indulgence from the pulpit. Sancroft was a mild-mannered man whose loyalty to established church-and-king Toryism was increasingly at odds with James's zealous promotion of Catholicism. Ken, made of sterner stuff, had once preached a sermon in the presence of Charles II which touched rather too severely on Nell Gwynn, one of the two royal *maîtresses en titre*. When the see of Bath and Wells fell vacant soon afterwards, Charles's sense of humour came to the fore when he suggested 'the little black fellow that was so hard upon poor Nelly' as the likeliest candidate for episcopacy.

The presence of an Anglican imprimatur, and a dedication to a bishop known for his inflexible constancy to a church many now supposed to be seriously in danger from the King's abuse of his prerogative in the name of Popery, gave an obviously Protestant slant to *Harmonia Sacra*, confirmed, though somewhat more obliquely, by Playford's introductory address to Ken. 'Now as to this present collection, I need say no more than that the words were penn'd by such persons as are, and have been very eminent for learning and piety; and indeed, he that reads them as he ought, will soon find his affections warm'd, as with a coal from the altar, and feel the breathings of divine love from every line.' With its beautiful engraving opposite the title page, by the Huguenot artist Simon Gribelin, a refugee in 1681 from persecution at Blois, showing a trio of musical angels against a landscape backdrop, and with a generally high standard of presentation in the musical text (though there is a list of 'erratas to be amended with a pen') the publication was surely intended in part as an English riposte to the seductiveness of Italian music by Innocenzo Fede and others, currently gracing worship at the Catholic chapels of Whitehall and St James's.

In purely musical terms, leaving aside its propagandistic importance, *Harmonia Sacra* (a succeeding instalment was published five years later) represents the last, most impressive monument to that Protestant devotional tradition of 'chamber piety' which we have noted earlier in connection with Purcell's Charterhouse motets. Henry Playford brought together for his anthology some of the finest works of this kind produced since the Restoration. 'As for the musical part,' he declared, 'it was compos'd by the most skilful masters of this age; and though some of them are now dead, yet their composures have been review'd by Mr Henry Purcell, whose tender regard for the reputation of those great men made him careful that nothing should be published, which, through the negligence of transcribers, might reflect upon their memory.' Matthew Locke was here, so too was Pelham Humfrey; John Blow was represented by an eloquent setting of George Herbert's 'And Art Thou Griev'd' as well as by a dialogue cantata whose text was based on the moment in Christ's parable of Dives and Lazarus when Dives pleads with Abraham to save him from burning in hell.

The character of several of these pieces, derived though their poetry is from English Protestant 'metaphysical' sources, leans nevertheless, in allusion if not in outline, towards continental styles, recalling the motets of French composers like Marc-Antoine Charpentier or the innumerable compositions in this genre which punctuated the ritual of cathedrals, palatine chapels, oratories and monastic foundations up and down Italy during the seventeenth century. Works such as 'A Dialogue between two Penitents set by Mr Pelham Humphryes and Dr John Blow', ending in a Latin chorus to the words 'O misere Jesu mi, Jesu indulgentissime', or indeed Blow's 'Dives and Abraham', belong to the dramatic dialogue type developed by Italian masters like Alessandro Grandi and Giacomo Carissimi. Drama in general, intense and unmistakable, conditions the religiosity of the entire collection, almost as if Playford and his editor Purcell (Blow may also have been involved) were seeking to challenge the Catholics in their own devotional idiom.

Purcell's contribution of twelve items to the 1688 *Harmonia Sacra* marks his presence more strongly than that of the other three composers. Among these dozen works are some of the most profoundly expressed religious compositions of his mature years. Though all are inward-looking rather than celebratory, none replicates another's individual world, and their range is a phenomenal testimony to the seemingly infinite expansiveness of their creator's musical inspiration. As with the Charterhouse psalms, the drive here may have been personal, related perhaps to the loss of his children. Interestingly, certain of these pieces belong to that earlier period, but were only now made available in print, though they had circulated in manuscript for some years.

One of these is 'Let the night perish', entitled 'Job's Curse' in the published source, setting a paraphrase of Old Testament verses from the Book of Job, which the scriptural original introduces with 'After this opened Job his mouth, and cursed his day'. The author was Jeremy Taylor, one of the most memorable writers of devotional prose during the mid-seventeenth century, whose *Rule and Exercises of Holy Living and Dying* long outlived his death in 1667. Rewarded with an Irish bishopric at the Restoration, he had spent the years of the Protectorate as an unofficial household chaplain and spiritual director in the family of Lord Carbery, living in north Wales, and it was here that this bleak malediction, in which Job asks why he was born and longs for the quiet of the tomb, was probably written. Purcell's treatment responds wholeheartedly to the inexorable grimness of Taylor's lines, snatching for their effective potential at phrases like 'the dark shades of an eternal night' and 'drop down into my tomb', and exploiting the grotesque horror in the idea of babies dying in the womb at the very mention of Job's birth. Throughout most of the piece the emphasis, melodic and harmonic, is on falling towards a desired nemesis of self-forgetfulness, and the same concept inspires the final section, a short triple-time duet evoking that favourite Baroque spiritual theme, the power of the grave to act as a social leveller.

The Anglican saint George Herbert was an older contemporary of Jeremy Taylor's, whose single book of verse *The Temple* was endlessly imitated by religious poets after his untimely death in 1633 at the age of forty. Two of his poems appear in *Harmonia Sacra*, 'And Art Thou Griev'd' to music by John Blow, and the abjectly despondent 'With Sick and Famish'd Eyes', a penitential outcry in which the soul finds no ultimate relief, given a heartfelt chromatic pictorialism by Purcell. Even in a setting like that of John Norris's 'The Aspiration', 'How Long, Great God', the stress is initially on languishing sadness, and only gradually does the music's thrust acknowledge the enabling power of love. This admirable poem was written by one of Herbert's successors as vicar of Bemerton near Salisbury, a distinguished Oxonian adherent of the so-called 'Cambridge Platonist' circle reconciling Christian and rational humanist ideas. Veering and plunging hither and thither, Purcell's musical line enacts the imprisoned soul's search for liberation before a brisk, airy close implies the triumph of divine grace.

The mood of prophetic sombreness is intensified in two more expansive Purcellian numbers in the collection, a version of the lines 'On Our Saviour's Passion' by Francis Quarles and a treatment of Abraham Cowley's astonishing paraphrase of a whole apocalyptic visionary chapter of the Book of Isaiah, 'Awake, Awake and with Attention Hear'. Quarles, described by the Oxford antiquarian Anthony à Wood as 'an old puritanical poet . . . the sometime darling of our plebeian judgment', had died in 1644, but his verse was still a favourite in sober Christian households, and Purcell's animation of his poem on the moment at which the crucified Jesus gave up the ghost lends the words a pathetic nobility, which is a good deal more than their rhetoric deserves. The Cowley setting, written in 1685, is much the most grandly conceived of the composer's religious solo songs, making deft use of formal variations between recitative and arioso and suggesting that the more nightmarish aspects of Isaiah as interpreted by Cowley, invoking a universal hecatomb, the Battle of Nature and Time, the sky shrinking and crackling 'like parchment in a fire', rotting corpses, lakes of blood, glutted vultures and unburied ghosts, sent Purcell into an exuberant creative spin which took little account of a singer's stamina.

Harmonia Sacra is not all dejection and despair, though critics tend to agree that a work like 'We Sing to Him Whose Wisdom Form'd the Ear' forfeits spontaneity almost by virtue of its relative jubilance in comparison with the other pieces. Even Purcell's account of the two morning and evening hymns by William Fuller, neither poem quite as dark as some of its companions, has a chiaroscuro quality, the vocal line touched throughout with prevailing harmonic shadow. In the case of the evening hymn, there is evidence that the composer rewrote Fuller's verses as published in Nahum Tate's *Miscellanea Sacra* so that he could get the more penitential tone with which he obviously felt most in sympathy when writing this kind of music.

In the summer of 1687 Mary of Modena had gone to take the waters at Bath – or 'the Bath' as it was often called – to recuperate from the shock of her mother's recent death, while King James made a pilgrimage to the Welsh shrine of Saint Winifred's Well, where he bathed in the spring and prayed fervently for a male heir, in the hope that this at least would endear him to his erring subjects. By the end of the year the Queen was pregnant, and at Bath a loyal Scottish peer Lord Melfort raised a commemorative monument to the fact, consisting of a dome supporting a cross, a crown of thorns and a dove, placed in the Cross Bath where regular bathing was held to have encouraged the royal success.

This was not Mary Beatrice's first pregnancy, but everyone seems to have guessed that after a sequence of childbed losses she was destined on this occasion to bear a healthy baby. The news was greeted nevertheless with such resentful scepticism that for once we can feel genuine compassion for James and Mary, as prospective parents whose claim to their own child was doubted from the outset. Princess Anne, soured by successive failures to produce a child, was enraged at the news and began immediately to foster the rumour that the whole business was an elaborate imposture. To her sister Mary of Orange, another disappointed would-be mother, she wrote slightingly of the Queen: 'Her being so positive it will be a son, and the principles of that religion being such that they will stick at nothing, be it never so wicked, if it will promote their interest, give some cause to fear there may be foul play intended.' So eager was the Princess to sustain this fiction – for such it at length turned out to be – that she even refused her stepmother's invitation to put a hand on her belly and feel the baby kicking inside the womb.

On 15 and 29 January 1688, days of public thanksgiving were ordained and special forms of prayer issued for worshippers in churches of whatever denomination, but few seem to have responded to the announcement with any particular enthusiasm. Going to St James's Piccadilly, Henry Hyde, Lord Clarendon wrote afterwards: 'this is the thanksgiving day appointed for the Queen's being with child; there were not above two or three in the church who brought the form of prayer with them . . . as if scarce anybody believed it to be true. Good God help us!' The Protestant Chapel Royal was plainly required to manifest some kind of open rejoicing, and an anthem *Blessed Are They that Fear the Lord* was commissioned for the occasion from Henry Purcell. The words were derived from the same marriage psalm, 128, which he had used for the anthem composed for his wedding to Frances Peters, but this time the emphasis was more obviously on what England was likely to gain in the way of peace and wealth from the assurance of a Stuart heir. The Chapel Royal violins were drafted into service for a hauntingly beautiful introductory symphony, whose slow section edges itself into place via some effective suspensions over a long-drawn pedal bass, and as in other Purcellian sacred works the text is dramatized through the assignment of different roles to various voices. The tenor is the abstract commentator, the bass becomes the worthy farmer eating the fruits of his labour, and twin trebles hover on high like the winged putto heads decorating the sculptured church monuments of the period, their cries of 'O well is thee' reiterated with something more like melancholy than jubilation from one end of the piece to the other.

It was during this fateful year of 1688 that a musical controversy in which Purcell was centrally involved at last reached its resolution. We have already seen how his judgment was courted in respect of the appointment of an organist to the church of St Katherine Cree, and as regards the quality of the instrument itself. The organ's builder, 'Father Smith', had been commissioned in 1682 by the resident lawyers of the Middle Temple – always known as 'benchers' – to set up an organ in the Temple Church, the handsome Gothic structure whose western end preserved the circular space which its founders, the medieval Knights of the Order of the Temple, always prescribed for their worship of God. Not to be outdone, the benchers of the adjacent Inner Temple engaged the services of Renatus Harris, whose unusual Christian name, the Latin original of René, derived from his birth in France, where his father had retreated as an apprentice to the great organ builder Thomas Dallam, a refugee from the Civil War when so many of his organs were destroyed.

In February 1683 both Smith and Harris were encouraged to assemble their respective instruments in one or other of the two inn halls, where they could be properly tested before a suitably discerning audience. Nothing came of this suggestion, but the following summer Harris was permitted to set up his completed organ in the Temple Church itself and Smith presumably did the same, since soon afterwards the musical contest began in earnest. Harris was a Catholic, who subsequently provided an organ for Queen Catherine's chapel, so not surprisingly he secured her chief organist, Giovanni Battista Draghi, to demonstrate his handiwork to best advantage. To make Smith's stops and pipes discourse, the Middle Temple benchers turned to John Blow and Henry Purcell, whose friendship with the Norths stood the latter in good stead here, since Roger North belonged to the inn and played a significant part in what fast became a wearisome dispute over respective technical merits. North strongly disapproved of the growing enthusiasm for forcing musicians in various fields to compete with each other – 'so much a mistake it is to force artists upon a competition, for all but one are sure to be malecontents' – and later observed that in the course of the present argument, 'the 2 competitors, the best artists in Europe, Smith and Harris, were but just not ruined'. In 1685, when he and his fellow benchers, tiring of 'the tedious competicion', declared for Smith's instrument, 'both for sweetnes and fulnes of Sound, besides the extraordinary Stopps, quarter Notes, and other Rarityes therein ... and that the same is more ornamentall and substantiall', their disgruntled Inner Temple counterparts proposed that an impartial jury, 'such as are the best Judges of Musick' be appointed by mutual consent.

North was quite correct in asserting that the two organ builders were placed under heavy financial stress by a contest which seems in the end to have had more to do with the know-all vanity of barristers than with the contrasted virtues of the organs themselves. Smith received an advance of £500 from the Middle Temple, designed either as a part payment if he should be the winner or as a compensatory *douceur* if he lost. Harris petitioned for £100 from his backers, adducing 'extraordinary charges of watchmen, besides the damage and loss of time in attendance and ineffectual working' which produced 'great straits and inconveniences for want of money to supply his occasions'. The watchmen were needed to prevent sabotage: writing almost a century later, the musical historian Charles Burney says that the organist Thomas Roseingrave told him that on the night before the reed stops were due to be tested, Harris's partisans punctured the bellows on Smith's organ, and that both sides were guilty of 'the most mischievous and unwarrantable acts of hostilities'.

The two instruments, one set up on the south side of the altar and the other in the west gallery (since removed), were played on alternate days by Draghi, Purcell and Blow before all three performed in succession on a single day. The Inner Temple benchers' insistence on independent arbitration, resulting in further delays, called for visits to the church by no less a figure than the Lord Chief Justice himself, the historically notorious 'Bloody Judge Jeffreys'.

An archetypal example of the ambitious Welshman jockeying for position and influence among the English establishment, Jeffreys has never been successfully vindicated by Tory revisionist historians of the period, against even the most vituperative Whig accounts of his career as a judicial bully and fixer on behalf of Charles II and James II. Both loaded him with favours in return for his gerrymandering operation of the law as the engine of their barely concealed drive towards recovering the executive power lost to the crown at the Restoration. Even Roger North, a natural conservative whose sympathies were always profoundly Tory, wrote of him with a kind of horrified absorption, relying heavily on the notes left by his brother the Lord Keeper, who had charted with evident alarm the sinisterly meteoric rise of this hard-drinking, foul-mouthed, scornfully hubristic creature, sulphurously fascinating to his more sober contemporaries in the continuous abuse of his authority and personal gifts.

In the early summer of 1688 Purcell's path thus briefly crossed that of Jeffreys, now at the zenith of his success and newly created

Lord Chancellor of England. Famous for the swiftness of his judgments, Jeffreys gave a decision in favour of Smith's organ, while Harris's work was divided between St Andrew's church, Holborn, and the cathedral of Christ Church in Dublin. On 21 June 1688 Smith signed the document transferring his 1,700-pipe instrument to the Temple in exchange for the sum of £1,000, the whole transaction overseen by a group of music-loving benchers led by 'the Honourable Roger North'. What exactly Purcell played as test pieces on the organ, with its '14 pipes Spittsflute of metal', '16 pipes Voice human', '17 pipes Gedackt of wood' and '22 pipes Sequialtera', we cannot know, and it is in any case regrettable that so little music of any significance written by him in his incarnation as an organist survives for us to judge what his skill must have been. The most substantial of the organ works attributed to him, a Toccata in A major, now has a question mark hanging over it regarding authorship, some musicologists maintaining that it was probably composed by one of his contemporaries in the North German style of Nicholas Bruhns and Dietrich Buxtehude, though it would be gratifying to discover that this exuberantly confident essay in the form was in fact by Purcell himself.

The spring and summer months of 1688 which witnessed the build up to the last round of the Temple benchers' Battle of the Organs saw Purcell returning, after a prolonged absence, to the stage. This time he was writing for the Theatre Royal in Drury Lane, where Thomas D'Urfey's play *A Fool's Preferment or The Three Dukes of Dunstable* was licensed for performance at the end of May. The play is an adaptation of an indifferent Jacobean comedy, *The Noble Gentleman* by John Fletcher, on which D'Urfey considerably improved, sharpening the main plot involving the socially ambitious Aurelia and her husband Cocklebrain. The former takes the latter to town and engineers a bogus dukedom for him so that she can continue to indulge her addiction to the fashionable new card game of basset. The underplot, surrounding the madness of Lyonel, who, rightly as it turns out, suspects his sweetheart Celia of receiving the king's favours, was also refashioned to suit the talents of William Mountfort, a protégé of Judge Jeffreys and much commended both for the ardour with which he played tragic lovers and for the relaxed elegance and good taste he brought to 'fine gentleman' roles in comedy.

Six of Purcell's songs for *A Fool's Preferment* were printed separately as an addition to the published quarto of the play, whose title page advertises 'Together with all the SONGS and NOTES to 'em, Excellently Compos'd by Mr Henry Purcell'. One is a Scotch song, 'A Dialogue by Jockey and Jenny', a folk parody of the kind of pastoral colloquy between Thyrsis and Dorinda or Damon and Phyllis popular with seventeenth-century poets and songwriters. The other items all spring directly from the occasions of the drama, being written specifically for William Mountfort who, so Colley Cibber tells us, 'sung a clear counter-tenor and had a melodious warbling throat'. Each is couched in a different mood, reflecting the shifts in Lyonel's mad humours. In 'I sigh'd and I pin'd', the lover, with mock gaiety, arraigns himself for trusting 'a jilt that laughed at my pains', while in 'There's nothing so fatal as woman', the music matches the cynicism of the lyrics:

> There's nothing so fatal as woman
> To hurry a man to his grave,
> You may think, you may plot,
> You may sigh like a sot,
> She uses you more like a slave.

> But a bottle, altho' it be common,
> The cheats of the fair will undo,
> It will drive from your head
> The delights of the bed,
> He that's drunk is not able to woo.

'Fled is my love', sung by Lyonel in the depths of his frenzy, and its companion piece ''Tis death alone', are gem-like exemplars of Purcell's ability to etch in miniature the entire and convincing profile of a single human emotion and to make us feel that nothing more needs adding to the picture. Equally attractive is the tiny 'If thou wilt give me back my love', whose serene triple-time lilt falls somewhere between a minuet and a jig. But it is Lyonel's maddest effusion of all which has remained among the composer's most famous songs: 'I'll sail upon the Dog Star' tested Mountfort's skills to the utmost in the deliberate tension between Purcell's counterpoint and the crazy extravagance of Lyonel's ranting.

> I'll climb the frosty mountains
> And there I'll coin the weather;
> I'll tear the rainbow from the sky,
> And tie both ends together.

The play, though subsequently revived at Dorset Garden, was a failure at its first performance. Sir George Etherege, himself a dramatist and now Ambassador to the Imperial Diet at Ratisbon, wrote soon afterwards:

By my last Pacquet from England, among a heap of nauseous Trash, I received the Three Dukes of Dunstable, which is really so monstrous and insipid, that I am sorry Lapland or Livonia had not the Honour of producing it, but if I did Penance in reading it, I rejoyced to hear that it was solemnly interr'd to the Tune of Catcalls.

According to D'Urfey it flopped in part because of resentment among some of the audience at his mockery of basset. In his dedication to Charles Howard, Lord Morpeth, he says:

I knew Basset was a Game only proper for Persons of great Fortunes; and therefore I thought that a Wholsome Satyr of this kind might have oblig'd some Country-Gentleman, or Citizens of small Estates, whose Wives ne're heeding the approaching Ruin, took only care they might have the Honour to be seen at Play with Quality. But some certain, very nice, Persons, especially one, took it so to Heart that dear Basset should be expos'd, that my honest Intentions were quite frustrated . . .

Among them perhaps was Queen Mary Beatrice herself, a basset enthusiast who spent the night before the delivery of her child, on 10 June, playing the game with the King. At a quarter past eight next day she went into labour, in the presence of no less than sixty-seven people, including members of the Privy Council, three Protestant countesses, a score of ladies-in-waiting and of course James himself, whom she desired to conceal her face under the curls of his periwig. 'For she said she could not be brought to bed and have so many men look on her.' By ten o'clock she had given birth to a fine boy, to be christened James Francis Edward, and so delighted her husband with her success that he knighted the attendant physician Dr Waldegrave at the bedside and bestowed a purse of 500 guineas on the midwife Mrs Wilkes.

Besides the fact that the infant prince was almost killed as a result of his parents' foolish decision to feed him on brown bread and water in preference to hiring the services of a wet nurse, there was the whole question, as far as many Protestants were concerned, of his authenticity. Among the various rumours surrounding the Queen's pregnancy – it seems extraordinary that at the age of only twenty-nine she should have been judged too old to bear a child – none was more persistent than the notion that her baby had been smuggled into the crowded bedchamber inside a warming pan. This pernicious tarradiddle was enthusiastically accepted by Whig propagandists, and the venomous Princess Anne (another basset addict, incidentally) did her best to pour suspicion into the willing ear of Mary of Orange, whose husband William now waited at The Hague for his father-in-law to complete the process of political self-destruction begun so blindly three years earlier.

He would not have to wait long. Even King Louis of France, in his new access of Catholic fervour which had sent the Huguenots fleeing from his kingdom, warned against his cousin's imprudence in overturning the law so as to promote the faith. While the ejected President and Fellows of Magdalen remained in determined stand-off against the royal authority which had supplanted them with Jesuits, James also faced the refusal of seven Anglican bishops to promulgate his Declaration of Indulgence among their clergy, issued as it had been without Parliament's consent. Seven other bishops later added their names to the original petition submitted to the King at Whitehall, but only the first rebels were sent to the Tower of London for seditious libel. Rejecting hints that he might pardon them as a gesture of royal clemency following the prince's birth, James ordered their trial in Westminster Hall. That staggering imperviousness to reality which typifies leaders on the brink of catastrophic downfall meant that

163

when the bishops were acquitted on 29 June, to the jubilation of a mob which burned an effigy of the Pope on a bonfire in front of St James's Palace, and when his own guards gave loud 'huzza's at the verdict, his response was simply to dismiss the judges involved and to order a blacklist to be drawn up of the several hundred clergy who had refused to read the Declaration from their pulpits.

By the end of August James's son-in-law, William, Prince of Orange, had begun preparations to invade England, assured by a group of highly placed dissidents that his reception was likely to be most favourable. During the autumn, while the London mob began looting and burning popish chapels and religious houses and while most of the ambassadors from Catholic powers made haste to leave the kingdom, James hastily backtracked on his more extreme demonstrations of monarchical authority. A number of local officials, mayors, justices of the peace and lords lieutenant, who had originally been ousted in favour of Catholics, Dissenters or compliant Tories, were now reinstated, the rebellious Magdalen dons were restored to their college and the detested Earl of Sunderland, the King's chief minister, was dismissed.

Such measures came too late to convince the majority of James's subjects, whose mood of nervous expectation is potently conveyed in the notes John Evelyn wrote in his diary for 4 October. 'The King's birthday. No guns from the Tower as usual. The sun eclipsed at its rising. This day signal for the victory of William the Conqueror against Harold near Battle in Sussex. The wind, which had been hitherto west, was east all this day. Wonderful expectation of the Dutch fleet. Public prayers ordered to be used in the churches against invasion.' For once no birthday ode had been commanded from Purcell or any other composer, and the King and Queen busied themselves instead with preparing a grand tribunal to assert the legitimacy of the little Prince of Wales. Three weeks later, on 5 November 1688, William of Orange landed at Brixham in Devon, and by Christmas James had followed Mary Beatrice and her baby into perpetual exile.

5
Wayward Sisters

It was several months before William of Orange and his wife Mary, having arrived in London and taken up residence at White-hall, could be crowned King and Queen. As the eldest daughter of James II, Mary had a better right to the crown than her husband, and the two Houses of Lords and Commons, having taken care to legalize their action by declaring James unfit to rule, assembled in the Banqueting House at Whitehall on 13 February 1689 to make husband and wife a joint offer of sovereignty. The astute Earl of Halifax, whose memoirs and aphorisms afford such a fascinating glimpse into the late-seventeenth-century political mind, submitted the Declaration of Right, exacting a promise from both monarchs to be governed by the laws of England as enacted by Parliament, and the new King and Queen were then proclaimed to the ringing of bells and sounding of trumpets, 'though a great many looked very sadly upon it'.

Among these, perhaps not surprisingly, given her tendency to sombre reflection, was Mary herself. 'God knows my heart is not made for a kingdom', she confided to her private journal. She had already antagonized various people by her unfortunate determination to put on an air of self-assurance and cheerfulness at her husband's side, instead of showing the reluctance and self-doubt she actually felt on assuming a position to which even James's sternest critics believed she had no legitimate claim. She was not helped by William himself, a man whose qualities of remoteness and impatience, linked to an understandable contempt for the squalid parochialism of London's court and political life, made him instantly unpopular with his new subjects. A sexually ambiva-lent loner, adept at suppressing profound emotions under a veneer of cynical rudeness, William was never loved or appreciated by the English, and remains to this day the most seriously under-estimated of our monarchs.

Where Purcell is concerned, the standard cliché is that William cared nothing for music, and in any case had no artistic sensitivity. The latter assertion is unjust nonsense, if we consider both the embellishment of Hampton Court and Kensington Palace which took place under his direction, as well as the fitting out of the splendid palaces at Het Loo and Honselaarsdijk which he had left behind as a memorial to his innate good taste while still Stadt-holder of the Netherlands. The reality where William and music were involved seems to have been that he was not fond enough of it to want to maintain the court establishment at such a pitch of activity as that expected by his two Stuart predecessors, and the early years of his reign witnessed a gradual winding down of that great musical infrastructure of ceremonial and entertainment which had existed in the British monarchy's palaces and palatine chapels since the days of Henry VIII, an organization, indeed, never to be properly reinstated after William's death.

For the joint coronation on 11 April 1689 Purcell provided a crisply effective anthem, *Praise the Lord, O Jerusalem*, whose design, encapsulating both the awesome solemnity and the rejoic-ing inherent in the occasion, leads choir, soloists and string band from the self-consciously old-fashioned gravity of its G minor opening to a buoyant major resolution in billowing choral alle-luias. Narcissus Luttrell tells us that the service was performed 'much in the manner the former was', and from the manuscript order of ceremony we can assume that some of the anthems used for James II's crowning were recycled on this occasion. Reminders of the fugitive king made him a kind of Banquo's ghost at the day's celebrations: news was brought to William at dawn that James had landed at the head of a French army in Ireland, and while Mary was dressing to go to the Abbey she received a devas-tating letter from her father, calling down curses upon her for filial ingratitude and disobedience. She managed, however, to carry off the various stages of the not very well organized ritual without yielding openly to remorse. She must have been aware that she and her husband lay under the relentless scrutiny of courtiers and politicians whose trustworthiness could be measured by the number and degree of the bribes they received from the Jacobite court, now installed outside Paris at the château of St-Germain-en-Laye. Few of those present on the occasion could have failed to note the significance of the fact that the service was led by William Compton, Bishop of London. The saintly William Sancroft, Archbishop of Canterbury, who should have fulfilled the office, had simply refused to crown either of the sovereigns. When Mary asked for his blessing, he replied by bidding her ask her father's first of all.

Purcell's concerns regarding what William, in a letter to a Dutch friend, called 'these funny old Popish rites', were not so much to do with legality or religion as with the purely practical issue of whether or not he was to make any money from the coronation beyond what he might expect to receive as Chapel Royal organist. At James II's crowning he had been allowed to sell tickets for places in the specially constructed organ loft, together with Stephen Crespion, a 'petty canon' of Westminster and chanter of the choir. This perk was not enshrined in official regulations, but appears to have been accepted practice dating back nearly thirty years to Charles II's coronation in 1661. Even then, however, there had been some dispute as to who should be paid what for the building of extra scaffolds and galleries and the admission of spectators to such areas. A document in the Westminster Precentor's Book suggests that the choir, the vergers and the carpenter who erected the temporary structures in the Abbey churchyard should divide the takings between them, noting that 'the organist being a good gainer by his organ loft and scaffolds being erected, had no share with the rest of the choir'.

Evidently Purcell and Crespion assumed that the same privilege, enjoyed once more in 1685, could be taken for granted at this latest ceremony, but they probably did not know that Thomas Sprat, Dean of Westminster (an office he held *in commendam* with the bishopric of Rochester) had petitioned the joint sovereigns for confirmation of their right to 'several perquisites and advantages of very great value for their service and attendance' on the occasion. In reply, an order was given a fortnight before the celebrations 'that all such money as shall be raised for seats at the Coronation within the church organ-loft or churchyard shall be paid into the hands of the Treasurer and distributed as the Dean and Chapter shall think fit', but there is no proof that Purcell heard of this directive before 11 April.

A week afterwards he was ordered to hand over all the money made from ticket sales to John Needham, the Westminster Chapter Receiver, on pain of losing his organist's position, 'and it is further ordered that his stipend or salary due at our Lady Day last past be detained in the hands of the Treasurer until further order'. Purcell and Crespion having submitted £492 1s 1d, Needham, after several disbursements, including one to a woman who had cleaned the waxen effigy of Charles II which may still be seen today in the Abbey museum, divided the remaining sum of £414 4s 11d among petty canons, choristers, bell-ringers, almsmen, the butler, the gardener, the 'three choir widows' and 'the cloister porter', before giving £24 to Crespion and leaving Purcell with the relatively inconsiderable sum of £35. It is permissible to suppose that there was little joy in the Purcell household when the news arrived that the composer was to receive less than one-fourteenth of what he had assumed to be, in large part, his by custom. Given that his official salary was already overdue, that he had to wait nearly a year to be paid for his part in the coronation service and that it seems as though Needham probably fiddled the accounts to his own advantage in any case, the idea encouraged by some early Purcellian authorities that Henry was engaged in a little sharp practice is hardly sustainable.

Scarcely was the coronation over than he was summoned to provide an ode for Queen Mary's birthday on 30 April. Though there is no definite proof that *Now Does the Glorious Day Appear* belongs to 1689, since the manuscript in the British Library is undated, this appears probable, if only because other birthday odes exist for the six remaining years of Mary's life. The poet commissioned to supply the text was the distinguished comic dramatist Thomas Shadwell, unjustly if brilliantly satirized in Dryden's poem 'Mac Flecknoe' and for that reason written off by idle, incurious literary historians as a talentless hack. Those with a proper awareness of the Restoration theatrical scene will know him as a gifted and original creator of a series of comedies in which he consciously tried, not always unsuccessfully, to fulfil

Ben Jonson's idea of comic characters founded on 'humours', ruling passions providing a keynote in the idiom and mannerisms through which such figures engaged the audience. There is abundant evidence in Shadwell's plays that he was powerfully interested in music, in its techniques and in the fashions currently dominating musical style in performance and composition.

Regrettably, though he was now given the very laureateship which his old enemy Dryden had enjoyed under James II, Shadwell possessed no obvious poetic gifts. The system followed in *Now Does the Glorious Day Appear* is essentially no different from those of its precursors offered to the brothers Stuart. This, we are assured, is 'the mightiest day of all the year' and 'did the hope of liberty retrieve'. Mary, with what some may have viewed as staggering impiety, is portrayed literally as a saint on earth, enslaving all hearts, especially that of 'her hero too, t'whose conduct and whose arms/ The trembling Papal world their force must yield'. Her mingled zeal and benevolence 'must her above all former monarchs raise', even 'the great Eliza', so 'Io Triumphe let us sing/ And make Heaven's mighty concave ring'.

Musically the piece establishes new levels of inspiration and control of resources in Purcell's approach to the court ode genre, and it is possible to see the sequence of Queen Mary's birthday panegyrics as a distinctive group, rather like the late Beethoven quartets or Haydn's mature mass settings. The five-part string band is fully exploited in an overture of exceptional expansiveness, which shuns the traditional French dotted-rhythm slow section at the beginning in favour of a bustling andante. Though the choral sections are as significant as ever, especially in the expressive weight of the opening number and the final movement's overwhelming authority, there is a more obvious attempt at detaching the solo numbers, so that they seem more like Italian arias both in overall profile and in structure, a trend increasing throughout this last, hectically productive phase of the composer's career. The bass is still rewarded with one of those eloquent declamations for which, we might imagine, the singer must have felt tempted to ask expressly because Purcell was so good at writing them, but another standard feature, the alto air on a D minor ground, gains in distinctiveness because of its positioning between the bass arioso and a subsequent duet, none of these three numbers carrying a choral reprise as in certain earlier odes.

One by one during the summer of 1689 the various court musicians, apart from those who, like Innocenzo Fede, had followed James II and Mary of Modena to France, or were professed Papists like John Abell the countertenor, now embarking on a theatrical career, resumed their places in the Whitehall establishment. John Blow was appointed 'composer for the vocall musick' on 20 July, John Banister, Moses Snow and Robert King were reappointed, as was 'Mr John Gosling, clerk', while 'Henry Purcell, composer' was confirmed as part of the Private Musick. Noting the appearance of a warrant 'to swear and admitt Dr Nicholas Staggins master of their Majesties musick', we may be tempted to smile cynically at the idea of Dr Staggins continuing to enjoy a post to which merit scarcely entitled him, but his genius was doubtless administrative, and in that sense he was as serviceable at the court of the new monarchs as he had been at their predecessor's. As a footnote to Staggins's reinstatement, it is perhaps worth mentioning that a further warrant exists, dated 15 April 1690, to pay him the not inconsiderable sum of £25 16s as part of 'what is due to him as one of the musicians of the late Charles II'. Blow was also a beneficiary of this attempt at clearing the accounts of the most financially irresponsible of the Stuarts, to the tune of £30 13s 4d. Payment, however, was conditional on both men taking the oaths of allegiance to the new regime.

Purcell clearly had no problem in squaring his conscience with 'the change of crowns', a further small but significant piece of evidence that his Tory loyalty was not of a kind to lead him into the ranks of non-jurors or so far as Catholic conversion. There was a living to earn for Frances and their children. After the sadness of their earlier losses, they had finally been blessed, in 1688, with a healthy baby, a girl whom they named after her mother, and she was followed in September 1689 by a boy christened Edward for his uncle Edward Purcell, Henry's elder brother, who after a period at court as a gentleman usher had entered the army and was now an officer in an infantry regiment bound for Ireland.

Even with official entitlements secure, the prospects for displaying his musical talent to advantage were hardly enticing to Purcell
at a royal court existing more in name than in fact. William, never
the most gregarious of men, preferred the ruralities of Hampton
Court and Kensington as being better for his asthma to the bad
air of low-lying metropolitan Whitehall, and in any case hardly
cared to surround himself with the scatter of courtiers whose
gossip and ribaldry had relieved his uncle, Charles II, of boredom.
Palace society of a kind existed around Mary, whose vivacity at
first encouraged onlookers to imagine that the old Restoration
atmosphere of 'ease and fashion', gaming, dalliance and intrigue
might yet return, but she too had her serious side, jealously guard-
ing her moments of solitude, communing with her private journal
and composing prayers and religious meditations in an attempt to
sort out the ethical complexities of the position she now assumed.
Firmly founded as her spirituality undoubtedly appears, it was
not of the sort which delighted in tapping its foot to the rhythm
of an airy French symphony in the Chapel Royal or admiring the
vocal athletics of John Gostling praising the Almighty up and
down an impressive ladder of octaves.

Thus during the reign of William and Mary Purcell was forced
to look elsewhere, less for simple emolument than for the chance to
write music which would find an appreciative audience. One such
opportunity occurred during the summer of 1689, when he
received a commission to compose an ode on a text supplied by a
pupil at a school kept by Lewis Maidwell in the parish of St
James's, Piccadilly. A King's Scholar at Westminster School,
Maidwell had entered St John's College, Cambridge as a Bishop's
Boy in 1670 – that is to say, under the same dispensation that
Purcell was educated by at Westminster – and though they were
not exact contemporaries, it was perhaps this school connection,
possibly cemented by Dr Busby, which brought them together on
the present occasion. Purcell may also have heard of the prank
Maidwell had played while at Cambridge on an over-zealous
undergraduate named Perry, busy lodging information against suspected nonconformists. A forged document was sent to Perry,
purporting to bear the King's signature and seal, which was then

171

proudly shown to Dr Turner, Master of St John's. Turner at once guessed that Maidwell was involved,

> convented the boy and he could not then deny it. His impudence was inexcusable, but we are all satisfied that there was no malicious design, but pure roguery. This I must needs say for him: He has bin studious and inoffensive in all his carriage, except this great misdemeanor, and he is of excellent facultys. He comes to us from the top of Westminster Schools, and thoughte this but a Westminster trick, not considering the consequence.

Maidwell had also tried his hand at playwriting, with a comedy produced at Dorset Garden in 1680, *The Loving Enemies*, starring the greatly adored Elizabeth Barry (who spoke a bawdy epilogue specially written by Shadwell) and featuring at least one genuinely amusing character, Circumstantio, 'a formal Valet de Chambre very troublesome, with impertinent Rhetorick'. There was no impertinent rhetoric in the more than passable poem tendered to Purcell by Maidwell's unnamed scholar, and the composer rose keenly to the challenge of his elegant verses, appropriately suffused with allusions to the sort of classical learning which provided the basis for a decent seventeenth-century school education. Despite the composer re-utilizing the symphony from the 1685 coronation anthem *My Heart Is Inditing* – James II was now a safe distance away at St-Germain, so there was no concern over giving offence to royalty – *Celestial Music Did the Gods Inspire*, 'A song that was perform'd at Mr Maidwell's, a schoolmaster on ye 5th of August 1689 ye words by one of his scholars', remains among Purcell's freshest and most engaging works.

Again the chorus figures only in the first and last movements, the former introduced by a superb bass solo, building up the picture of music as both inspiring and sensual (the repeats of 'touch'd' in the line 'When at their feasts Apollo touch'd his lyre' are particularly effective), the latter constructed as a trio celebrating the charms of music as worked by Phyllis on Philander, in which Purcell gives a striking harmonic profile to the word 'ravish'd' and provides spirited Italianate passages for the first violin. Stretched between these two pieces are four deliciously varied numbers: a countertenor air with recorders and a lovely soprano evocation of the world of Virgil's eclogues, written over ground basses, a stirring Scotch jig describing Amphion's ability to make the stones of Thebes dance to his music, and, most haunting of all, the praise of Orpheus whose 'soft'ning lyre did cruel Pluto move', a countertenor aria in which the relaxed assurance of Purcell's genius generates a sublime spontaneity in the movement of the vocal line.

Lewis Maidwell was evidently a successful and respected schoolmaster committed to his profession, as can be seen in the *Essay upon the Necessity and Excellency of Education* he published in 1705, ten years after Purcell died. Acknowledging his debt to Dr Busby he disparages the mushrooming of cheap schools, 'too many little Parish Nurserys of the Latin Tongue', and suggests that England should emulate France in setting up a mathematical and navigational school. 'The Antients', he says of education, 'were ravish'd with her Charms, and in Raptures recommended her Incomparable Advantages to Posterity,' though the House of Commons, before whom he had set his proposals, was typically unenthusiastic for anything so organized and innovative.

In his petition to the House he mentions his 'Large Brick-House . . . situat in an Open Healthful Air, in the Parish of St James Westminster, Wel-wal'd about with Spatious Ground, and Out-houses and other Conveniencys . . .' and it was presumably here that *Celestial Music Did the Gods Inspire* was performed. Maidwell's anxiety over the growth of low-grade schooling was no doubt justified, but an increasing concern among Londoners at various social levels with securing an adequate degree of book-learning for their children meant that during the latter half of the seventeenth century a whole range of different educational establishments had sprung up around the fringes of the city. Among these were a number of girls' boarding schools, generally located in salubrious villages within convenient coach-driving distance of metropolitan London, but still sufficiently rural for disease, sanitation and the tiresome attentions of philandering rakes and gallants not to prove too much of a problem. Some of the most famous were in Hackney: at one of these Katherine Philips, 'the matchless Orinda', best-known woman poet of the early Restoration years, received what was obviously an excellent schooling. Other establishments opened their doors in Clapham, Bloomsbury, Kensington and Mortlake, while the one in Islington was kept by the wife of John Playford the elder.

Their popularity made them an ideal target for a comic dramatist like Tom D'Urfey, whose *Love for Money or The Boarding School*, first produced in 1691, features some splendid fun at the expense of over-ambitious parents, lax discipline and the noisy girls themselves in the persons of Miss Jenny and Miss Molly, 'two tawdry, hoyden, over-grown romps of the boarding school'. The scene of the play is 'Chelsey, By the River', and it was here that one of the best-known of all the London girls' schools had originally been opened, in a house overlooking the broad sloping bank of the Thames on what is now Cheyne Walk, during the 1670s by Jeffrey Banister, one of the royal violinists, and his fellow musician Thomas Lowe, who had been a gentleman of the Chapel Royal before the Civil War. The school stood next door to the residence of the Earl of Lindsey (a house still existing), noted as a Royalist commander, and it was the social cachet of Chelsea which no doubt appealed to aristocratic parents in search of a place which might give their daughters a decorous polish before turning them forth on to the marriage market.

In 1680 the school was taken over by Josias Priest, who had made a successful career for himself as a dancing master and what would nowadays be called a choreographer at the London theatres. This explains why *Love for Money*, which contains a lecherous dance teacher among its characters, was hissed by members of Priest's profession at its first performance. The school's day-to-day running was managed to a large extent by Mrs Priest, whose name was often attached to it, and though the general atmosphere may well have smacked somewhat of the academy portrayed in D'Urfey's farce, the place was evidently well considered and offered a full range of genteel accomplishments. One parent who thought highly of it was Sir Edmund Verney of Claydon, son of that very Sir Ralph who had once employed Purcell's grandfather as a carpenter. His daughter Molly, at eight years old, was whisked off to 'Mrs Priest's school at Great Chelsey' in her Aunt Elizabeth's 'chariot', after her father had spent some days in London

with her. One of his letters makes reference to a sophisticated extra included in the curriculum for which he had to pay 'a Guiney entrance and some 40s more to buy materials to work upon', the newly popular art of japanning, working in lacquer on wooden boxes and furniture:

> I find you have a desire to learn to Jappan, as you call it, and I approve of it; and so I shall of any thing that is Good & Virtuous, therefore learn in God's name all Good Things, & I will willingly be at the Charge so farr as I am able – tho' They come from Japan & from never so farr & Looke of an Indian Hue & Odour, for I admire all accomplishments that will render you considerable & Lovely in the sight of God & man . . .

Molly Verney inevitably perfected her dancing while she remained at the Priests' – her aunt, little more than a child herself, admired her skill in a 'Grand Ball at Chelsey School', and she must surely have taken part in some of the theatrical entertainments which this and other seminaries of the time were accustomed to peform as a seventeenth-century equivalent of 'the school play', which forms such a hallowed fixture in our own day. The annual Westminster Latin comedy was well known, but we read of other diversions, such as James Shirley's masque *The Triumph of Beauty*, performed at the school he himself managed in 1645, and Thomas Jordan's play *Cupid His Coronation* given in 1654 at a girls' school in Spitalfields; while on 26 April 1663 Samuel Pepys noted in his diary that out walking with his wife her maid Ashwell diverted them with passages from a masque in which she herself had taken part some years earlier.

The tradition of presenting a musico-dramatic *divertissement* of some sort had been initiated at the Chelsea school before the Priests took over. In 1676 *Beauty's Triumph*, a masque by Thomas Duffett, who specialized in musical parodies and burlesques, was given 'by the scholars of Mr Jeffrey Banister and Mr James Hart, at their New Boarding School for Young ladies and Gentlewomen kept in that House which was formerly Sir Arthur Gorges, at Chelsey'. The subject was mythological, the story of the Judgment of Paris, and classical antiquity, indeed, provided the source of every other school entertainment for which the period offers us any clue.

Much more significant where Henry Purcell was concerned was the production of John Blow's *Venus and Adonis* which took place under the Priests' supervision on 17 April 1684. The recently discovered libretto, specially printed for the occasion, describes the work, which musicology still prefers to call a masque – it is not – as 'AN OPERA Perform'd before the KING. Afterwards at Mr JOSIAS PRIEST's Boarding School at Chelsey. By Young Gentlewomen'. Since this word-book was discovered among the papers of Sir John Verney, we may suppose that Molly herself watched or maybe even took part in the performance.

Venus and Adonis had been given its première at some stage during the 1680s as a piece written for presentation at court. Charles II's illegitimate daughter Lady Mary Tudor sang the part of Cupid and her mother, the actress and dancer Moll Davis who had partnered Priest in the dances for Dryden's comedy *Sir Martin Mar-All*, took the role of Venus. Blow's work is a miniature opera, of a kind not unique to Restoration England (Marc-Antoine Charpentier, his French contemporary, wrote several fine examples), and was clearly meant to capitalize on the enthusiasm for the genre created by compositions such as Shadwell's *Psyche*, produced at Dorset Garden in 1674 with music by Matthew Locke, and John Crowne's *Calisto or The Chaste Nymph*, given at court in the next year with a score by Nicholas Staggins. *Calisto* had been an expensive one-off affair, in the manner of the old court masques of Charles I's time, harnessing the talents both of professional musicians and of royal and aristocratic amateurs, including the Princesses Mary and Anne and the Duke of Monmouth.

Opera in the French vein had already been presented in London by the indifferent composer Robert Cambert, a refugee from Lully's ego-boosting machinations in Paris which had succeeded in securing to the ex-Italian the sole rights to perform French lyric drama, and in 1673 Louis Grabu made his own setting of Perrin's *Ariane et Bacchus* to honour the marriage of James II and Mary of Modena. In 1683, what is more, Blow and Staggins petitioned the King to establish 'an Academy or Opera of musick for performing or causing to be performed therein their musicall compositions', an initiative which prompted Charles to send the actor-manager Thomas Betterton to Paris with the idea of bringing home another French company to gratify the royal taste for all things Gallic and, by implication, to put English musicians in their place.

Betterton returned with Louis Grabu, who had quitted England ten years previously but was now prepared to collaborate with no less a poet than John Dryden on a full-scale English opera. *Albion and Albanius* was a celebration of the triumphant Toryism of Charles II's final years, and as such left no possibility unexplored in the use of dramatic allegory. Puritan values were represented by Zelota, London figured as Augusta, the River Thames made a personal appearance, and Tyranny and Democracy were represented alongside dances of Watermen, Sectaries and 'Property Boys' (Whigs who invoked that time-honoured English votecatcher, scaremongering about likely menaces to individual property by their political and religious enemies). From among the Olympian deities, Apollo, Juno and Iris contributed their share, and the action included a procession of Knights of the Garter, the fomenting of the Popish Plot, and a scene at Dover in which Proteus, among other transformations, briefly became a crocodile.

If not the worst of Dryden's achievements in a life of amazing fecundity and versatile inventiveness, *Albion and Albanius* deserves Edward J. Dent's description of it as 'this monument of stupidity'. Though Grabu's music, courageously marrying the appropriate French idioms with the English text, is by no means as bad as certain commentators have suggested, the work was doomed to failure, partly because Charles II died while it was still in rehearsal but also for reasons more obviously linked to the opera's artistic shortcomings. As a scurrilous contemporary pasquinade expressed it:

> Betterton, Betterton, thy decorations
> And the machines were well written, we knew;
> But all the words were such stuff we want patience,
> And little better is Monsieur Grabu.

Whether Purcell attended any of the opera's rehearsals or performances we do not know, but he obviously managed a close and

thoughtful inspection of Grabu's score. The extended choruses
with solo episodes and instrumental ritornelli were formally not
unlike those he himself produced for the early court odes, and he
was later to use them as a dramatic model in the semi-operas of
the 1690s. Another device taken over from Grabu and the French
manner in general was the use of small linking passages in the
continuo line between sections in different keys, as in the Sorceress's address to the two witches in the closing scene of *Dido and
Aeneas*. Most significant of all was Grabu's provision, at the close
of Act II of *Albion and Albanius*, of an elaborate chaconne, involving the full choral and orchestral forces. Purcell overhauled this
concept, handled without special distinction by the foreigner, in
King Arthur and *Dioclesian*, to produce some impressive examples.

In purely musical terms the most successful opera produced
during Charles II's reign was undoubtedly *Venus and Adonis*.
Traditionally the relationship between Blow and Purcell has been
seen in terms of the learned master stepping aside to allow his
brilliant pupil to blaze in a brief splendour before quietly resuming
his place after the latter's untimely death. In fact the creative
exchange between both men was on a much more equal scale, and
the modern recovery of Blow's work via the concert platform
and the record catalogue has enabled us to appreciate how much
the two composers owed to each other in terms not just of idiom
and style, but also of individual character for their various pieces.

Since Blow's opera had been performed at court with a mere
child taking Cupid's part, the Priests would have had few qualms
in mounting it at the Chelsea school. Adonis, sung by a high bass
(the baritone was not an acknowledged operatic life form before
the nineteenth century), was transposed and given to 'Mr Priest's
Daughter'. A certain 'Mris Baker a Dutch young Gentlewoman'
sang the role of Venus. As there are dances at various points in
the work, Priest's talents as professional choreographer would
have been called into play, and his considerable experience of being
what was punningly known as a 'hop-merchant' in the London
theatre must have lent valuable polish to the amateur performance
by his well-bred pupils.

No doubt emboldened by the success of this and other entertainments whose details have not yet come to light, the Priests, at

some point during 1689, mounted another opera, a work which in style and character strongly resembled *Venus and Adonis*, but which so far excelled Blow's 'masque' as to become the most famous and well-loved of all English musical works for the stage. Though controversy continues to rage as to whether the perform- ance of Henry Purcell's *Dido and Aeneas* at Mr Josias Priest's boarding school in Chelsea was its very first, this is the only one of which we have any evidence until the work's revival during the late nineteenth century. I may as well say, since this is such a notorious subject of Purcellian argument, that though there is a distinct possibility that *Dido* may have been written for earlier presentation at court and though it appears superficially unlikely that Purcell would have composed it simply to gratify the staff, pupils and parents of a girls' boarding school, none of the argu- ments marshalled against the 1689 dating is so entirely compelling as to encourage wholesale rejection of the traditional view. Several points, indeed, would seem to uphold it.

The libretto of *Dido and Aeneas* was provided by Nahum Tate, whose words Purcell had set elsewhere and who was perhaps personally known to him. In devising the drama, Tate had drawn on his own earlier play *Brutus of Alba or The Enchanted Lovers*, licensed for production at Dorset Garden on 15 July 1678, and based on the fourth book of Virgil's *Aeneid*. The tragedy's intended title had been *Dido and Aeneas*, but friends had persuaded the poet, perhaps wisely, not to risk comparisons with the epic gener- ally regarded as one of the benchmarks of polite learning through- out Europe. Tate swiftly changed the names of the principal characters by resorting to Geoffrey of Monmouth's *Historia Bri- tonum*, that bracing medieval confection of legend, tradition and folk memory intermingled with a smattering of history, which claimed, among other things, that Britain had drawn its name from Aeneas's grandson Brutus, and that London had originally been styled 'Troia Nova' – New Troy. Though by no means a direct anticipation of the libretto for *Dido and Aeneas*, *Brutus of Alba* certainly foreshadowed one or two of its more important features. The errant hero in both dramas pauses, on his way to found an empire, to indulge in dalliance with a beautiful queen, their love develops under a sorceress's baleful glare, and the queen becomes the tragic victim of her lover's imminent destiny.

Where *Dido and Aeneas* was concerned, Tate had no apparent reservations as to a direct engagement with the Virgilian theme or with boiling down the best-known episode in the *Aeneid* to make an opera. He retained the love story, the character of Dido's sister and confidante Anna, whose name, doubtless because it seemed hard on the ear, was changed to Belinda, and the famous 'royal hunt and storm' known to devotees of what used to be called 'grand opera' from its presence in Berlioz's longer, more orthodox Virgilian version, *Les Troyens*.

The supernatural motivation, on the other hand, entrusted by the Roman poet to a scenario plotted by the immortal gods, is here largely in the hands of a coven of witches, whose hatred of Dido is vaguely ascribed to what modern right-wing newspapers like to call 'the politics of envy':

> The Queen of Carthage whom we hate,
> As we do all in prosp'rous state

sings the Sorceress, having invited her 'wayward sisters' to 'share in the fame/ Of a mischief shall make all Carthage flame'. Watching *Lucia di Lammermoor* in E. M. Forster's *Where Angels Fear to Tread*, Harriet Herriton exclaims: 'Call this classical? It isn't even respectable!' The uncanonical, unrespectable nature of the witches in *Dido* has proved curiously distressing to those who would prefer the opera to be an unsullied vessel of the pure antique, and to listeners reluctant to tap into the rich veins of Restoration theatrical inventiveness. Witchcraft, by the time Tate prepared his text, had entertained London audiences in such plays as Davenant's revamping of *Macbeth*, a spectacle for which Locke had originally provided some vivid music, and Shadwell's potboiling anti-Papist comedy *The Lancashire Witches*, produced at Dorset Garden in 1681, in which Mother Demdike, Mother Chattox and the rest had actually flown across the stage with the aid of machinery. The witches in *Dido*, cackling and scarcely genteel – 'Our plot has took/ The Queen's forsook' is surely more than just standard colloquialism – are essentially figures from late-seventeenth-century low life, analogous to the bawds, bunters, keepers of various sorts of disorderly house, go-betweens, sellers of 'china oranges' and female knick-knackery who people the literature of the period.*

The Sorceress is nevertheless a majestic creature when clothed in the splendid music Purcell wrote for her – to such an extent indeed that she has been interpreted as representing the 'dark side' of Dido herself. Such grandeur relates to a possible allegorical function postulated by certain writers on the opera, who see the witches as embodiments of malign popish resistance to the Protestant settlement of 1688–9. While couplets like

> When monarchs unite, how happy their state,
> They triumph at once o'er their foes and their fate

are surely connected directly to the recent coronation of William and Mary, we look in vain for any direct allegory in the central drama. What Tate seems to have done instead is to purge Virgil's story of anything which might reflect too closely on the situation of the new Queen of England herself, and to tone down the dramatic intensity, not to speak of the heightened, doom-laden sexuality implicit in Virgil's handling of the story. To believe that Mary, assuming that she knew anything of the opera (and it is faintly possible that she may have attended its first performance), would have taken offence at the spectacle of a queen forsaken by a warrior husband is to misunderstand her clear grasp of political realities. Even if she missed William on his annual campaigning, she had been married to him long enough to know that his soldier- ing was no mere cosmetic performance, but inspired by a driving determination to overturn French dominance in Europe. Her own task was to manage the inner circle of government while he was away, a job made more difficult by the self-seeking and faithless- ness of those in high office.

Setting aside the fairly light superstructure of contemporary political allusion, what are we to make of the drama which runs beneath it? Critics have been less than generous to Tate and his 'wretched couplets', and it is now customary to dismiss the text

---

*Note however that the earliest printed libretto (1689) calls them 'enchantresses' rather than 'witches'.

of *Dido and Aeneas* as little better than claptrap. Closer inspection induces a more positive view: lines such as Dido's notorious

> Thus on the fatal banks of Nile
> Weeps the deceitful crocodile

seem, to this writer at least, consistent with late Baroque decorum in being appropriate to the situation of a frantic woman berating the lover who is trying his hardest to make a dignified getaway. The dramaturgy is sound throughout, there are skilful alternations of mood, the characters – even the vacillating Aeneas – are sharply drawn, and some at least of the poetry is genuinely beautiful:

> Wayward sisters, you that fright
> The lonely traveller by night,
> Or like dismal ravens crying,
> Beat the windows of the dying ...
>
> With drooping wings you Cupids come
> To scatter roses on her tomb.
> Soft and gentle as her heart,
> Keep here your watch and never part.

To turn up our noses at verse like this is either pedantic or else curmudgeonly, or perhaps merely snobbish. Could we have done any better? We have already noted the composer's ability to make a silk purse out of a sow's ear where poor textual material was involved. The success of *Dido and Aeneas* is owing mostly to Purcell himself, but it needs saying that it would hardly make the impact it does on modern audiences without the contribution of Tate's serviceable drama.

Some of the original score has been lost, assuming this portion was actually set to music by Purcell. The 1689 word-book contains a prologue, in the manner of French and Italian opera of the period, involving the Olympian deities Phoebus and Venus, but no Purcellian music for this has ever been discovered, neither has an adequate solution been found to the curiously lame conclusion to Act II, as it now exists in a musical text based on the earliest manuscript scores. Aeneas, having accepted the command apparently sent from Jove via Mercury (impersonated by the Sorceress's 'trusty elf'), ends the act with an arioso blaming the gods for his dilemma. Once again the word-book tantalizes us with the presence, immediately following this, of a witches' chorus:

> Then since our charms have sped,
> A merry dance be led.
> By the nymphs of Carthage to please us,
> They shall all dance to ease us,
> A dance that shall make the spheres to wonder,
> Rending those fair groves asunder.

Since we know that Purcell's score was used as an entertainment inserted into Charles Gildon's adaptation of *Measure for Measure* in 1700, we must suppose that the music for this chorus and the ensuing 'Groves Dance' disappeared soon afterwards, as both items figure in Gildon's version, attached to a moralizing duet on fame and honour for two of Aeneas's companions, set by John Eccles.

The opera we know as *Dido and Aeneas* owes much to the example set by Blow in *Venus and Adonis*. Both works share the same tragic core involving the heroine's loss of the man she loves, both make use of lighter episodes to heighten the tragedy. In each opera the composer has been careful to accentuate, through the prevailing tonal scheme, the inevitability of a sad fate, and each is initiated by a prologue and an overture in the approved Parisian manner. There is even a direct allusion to the earlier work in Act II of *Dido and Aeneas*, where the Trojan hero, showing off the wild boar he has just killed, draws Dido's attention to its

> tushes far exceeding
> Those did Venus' huntsman tear.

Like Blow, Purcell makes use of key identification: the opening act of *Dido* shifts from C minor to a positive C major in the hubristic triumph of 'Let the hills and the vales'; the Sorceress and her fellow witches move out of the sinisterly bleak F minor to the Echo dance's F major; while in the last scene we come to rest, after the anguished parting of the two lovers, in the melancholy G minor of 'When I am laid in earth' and 'With drooping wings'.

It is not by its musical structure alone that *Dido and Aeneas* has gained for Purcell an international reputation he never properly enjoyed during his lifetime. We can praise the work for that almost indefinable beauty which invades the ears from the overture's first bars and 'Shake the cloud from off your brow' to the heartstopping chromatic slide from c" to d' accomplished in 'Thy hand, Belinda'. We can admire the deftness of its musical characterizations, more especially in the contrasted figures of Dido and her incomparable foil, the irrepressibly optimistic Belinda. Yet in the end what we are actually celebrating throughout the piece is the Purcellian synthesis, the composer's remarkable ability to weld together three musical idioms, English, French and Italian, in the service of his own individuality. Whatever the formal indebtedness of his declamatory style to the French *tragédie lyrique* or his Italianate use of identifiably separate musical numbers, there is no sense of him trying, at any point in the opera, slavishly and self-consciously to imitate a foreign model. The recitative, rhythmically and instrumentally far more varied than those of Lully and Charpentier, owes as much to Purcell's rootedness in English seventeenth-century traditions as the dramatically diversified choruses do to his mastery of writing for mixed voices in the Chapel Royal anthems and court odes. At the risk of sounding too resonantly nationalistic, it should be said that we are sometimes in danger of ignoring *Dido*'s English inheritance in our zeal to rescue Purcell from charges of provincialism.

Ironically it is this issue which forms part of the prevailing battle about the date of the opera's first performance. The 1689 Chelsea boarding school context has recently been spurned in favour of a presentation several years earlier before an aristocratic adult audience at the court of Charles II. Since *Venus and Adonis* had been specially revived by the Priests for their schoolgirls, why should not *Dido and Aeneas* have been the object of a similar exercise? In addition, the prevailing style, it is argued, implies an earlier period in Purcell's creative output than the end of the 1680s. The wide choral spacing, the running ground bass in a piece like 'Oft she visits this lov'd mountain', the declamatory writing in the manner of Locke and Humfrey, Blow's influence in the various bursts of arioso and the assignment of instruments to accompany the individual chorus lines are all features invoked in support of a dating somewhere around 1684. What is more, say these 'early-ists', would not Purcell, so heavily committed in the spring of 1689, what with the composition of *Praise the Lord, O Jerusalem* for the coronation and of *Now Does the Glorious Day Appear* for the royal birthday, have found himself more than a little over-burdened with the writing of a complete mini-opera?

This last objection is more easily dealt with than the others. There is no reason why a composer with such an evident gift for rapid invention should not have begun work on *Dido* at the beginning of the year or even at the close of 1688. Nothing neces-sarily ordains that its creation must have been uninterrupted by other projects, especially in so busy a life as Purcell's now was. As for the stylistic argument, it has been convincingly shown that however much his musical idiom may have altered with maturity and changing currents in the increasingly cosmopolitan world of London music-making, several aspects of it remained constant throughout his career.

A much more convincing view seems to support the 'late-ist' position, though not, alas, to the extent of clinching the argument. Quite simply, since not a shred of evidence exists for a court performance of *Dido and Aeneas*, and since the printed libretto would surely have mentioned this had it taken place, the work must indeed have been composed expressly for the Priests' school. The fact that *Venus and Adonis* had already been given there merely reinforces this belief. Purcell must have been aware that if the boarders were equal to singing Blow's music, then they were gifted with considerable versatility. Interestingly, when the earlier opera was performed by the girls, the part of Adonis was sung by the Priests' daughter, so if she was still a pupil in 1689 she may have taken the role of Aeneas. Considering that, apart from the Trojan hero, the only other males in the work are the sailor in the final act and the false Mercury sung by the 'trusty elf' (whose sex is not specified), and that both their contributions are extremely brief, it seems more than likely that Purcell, seasoning his score with dances for Priest to choreograph, wrote the whole piece, as much of it as has come down to us, for the Chelsea girls of 1689.

A special epilogue for the occasion was provided by Thomas

D'Urfey, who probably gleaned some of his material in *Love for Money* during his visits to the Priests in connection with the *Dido* performances. Making jocular reference to the girls' virginity,

> Great Providence has still more bounteous been
> To save us from those grand deceivers, men,
> Here blest with Innocence and peace of Mind,
> Not only bred to virtue, but inclin'd

the poet also stressed the fact that whatever their families' politics they were all of the right religion:

> Rome may allow strange Tricks to please her sons,
> But we are Protestants and English nuns;
> Like nimble fawns and birds that bless the spring,
> Unscarr'd by turning times we dance and sing.

The point of such allusions would hardly have been lost on adult members of the audience, more particularly since the speaker of D'Urfey's epilogue was the sixteen-year-old Lady Dorothy Burke. Her father, the Earl of Clanricarde, was an Irish peer from a respected Papist clan, but in 1680, while still Lord Dunkellin, he had conformed to Anglicanism for reasons which doubtless had something to do with political expediency, and sent his son Ulick to Oxford to be educated as a Protestant. Charles II, it should be noted, wrote personally to Dunkellin to thank him for his adherence to 'the true Protestant religion', and enjoined his father the 7th Earl to make him a proper allowance for the support of his family. When James II came to the throne, Dunkellin* slipped back to Catholicism and sent Lady Dorothy to a Benedictine convent school in Dublin. By 1689 the nuns had left hurriedly for the Continent, and Lady Dorothy was transferred to the Priests at Chelsea, where her fees were paid with the help of a pension from Queen Mary.

Not everyone approved of the amateur dramatics on Thames-side. The following year a Mrs Buck, commissioned to look over the London girls' schools on behalf of her friend Mary Clarke,

---

*He succeeded to the earldom of Clanricarde at the death of his father in 1687. His younger son John rejoiced in the courtesy title of Lord Boffin.

wife of a Whig Member of Parliament and living at Chipley in Somerset, wrote censoriously: 'I went my self to three schools. Preists at Little Chelsey was one which was much commended; but he hath lately had an Opera, which I'me sure hath done him a great Injury; & the Parents of the Children not satisfied with so Publick a show . . . Att present all schools are redicul'd: they have latly made a Play cal'd The Boarding School.'

However Priest might have suffered from such parental starchiness, Purcell's fame remained undimmed. For the previous two years he had been writing and publishing a wide variety of single songs, mostly issued by Henry Playford and John Carr, and covering a wealth of different moods. Early in 1688 Playford had issued *The Banquet of Musick: or a Collection of the Newest and Best Songs Sung at Court, and at Public Theatres*, intended to initiate a companion series to the firm's four-volume *Theatre of Musick*, and followed up this first instalment with a new collection issued under the same title that summer. Purcell's songs in these two anthologies ranged from airy trifles such as 'Sylvia, Now Your Scorn Give Over' and the lilting 'Ah, How Pleasant 'tis to Love', a ditty which shows how well attuned his music was to popular taste, to the more substantial fare offered in 'This Poet Sings the Trojan Wars'. Here is a splendid setting of a translation from the Greek of Anacreon, always a favourite with Restoration rakes and topers for his cult of fleshly pleasures. One of comparatively few songs Purcell wrote specifically for a bass, it falls into four clearly defined episodes, opening with a spirited fling at epic bards with whom the poet wants nothing to do – the composer has fun with a dotted rhythm for 'rattling numbers' – softening thence into the minor to evoke 'Anacreon's Defeat' (the song's alternative title) in the wars of love, and ending with a comic contrast between 'all your artillery companies' and 'those encamp'd in killing eyes'.

Further songs appeared in 1689 in the latest instalment of *Comes Amoris or The Companion of Love*, the collection John Carr had started from his shop tucked so snugly into the right side of Roger North's Middle Temple Gate. The first volume, issued two years earlier, had been prefaced with 'A Catch by Way of Epistle' set by Purcell himself:

To all lovers of musick, performers and scrapers,
To those that love catches, play tunes and cut capers:
With a new catch I greet you, and tho I say it that shouldn't,
Like a fiddle, 'tis musick, tho' the words are but wooden.
But my brother John Playford and I shall present you
E'er long with a book I presume will content you.
'Tis true we know well the sale of good musick,
But to hear us perform would make him sick or you sick!
My maggot-man Sam, at the first Temple-Gate,
Will further inform you, if not, my wife Kate;
From between the two devils near Temple Bar,
I rest your friend and servant John Carr.

'My maggot-man Sam' was Carr's partner Samuel Scott, presumably given to fanciful ideas (a 'maggot' was a whim or a caprice) who provided a rather pompous introductory epistle to a songbook which featured one of Purcell's most winning compositions for solo voice and continuo, the setting over a ground bass of 'O Solitude, My Sweetest Choice' by Katherine Philips, 'The Matchless Orinda', whose Hackney boarding school education we referred to earlier. Born in London, the daughter of a merchant in Bucklersbury who died while she was still a girl, she moved to Wales when her mother married a Mr Hector Philips of Denbighshire, and at sixteen years old Katherine herself was engaged to her stepfather's son James. Dividing her time between a Welsh country retreat and literary London, she built up a circle of likeminded friends to whom she gave classical nicknames, Sylvander, Lucasia, Rosania, etcetera, and addressed a series of intense Platonic verses to them under the *nom de plume* Orinda.

Incomparably the best woman poet of her age, Orinda was also an accomplished French speaker – among other achievements she produced an admired version of Pierre Corneille's tragedy *Pompée* – and her divided life between wild mountains and the populous city must have encouraged her to translate one of the finest of all Baroque celebrations of rustic solitariness, the ode 'O Que J'Ayme la Solitude' by the French poet Antoine Girard de Saint-Amant, a contemporary of hers who had spent some time in London and was greatly favoured by English writers of the period. Philips's work is a shortened paraphrase of a poem so deliciously prodigal in details drawn from nature that it reads like the verbal equivalent of some seventeenth-century landscape painting, though she understandably preserves the spirit of its closing stanza, hymning a passionate friendship:

> For thy sake I in love am grown
> With what my fancy does pursue;
> But when I think upon my own
> I hate it for that reason too,
> Because it needs must hinder me
> From seeing and from serving thee.

Purcell's setting of 'O Solitude, My Sweetest Choice' shortens the poem still further, but so far from destroying its effectiveness, he reduces it to its contemplative essence through the use of a twelve-note ground, reiterated twenty-eight times, over which he skilfully throws Orinda's text in such a way that the rhythmic regularity of the ostinato is constantly at odds with the poetic line. At the same time, being Henry Purcell, he is aware of having to paint a picture, whether on the word 'restless' with its edgy dotted melisma, or in the evocation of 'these hanging mountains', which, according to Saint–Amant as rendered by Philips, 'th' unhappy would invite/ To finish all their sorrows here'. Purcell lets 'hanging' slope down a four-crotchet phrase before rising an octave to 'mountains'. The whole conception, using the hauntingly inexorable bass he had earlier employed in the anthem *In Thee, O Lord, Do I Put My Trust* to underpin subtle harmonic shifts in the vocal line, is another of those Purcellian touchstones, proof of his genius if ever we were to doubt it.

Scattering songs from his pen, Purcell was also continuously engaged in writing keyboard music, some of it for his private pupils. There is plenty of evidence that he earned part of his living as a teacher – the letter to the Dean of Exeter about 'Hodg' provides one such example. Several of his students went on to become composers themselves, following in Purcell's professional footsteps either as cathedral organists or as theatrical musicians. The highly accomplished John Weldon, for example, to whom the music for *The Tempest* formerly attributed to Purcell is now assigned, began his period of study while still an Eton scholar before going on to become organist of New College, Oxford, and John Blow's successor at the Chapel Royal, Jeremiah Clarke, known nowadays for having written what used to be called 'Purcell's Trumpet Voluntary' (its title is in fact 'The Prince of Denmark's March') learned his craft from Purcell as a Chapel boy.

Several of the composer's pupils were talented amateurs, drawn from the families of the nobility and gentry with whom he came into contact through highly placed acquaintances such as Roger North and his coterie of music-loving lawyers. The dedicatee of the posthumously published 1697 trio sonata collection, Lady Rhoda – or Rhodia – Cavendish, had herself studied with Purcell, and the composer's widow specifically refers, in the opening epistle, to 'the wonderfull Progress You have made (beyond most of either Sex) in all Ingenuous [sic] Accomplishments, and particularly in this of Musick, for which you have often been Admir'd by the dear Author of these Compositions; whose Skill in this Science is best recommended to the World by telling it, that He had the Honour to be Your Master'. Before her marriage to Lord Henry Cavendish, son of the Duke of Newcastle, Rhoda Cartwright of Aynho in Northamptonshire had taken lessons at £2 a month with 'Mr Henry Purcell the spinet master' while she lived in London, perhaps as a pupil at one of the suburban boarding schools.

Another of Purcell's students whom his wife honoured with a dedication was Princess Anne's maid of honour Annabella Dyve, who in 1692, aged eighteen, married the 66-year-old Sir Robert Howard, brother-in-law of the poet John Dryden. Howard's career had followed the typical Restoration pattern of profitable government service (his financial acumen enabled him to milk the Treasury to considerable effect) combined with a taste for literature. His three brothers all wrote plays, and he followed suit with success both in comedy and tragedy, culminating in a scandalously mordant satire, *The Country Gentleman*, written in 1669 in collaboration with the Duke of Buckingham. The comedy was taken off before it could be performed, owing to its blatant but delicious caricature, in the figure of Sir Cautious Trouble-all, of Sir William

Coventry, Commissioner of the Treasury and friend of Samuel Pepys.

Howard was known to Purcell, who set some of his not very distinguished lyrics to music and more famously provided the superlative score adorning the revival of his tragedy *The Indian Queen* in 1694, a play to which Dryden had contributed a share. Annabella, as 'the Honourable Lady Howard', received the dedication, three years after Purcell's death, of the great song collection *Orpheus Britannicus*, in which Frances Purcell not only drew attention to earlier studies with 'that dear person, who you have sometimes been pleased to honour with the Title of your Master', but flattered the pupil still further by emphasizing the good opinion he had always had of her skill. 'For I have often heard him say, that as several of his best Compositions were originally design'd for your Ladiship's Entertainment, so the Pains he bestowed in fitting them for your Ear, were abundantly rewarded by the Satisfaction he received from your Approbation, and admirable Performance of them.'

Well, perhaps. At any rate Frances's introduction hints that Annabella extended her protection to the Purcell family after Henry's death, so the sense of mutual esteem between the musician and his young scholar may have been genuine. It seems, what is more, to have found him another pupil in the family, in the shape of Sir Robert Howard's granddaughter by an earlier marriage, Diana, a very little girl when she started going to Purcell for lessons in 1694 at £2 3s 6d a month.

What did these smart young misses learn from their 'spinet master'? Like many another teacher at that time Purcell wrote pieces for use as exercises or arranged items from his theatre music, odes and other sources expressly for the purpose of providing keyboard lessons. The word 'lesson' was applied to harpsichord music in the double sense of a practice piece from which beginners could learn, or simply of something which was read, like the lesson in an Anglican church service. We can assume that at least some of Purcell's miscellaneous works for keyboard were designed for this purpose, or perhaps given their harpsichord reductions from the vocal and orchestral originals at the request of particular friends.

Several of these pieces appeared in Henry Playford's *The Second Part of Musick's Hand-maid*: 'Containing the newest lessons, grounds, sarabands, minuets and jiggs, set for the virginals, harpsichord, and spinet', published in 1689. The first part had been issued by Playford's father as long ago as 1678, and the object of the present volume was to extend the range of the earlier collection with 'a collection of new lessons for the practick part . . . consisting of the newest tunes and grounds, composed by our ablest masters Dr John Blow, Mr Henry Purcell &c'. Himself an editor of the collection, Purcell contributed no less than seventeen items, ranging from minuets, marches and one-off trifles like *Sefauchi's Farewell* to weightier fare in the form of suites and overtures transcribed from elsewhere among his works.

At least one of the lighter pieces had already gained him fame among the supporters of William and Mary and the Protestant army currently engaged in mopping up James II's forces in Ireland. Did Purcell actually write the tune we now know as 'Lilliburlero', first appearing in a flute tutor printed by Playford in 1686 and now making a return as 'A New Irish Tune' in *Musick's Hand-maid*? The answer is that it probably existed already, and that his contribution was the accompanying harmony. Nevertheless he received the credit for this lilting ditty, which is probably as much English as Irish. With a set of jeering verses tacked on to it, referring to James II's unpopular appointment of Lord Tyrconnel as viceroy of Ireland, and the mock-Irish refrain which gave it a name, 'Lilliburlero' became known as the song which had 'drummed the king out of his three kingdoms'. Ardent Jacobites and Catholics in our own day may perhaps resent its use as a signature tune for the BBC World Service.

The keyboard suites, three of which appeared in the *Musick's Hand-maid* volume (they were reissued with five others in a separate collection after Purcell's death), represent his finest achievement in a field where improvisations now inevitably lost to us were sometimes better calculated than his surviving manuscripts to represent a musician's flair and science at the instrument. The traditional view of these suites has been somewhat condescending. Musicologists have tended to assume that because most

of the movements are fairly short – in the case of one of the two
G major suites, positively epigrammatic – this must imply a lack
of sophistication on the composer's part, and that therefore we
need not really take them seriously.

This is both unjust and short-sighted. Not only were the eight
suites, published on Frances Purcell's initiative in 1696 under the
title *A Choice Collection of Lessons*, powerfully influential on
English keyboard composers of the early eighteenth century and
widely disseminated among amateur performers who made copies
of them, but they embodied, in however narrow a compass, all
that Purcell had learned as a harpsichord player from native masters such as Locke and Blow or from the continental styles brought
to England by foreign artists such as Froberger and Draghi.

The suites themselves consist mostly of short dance movements
introduced by toccata-like preludes, but there is never any sense
of mood and character growing stale. Variety, both melodic and
harmonic, empowers the set throughout, and we can easily understand why, for all their brevity – number one in G major lasts
barely four minutes – they remained popular and may indeed
have been known to musicians abroad, in continental northern
Europe.

One native instrumental composer with whom Purcell had been
professionally associated was the youthful Thomas Farmer, a near
neighbour of his in Westminster. Farmer had been a violinist in
King James's Catholic chapel, as well as writing songs and publishing an important instrumental collection of *33 Lessons beginning
with an Overture*. His death in late 1688 had evoked an ode from
Nahum Tate, *Young Thirsis' Fate*, which Purcell set as a beautiful
multi-sectional song, whose principal episode involves a mournful
ostinato bass, before the soloist combines with a second voice in
a chorus proclaiming:

> While thus in dismal notes we mourn
> The skilful shepherd's urn;
> To the glad skies his harmony he bears
> And as he charm'd the Earth, transports the Spheres.

A more fortunate destiny than Farmer's had favoured John

Gostling, who was now given a prebendal stall at Lincoln and made a minor canon of St Paul's. Pluralism of this sort was increasingly common in the Church of England, and it comes as no surprise to find Gostling also being appointed chaplain to King William. The pervasive effect on court musical life of the King's reluctance to attend sung services at the Chapel Royal must have had its influence on Gostling's move to St Paul's. Though he retained his official place in the Chapel establishment, the days of specially composed showpieces for 'that stupendious bass' in the context of a matins or an evensong complete with the string band and Purcell or Blow at the organ were more or less consigned to the realms of professional nostalgia.

The Dean of St Paul's, in whose cathedral Gostling now sang, was John Tillotson, a hugely gifted and intelligent man whose humane theology (he was said to doubt the truth of eternal damnation) informs his sermons, rightly taken as models of clarity and unforced eloquence by generations of later Anglican preachers. In 1677, as Dean of Canterbury, he had shown great practical kindness to the newly married William and Mary when, *en route* to Margate where the royal yacht was waiting to take them across to Holland, they found themselves without money to pay for a night's lodging at an inn. Now high in royal favour, he was a likely candidate for Archbishop of Canterbury, and indeed became primate in 1691.

Tillotson's native county was Yorkshire, and among his early sermons we find one preached at the so-called 'Yorkshire Feast', the banquet held annually in London for distinguished Yorkshiremen living in the city, many of them involved in the cloth trade which underpinned the prosperity of the West Riding. Such county-linked demonstrations of solidarity were not uncommon – London hosted feasts for the men of Gloucestershire, Kent and Norfolk – but Yorkshire has always been, and notoriously remains, tub-thumpingly chauvinistic, a state within a state as it were, and the yearly get-together was merely another example of that deep feeling for native turf displayed in our day by professional Yorkshiremen in sport, the theatre and the media.

The festival of 1690 had originally been scheduled for 14 February, but was put back to March to avoid a clash with a general election to Parliament then taking place. On 20 March, the *London Gazette* announced that 'The Annual Yorkshire Feast will be held the 27th instant at Merchant-Taylors' Hall in Threadneedle Street; with a very splendid Entertainment of all sorts of Vocal and Instrumental Musick'. Yorkshire, with its farms and mills, was a rich county and the London Yorkshiremen, doing well out of recent government attempts to promote the woollen industry, could afford something handsome in the way of a musical paean to their home patch and its eponymous Roman city. No wonder Thomas D'Urfey, who furnished the text for the specially commissioned ode, cheerfully described Purcell's setting of his words as 'One of the finest Compositions he ever made, and cost £100 the performing'.

Purcell's *Yorkshire Feast Song* has suffered from the same sort of faintly contemptuous treatment as that meted out to the harpsichord suites. One standard work goes so far as to say cynically that 'much of it seems to have been written with the consoling reflection that an audience that had dined well would not be too critical'. We need only look at the score to see how preposterously dismissive a judgment this is. Not merely is the ode one of its composer's most elaborate celebratory pieces, the longest such apart from *Hail, Bright Cecilia*, but there is abundant evidence throughout that Purcell had thought carefully about problems of balance and variety in setting a text which concentrates so emphatically on Yorkist pugnacity and on toeing the Glorious Revolutionary party line.

For the first time in his orchestral writing the composer made more than token use of trumpets and oboes. Those who sometimes complain that Baroque music relies too heavily on the sonorities of a string band and deplore the absence of woodwind and brass to thicken the textures need reminding that seventeenth- and eighteenth-century masters had to use what resources lay to hand and, in certain cases, what they or the impresario who engaged them could afford. In Purcell's London there had of course always been trumpeters – sixteen of them were officially attached to the court musical establishment – and oboes, popularized by visiting French composers and players in the 1670s, formed part of the bands of the respective Guards regiments created by Charles II, but it was a happy combination of foreign influences and convenient availability of talent then and there which encouraged Purcell, in his music of the 1690s, to exploit trumpets and oboes more fully than ever before.

Italian composers like Antonio Stradella and Alessandro Scarlatti were writing for trumpets and strings in their operas, oratorios and other pieces, while in Paris the oboe, once noted for its gravity, was being re-educated as 'an absolute monsieur', to be employed in opera bands and dance music as much as in the more solemn ceremonial of church services. Ready to hand for Purcell's purposes lay a fine family of English trumpeters, the Shores, who were in the King's service, best of them surely being John Shore, who joined the royal band in 1688, and 'by his great ingenuity and application had extended the power of that noble instrument [the trumpet] beyond the reach of the imagination, for he produced from it a tone as sweet as an hautboy'. As for the hautboys themselves, these were mostly still played by foreign performers such as the Frenchman Jacques Paisible or the Moravian composer Gottfried Finger, on the improved instruments being made at this period by the Huguenot Pierre Bressan at his shop near Somerset House, but a work such as John Banister's *The Sprightly Companion*, published in 1695, shows how swift a gain in popularity the instrument had made in England during recent decades.

Both oboe and trumpet show to brilliant advantage in the *Yorkshire Feast Song*'s introductory symphony, not so much an overture as a throwback to the earlier Italian canzona form, demonstrating Purcell's eclecticism in his approach to shaping a personal style. The bass soloist, assuming that ceremonial role Purcellian wisdom often chose to assign to this register, ushers in the Yorkshire eulogy with an arioso in praise of the Celtic tribe the Brigantes, whose former territory the county embraces, confronting the Roman invaders (D'Urfey's text is touched here by the period's mounting interest in antiquarianism and archaeology). The solo converts, via a ritornello, into a duet with tenor celebrating the birth at York of the Emperor Constantine:

> Whose colony, whilst planted there,
> With blooming glories still renewed the year.

Recorders evoke the 'drooping' and 'puny' character of Roman London in comparison with its northern counterpart, 'tho' now she rears her towering front so high', and the Wars of the Roses are summed up, not with a martial chorus, but in an alto air of subtle rhythmic slyness in which the melody, first taken up by the oboes, is laid over a bass in each bar of which the first beat is omitted, a pattern later picked up by the full string ensemble.

For immediate contrast, what better than the exhilarating duet which follows, fortified with a full choral reprise? D'Urfey shamelessly plays on the double significance of the word 'Rome' here, in the line 'Princes that hate Rome's slavery'. The city of legions and eagles becomes the detested capital of Popery. At this point the opening symphony reappears to divide the ode in two, and as an indicator of the poem's increasingly combative mood the paired trumpets are drafted into service in praise of 'renown'd Nassau' (King William, whose family surname was Oranje–Nassau). Yet neither composer nor poet is prepared to throw everything away in the name of a political eulogy, and as ardent Purcellians, whether Yorkshiremen or not, we should have felt cheated without at least one air on a ground.

When it arrives, to some better-than-average lines using a metaphor of the sun breaking through darkness, the result is awe-inspiring in its economy and authoritativeness. As so frequently in Purcell's work, we have the sense of a creative genius who knows exactly what he is doing, something which cannot always be said of great composers at the height of their powers. Above the five-note ground, the vocal line, taken by a tenor, simulates the gradual onset of light through shade, as the bass moves briefly into the dominant, even more briefly releases its hold so as to lend extra emphasis to the word 'brighter', then resumes its soft downward march like muffled or distant bells.

Whether D'Urfey was right to say, in the final chorus of the *Yorkshire Feast Song*, that the plot to bring William of Orange to England had been hatched in York and its county, is doubtful. Two at least of the so-called 'Immortal Seven', 'the heroes [that] invited him in', Viscount Lumley and the Earl of Danby, were Yorkshiremen, while another county peer, Lord Halifax, made him the formal offer of the English crown on his arrival in 1688.

Their loyalty was still unwavering in 1690, which could certainly not have been said of many of the time-servers and sycophants who held official positions of trust under William and Mary but who had no scruple about keeping a provident hand in with the exiled court of James II, now living on Louis XIV's charity at St-Germain.

During the early months of 1690 these allegiances were being tested by the sharp-witted, politically cynical Queen Mary, who, whatever the tremendous strain placed upon her as William's partner in government, showed herself more than equal to the task of managing the various ministers during his prolonged absences on campaign. 'Though I cannot hit on the right way of pleasing England, I am confident she will,' said William to one of them, and they were soon to discover how firmly her finger was on the pulse of popular feeling and how much she understood the realities of the intensely volatile atmosphere now prevailing in a country which half wanted the new reign but disliked the King and felt guiltily uncomfortable at having unseated his predecessor.

With remarkable swiftness and aplomb Mary organized the suppression of a Jacobite conspiracy in a series of arrests and imprisonments, and went on to busy herself with shaking up the navy after its defeat at Beachy Head under the spectacularly incompetent Lord Torrington. What with these matters, together with reviewing troops in Hyde Park, issuing new charters to city livery companies, crushing minor revolts in Berwick and Rye, receiving a deputation of Cornish tin miners who had formed a local defence force and looking after wounded sailors from the Dutch ships at Beachy Head (they had fought a good deal better than the British), it is a wonder she found time, in the crowded spring and summer of 1690, to celebrate her own birthday.

Custom nevertheless was inflexible on the point, and the commission for the ode duly went ahead, assigned on this occasion to Thomas D'Urfey, with the music provided by Purcell. It is hard not to surmise that poet and composer must by now have been firm friends, and tempting, what is more, to believe that it was Purcell who suggested D'Urfey rather than laureate Shadwell to furnish his words. One at least of D'Urfey's images from the *Yorkshire Feast Song* surfaces again when he compares William III to the sun, a fling, perhaps, at Louis XIV, but more obviously an allusion to the colour orange, now of course so politically apt. Despite such recycling, D'Urfey's Pegasus was sprightlier than Shadwell's, and the new ode, *Arise, My Muse*, has his usual negligent elegance of tone, to which Purcell responded keenly elsewhere.

The composer's invention, on the other hand, was rather less consistent here than it had been in the cause of Yorkist triumphalism. It is true that he lavished considerable care on the orchestration, doubling the violas in the string band and making use of paired oboes and trumpets, as well as two recorders. He also strove more pointedly than in earlier odes to vary the vocal textures as much as possible through alternations of solo and ensemble in successive numbers, and by combining different voices in duets and trios with concluding choral sections. Yet throughout the piece lingers a sense of half-heartedness and near bombast. Though not quite a case of W. S. Gilbert's 'nonsense, yes, but ah! what precious nonsense!' *Arise, My Muse* reveals a great artist unenthused by his material and often seeming to trifle with the abundant resources at his disposal. It is with some relief that we listen to the alto's genuinely moving intervention on behalf of 'Eusebia, drown'd in tears', allegorizing the Church of England in dejection over William's departure for Ireland, a magnificent moment in which Purcell deliberately welded together the glacial D minor melancholy of the high voice accompanied by recorders and the bass's D major exhortation, coloured by two solo violins, 'But Glory cries "Go on, illustrious Man"'. This is in fact the last movement of the ode as it now stands in the earliest original score, though there must surely have been music for D'Urfey's two concluding verses which has alas not come down to us.

Purcell was to re-utilize the trumpet symphony at the opening of *Arise, My Muse* in his semi-opera *King Arthur*, produced a year later. By now he must have realized that the official policy regarding court music was, if not to marginalize the Chapel Royal, at any rate to scale down the pomp of its services. Soon after the 1690 ode was performed, a royal ordinance decreed that the number of musicians on official retaining fees in the various bands and palatine chapel was to be cut to twenty-four, with only the martial instruments being kept to their original strength. The single anthem Purcell produced for the Chapel Royal that year, *My Song Shall Be Alway*, vivid though its individual episodes appear, seems a mere ghostly outline of its noble predecessors, with the full strings used only in the opening symphony (repeated half way through the piece, as in *My Heart Is Inditing*), the choir contributing little to the proceedings, and a predominance for the bass soloist as virtuoso in recitative and aria sections. Perhaps the occasion, William's triumphal return to Windsor on 9 September fresh from his Irish campaign, allowed Purcell to turn a blind eye to the order issued by Queen Mary the previous year prohibiting the use of instruments in the Chapel, but soon enough William himself was to command that 'the King's Chappell shall be all the year through kept both morning and evening with solemn musick like a collegiate church' – that is to say, with choir and organ only. Though *My Song Shall Be Alway* was not Purcell's swansong as a religious composer, his professional activities were henceforth directed towards a far more uncertain sphere than the Chapel Royal – an area whose confines he had briefly touched upon during earlier years as a court musician – the contentious, mercurial but infinitely stimulating world of the London stage.

6

Bringing Home the Indies

The 1690s, witnessing the last phase of Purcell's short and crowded life, formed a decade of crucial significance in the development of England's modern identity, both where the nation's self-awareness was concerned, and in terms of the response made by intelligent foreign observers to what were seen, for better or worse, as specifically English values. Its importance can be measured not simply by the way in which so many of those dimensions of political and commercial life we now take for granted came into existence during the period. Regular sessions of Parliament, the growth of that mythical system of checks and balances upon which our phantom constitution has, until recently, been held to depend, the hands-off role of the monarchy, the creation of a national bank, a financial culture of stock market investment and speculation, and the presence of a free press, all belong to the age of William and Mary. Just as profound in their implications were the changes overtaking English society and its lifestyles, whether as a result of the increase in the nation's wealth or of a burgeoning cosmopolitanism against which even the sturdiest Britannic xenophobia fought in vain. Powerful too in ways only partially admitted at the time was the influence of William and Mary themselves, bringing with them to England that uncluttered awareness of the visual, that sense of order, comfort and cleanliness within the house and that tolerant attitude to religious and philosophical opinion which made Holland the most civilized of seventeenth-century European nations.

It was the age when we learned to live peaceably in brick houses in towns, to grow flower bulbs in pots, to dine off blue-and-white china dishes, to drink tea, chocolate and coffee, to take toast and marmalade at breakfast and to read the newspapers. It was a time when that quality loosely known as wit, encompassing everything from pure buffoonery to the labours of scholarship, became leavened with politeness and civility, as opposed to the swaggering coarseness which gave it a context during the reigns of the brother Stuarts. Above all the 1690s form a period when, by virtue of the international role in trade and politics thrust on England via William's commitment to challenging French hegemony in Europe, Englishmen became more fervently and cohesively patriotic than at any time since the days of the Spanish Armada over a hundred years before.

Purcell is located firmly in this world, not just because it gave him a living, but because his later scores are in many cases inalienably tied to words or images expressing these contemporary values. Some at least of their music implicitly dramatizes the tension between his audience's robust new nationalism and the eager embrace of foreign sophistications which its growing riches were able to purchase. The 1690s saw him becoming inevitably a more public figure, writing music for less exclusive or musically learned audiences, and publishing his songs in the magazines which sprang up in the rapid mushrooming of popular journalism, forming yet another of the decade's distinctive features. At the same time he was able to consolidate the professional reputation he had earned among fellow composers and performers throughout the 1680s, and there is certainly no evidence to suggest that any of his contemporaries would have seen a commitment to work in the theatre, uneven though some of his productions for it appear, as being a mere squandering of his proven gifts.

The fact that he had written nothing of any significance for the London stage since the songs for *Sir Barnaby Whigg* in 1681 may have something to do with the amalgamation of the Drury Lane and Dorset Garden companies in November 1682 as the so-called United Company, for reasons connected as much with theatrical ambition as box-office receipts. Colley Cibber gives us his version of events as follows:

> I shall content myself with telling you that Mohun and Hart now growing old (for, above thirty Years before this Time they had severally born the King's Commission of Major and Captain in the

Civil Wars) and the younger Actors ... being impatient to get into their Parts, and growing intractable, the Audiences too of both Houses then falling off, the Patentees of each, by the King's Advice, which perhaps amounted to a Command, united their Interests and both Companies into one, exclusive of all others, in the Year 1682.

It was by no means a perfect arrangement, and would eventually come undone altogether some dozen years later in the immemorial clash of theatrical egos, but for the time being the new troupe was able to mount a respectable sequence of revivals and premières, leavened with occasional ventures such as Dryden's *Albion and Albanius*, with its music by Louis Grabu. Other composers, Draghi for example, and Simon Pack who, as well as being the company's in-house music director, briefly joined the army during Monmouth's rebellion in 1685, provided vocal and incidental pieces, but though Purcell himself that year wrote a song for Nahum Tate's farce *Cuckold's Haven*, nothing on the scale of the *Theodosius* commission had yet drawn him more closely into the theatrical orbit.

In 1689 and 1690 the company chose to revive Charles Davenant's ambitious heroic tragedy *Circe*, first produced in 1677 and based on an ingenious conflation of the story of Euripides's *Iphigenia in Tauris* with Orestes's madness from the *Eumenides* of Aeschylus, and featuring the Homeric sorceress from the *Odyssey* as its eponymous heroine. The play originally contained a sequence of masques for which John Banister provided the music, but for the revivals Purcell contributed a single scene – evidence, perhaps, of a movement towards the semi-operatic form he was to make powerfully his own in succeeding years. Like other musical opportunities afforded by the play, the moment in Act I at which Circe conjures up the spirit of Pluto for prophetic consultation is fully integrated with the action. A sombre sense of ritual is generated by an introduction for the string band and the use of a bass soloist and chorus (straight out of the Chapel Royal, as it were). The insidious key change from C major to C minor at the tenor's 'The air with music gently wound' over a slithering ground bass, on the other hand (together with the festive French bounce of the ensuing airs and choruses), suggests a distinctly pagan context, culminating in the gloomy solemnity of the moment when Pluto, in his chariot drawn by black horses, is conjured from the underworld.

Purcell was to manage this sort of thing more effectively in *The Indian Queen* five years later, but the *Circe* music may well have drawn the United Company's attention to his gifts both as a dramatic composer and, on a simpler level, as a likely provider of the complement of act tunes, symphonies and songs without which no Restoration play was complete. His real opportunity to re-enter the theatrical arena arrived in the summer of 1690, when Thomas Betterton took in hand a revision of an old play, *The Prophetess* by John Fletcher and Philip Massinger, with the aim of turning it into a crowd-pleasing spectacle, incorporating songs, dances, lavish costumes and scenic effects. It was, says a contemporary witness, 'set out with Costly Scenes, Machines and Cloaths; the Vocal and Instrumental Musick, done by Mr Purcel; and Dances by Mr Priest; it gratify'd the Expectation of Court and City; and got the Author great Reputation'.

The dramatic organism we loosely refer to nowadays as 'Beaumont-and-Fletcher' – that is to say, the works of the Jacobean playwright John Fletcher, author of some fifty plays, some written in collaboration with Francis Beaumont, many others together with writers such as Shakespeare, Middleton and Webster – had remained enormously popular on the Restoration stage, notwithstanding contemporary critical attacks on their dramaturgy. Revivals of plays like *Rule a Wife and Have a Wife*, *The Chances* and *A King and No King* persisted until well into the eighteenth century. Notwithstanding the clumsiness of Fletcher's verse, with its incessant feminine endings, these pieces were seen for what indeed they were, well-crafted dramas making skilful use of character and situation in tightly-woven plots, not calculated to give offence by glancing too shrewdly at great offices and institutions of state.

An old play was an old play however, and if the company was happy enough to fall back on Fletcher as a dramatic staple, it had no scruples over revamping his work whenever this should prove advantageous to the box office. The plot of *The Prophetess* as originally written is based loosely on late Roman imperial history.

In a story dismissed by Gibbon as 'founded on a prophecy and a pun as foolish as they are well known' the Roman legionary officer Diocles, serving with his regiment in Batavia (modern Holland) had occasion to query the reckoning at an inn. The hostess, happening also to be gifted with second sight, taxed him with meanness, to which he jestingly rejoined, 'I shall pay you when I am Emperor.' She told him that he would indeed wear the purple, but only when he had 'killed the boar'. Having indulged in a series of fruitless hunts after wild pig, he finally succeeded in putting to death the praetorian guard captain Aper, whose name means 'boar' and who was accused of murdering the former Emperor Numerianus.

In Fletcher and Massinger's play the prophetess Delphia has a niece, Drusilla, whose consuming love at first sight for Diocles drives her to follow him to Rome, where to her horror, when he receives a share in the empire and alters his name to Dioclesian, he also accepts an offer of marriage with the noble Aurelia. In revenge Delphia contrives his defeat in battle; he repents, then returns victorious, deciding now to abdicate in favour of his ambitious nephew Maximian, a character apparently based on Massinger's often highly imitative reading of Shakespeare (in this case *Macbeth*). To surmount the problem of digesting a long imperial reign in a single play the dramatists suddenly introduce a chorus, who announce that Dioclesian 'weary of pomp and state' has retired to a country life in Lombardy. Maximian, having now married Aurelia, who promptly becomes his Lady Macbeth, plots to kill Dioclesian while he and Drusilla are watching shepherds and shepherdesses dance, but Delphia calls down thunder and lightning, the would-be murderers grovel for pardon and the play ends in a fine show of princely magnanimity.

The real Dioclesian did indeed retire from government, not to Lombardy but to Split in Dalmatia, where the ruins of his vast palace survive and where he famously proposed to spend part of his leisure growing cabbages. The Jacobean play is thus superficially consistent with ancient history, but commentators on Betterton's adaptation have been tempted to search instead for parallels with events and characters closer to Purcell's own time and look for direct links with the Glorious Revolution in this opulent Dorset Garden revival. Their interpretations do not really convince. Purcell and Betterton may indeed have had half an eye on attempting, from a purely artistic standpoint, to outdo Dryden and Grabu in the recently performed *Albion and Albanius*, but it would surely be wrong to detect a deliberate anti-Jacobite myth-history in a work where the extremely light retouching of the original text involves simplification rather than the sharpening of any possible allusion to the slippery turns of contemporary politics.

That *Albion and Albanius* was the musical 'beast in view' – more appropriately, in the case of *The Prophetess*, a boar in view – is made clear by Purcell's attempt to emulate Grabu's publication of his own full score (itself a gesture modelled on Lully's similar enterprises across the Channel) in 1687. The edition of *The Vocall and Instrumental Musick of the Prophetess, or the History of Dioclesian* which appeared in 1691 was not a commercial success, and music publishers grew wary of issuing comparable scores, despite the vogue for English 'opera' the work created. Writing an introduction to the score of the winning entry for a competition to set Congreve's masque *The Judgment of Paris* in 1702 – the winner in this case being Henry's brother Daniel Purcell – the bookseller John Walsh spoke of 'the ill Success which Publishers of Musick have mett with in other approved pieces', and noted 'the celebrated Dioclesian of Mr Henry Purcell' as 'an Instance of that Nature, which found so small Encouragement in Print, as serv'd to stifle many other Intire Opera's, no less Excellent'.

The point was made, nevertheless, by the presentation at Dorset Garden of the piece itself. In a preface to *Dioclesian*, as it is now generally known, addressed to the Duke of Somerset (whose Italian duchess would have had some experience of opera in its more sophisticated continental guise), Purcell, perhaps with some assistance from Dryden, puts a coherent case for his own polyglot style within the context of English musical culture. He declared,

Musick is yet but in its Nonage, a forward Child, which gives hope of what it may be hereafter in *England*, when the Masters of it shall find more encouragement. 'Tis now learning *Italian*, which is its best Master, and studying a little of the *French* Air, to give it some-

206

what more of Gayety and Fashion. Thus being farther off from the Sun, we are of later growth than our Neighbour Countries, and must be content to shake off our Barbarity by degrees.

With the exception of the masque in Act V, the musical episodes inserted into *Dioclesian* are by no means integral to the drama, but it is being rather too harsh towards Purcell and Betterton to suggest that the play cannot seriously find room for them all. So profuse, so abundant is the composer's invention that we might sometimes feel that he has seized his various opportunities rather too fully, but the sense of him giving everything he possesses to the task in hand is potent enough to turn the *Dioclesian* score into one of the most radiant and thrilling he ever created. We are easily seduced into acceptance of the two principal operatic sequences, the masque already referred to and the sequence of numbers in Act II which follows Diocles's murder of Aper and assumption of the purple (half of it at any rate) as forging their own musico-dramatic language from the various numbers, however irresponsible so extended a victory celebration may seem in the context of the spoken drama unfolding around it. The mood, what is more, does not rest exclusively with the new Emperor's personal triumph. A ringingly authoritative symphony for two trumpets, for example, is preceded by a mournful soprano air in G minor, with a nudge towards a ground bass and paired recorders furnishing the accompaniment. After the trumpeting, progressively more sombre pieces close in the remarkable chorus 'Let the priests and processions the hero attend'. Here, as in *Circe*, the priestly allusion triggers off religious associations, and what we are given is a fine morsel of sacred contrapuntal writing fraught with archetypally Purcellian dissonances.

That he had forgotten nothing of his early study of Matthew Locke is shown by the wonderfully creepy string symphony which evokes the monster summoned by Delphia to frighten Diocles when he shows rather too much interest in the charms of Aurelia. No seasoned London theatregoer could have failed to catch the allusion to the *Tempest* music which Locke had composed for the 1674 revival in this very same Dorset Garden playhouse. Those in the audience wanting something more blatantly accessible in the musical way, however, could catch hold of the Act III song 'What shall I do to show how much I love her?' which became an instant popular favourite and eventually found its place, some thirty years after Purcell's death, among the tunes used by John Gay and Johann Christoph Pepusch in *The Beggar's Opera*.

The Act V entertainment was designed to conclude the spectacle on the grandest possible scale, involving the winching down on to the stage of a 'machine' showing 'the Pallace of the Sun' surrounded by a sunburst. The proceedings were ushered in by a summons from Cupid to a mingled crowd of mythological attendants, after which a series of 'entries' took place on successive levels as the stage gradually filled to create what must have been rather like the finale of one of the more lavish modern Christmas pantomimes. Purcell did his utmost, as number followed number, to alternate them through varying touches of harmony, rhythm and instrumentation, and in a piece like the utterly winning soprano duet 'Oh the sweet delights of love' he transcended that over-egged-pudding quality which shows of this kind, viewed without the advantage of first-hand experience and a contemporary aesthetic, tend to suggest. Little in this masque quite rises to the level of inspiration shown elsewhere in the score, and we are left with the sense of *Dioclesian* as a kind of Purcellian bran tub crammed with brilliant individual artefacts, rather than as something carefully thought through in terms of balance and proportion.

Not everyone had shared in the generally favourable reception of Betterton and Purcell's opera – or semi-opera or 'ambigu' or play with music, since a suitable term for this particular type of dramatic entertainment, so favoured by theatrical managements of the 1690s, has never been conclusively applied. One anonymous critic, writing ten years later but still spluttering his disapproval of the flawed dramaturgy, damned as

> ridiculous . . . that Scene in the *Prophetess*, where the great Action of the *Drama* stops, and the Chief Officers of the Army stand still with their Swords drawn to hear a Fellow Sing – *Let the Soldiers rejoice* – faith in my mind 'tis as unreasonable as if a Man should call for a Pipe of Tobacco just when the Priest and his Bride are waiting for him at the Altar.

Dioclesian had succeeded, all the same, in capturing the spirit of the times, especially in the military flavour of some of its words and music. Nobody investigating the arts in the reign of William and Mary can fail to appreciate the sudden rise in the number of soldierly images and icons during this period, an obvious result of England's involvement in a prolonged continental war. However unpopular it may have been, William's exploitation of his new kingdom's resources in order to strike back at his old enemy France made an inevitable and lasting impact on English life, and the beginnings of national militarism can be found mirrored in everything from Kneller's portraits of dashingly periwigged generals wearing their cravats *à la steinkerque** to the appearance of a whole troop of colonels, majors and captains among the cast lists of London plays. As for the martial allusions in the song lyrics of the time, whether set by Purcell and Blow or by such rising talents as John Eccles and William Croft, these tell their own story. Marches found their way into collections of keyboard pieces and the trumpets in Purcell's later scores are authentic echoes of a warlike age. If he ever needed first-hand knowledge of battles and sieges, his brother Edward, first commissioned an officer under James II, could have given him all the necessary details.

The new opera had made its mark on a writer to whose fortunes the Glorious Revolution had dealt a serious blow. John Dryden, poet laureate until King James's flight into France, and a convert to Catholicism, now found himself officially disgraced. A lesser genius might well have followed the example of others in varying spheres of public life by hurrying to rejoin the Church of England, but to his eternal credit Dryden stayed constant to his new faith and made no secret of the political allegiance which went with it. Modern literary historians, though they can scarcely deny

---

*The 'Steenkirk' collar was named after the battle of Steinkerk (1692), in which the French defeated the English forces. English officers, hurrying to horse in the early morning, had hastily secured their cravats by passing one end through a coat buttonhole. The style remained in fashion for several years, and the small bust of John Blow, on his tomb in Westminster Abbey, is shown wearing a steenkirk.

Dryden's significance as a major creative force in the fields of verse satire, drama, translation and critical prose, are nowadays at pains, for whatever reason, to belittle his achievement, comparing him disadvantageously with the Earl of Rochester, whose glamorous 'bad boy' image makes a more blatant appeal to the twentieth-century imagination. Even without the saving grace of scurrility, Dryden's immeasurable superiority, both as artist and man, showed itself now, when, old, poor and politically suspect, he embarked on his great translation of Virgil's *Aeneid* and the series of versions and paraphrases of Chaucer, Boccaccio and classical authors eventually to be published as *Fables Ancient and Modern* a few weeks before his death in 1700.

He had not always been prudent, however, in the exercise of his gifts and the management of his literary career, and his detractors have seized avidly on the failures and embarrassments marking the course of his voluminous *oeuvre*. His courage as a writer lay in a readiness to experiment, to make mistakes and pick himself up again, and in this creative toughness and resilience he was assisted by the astonishing breadth of his reading in at least six languages and by an intellectual curiosity which drew on science, philosophy and theology for additional stimulus. Fond of music – his plays are strewn with deliciously pliant lyrics and his 1687 Ode on Saint Cecilia's Day', 'From Harmony, from Heav'nly Harmony', had been written expressly for Draghi's setting, to be performed at that year's London celebrations – Dryden would inevitably have been drawn to his friend Thomas Betterton's new Dorset Garden entertainment. The actor had followed a well-trodden path in soliciting from the poet a special prologue for *Dioclesian*. Dryden's prologues and epilogues are some of his wittiest, most perceptive glosses on the contemporary world, and to secure one of them was considered a mighty advantage by Restoration dramatists, so much so indeed that he felt himself justified in charging a little extra for the honour.

The *Dioclesian* prologue added a hint of scandal to the production. A glance at this typically challenging, combative address suggests that it must have seemed politically rather too near the knuckle. We know that London theatregoers listened eagerly to pieces of this kind, partly in the hope of catching some allusion to current town gossip or a fling or two at the latest fashionable crazes. Dryden's prologue did not disappoint them. A line such as 'When will our Losses warn us to be wise?' could easily be taken to refer to the loss of James II and Mary of Modena, let alone its more obvious criticism of the needless expense of a foreign war, pursued later in these verses. Resuming a theme developed earlier in *Absalom and Achitophel*, Dryden taxed his countrymen with their political slipperiness:

> Never content with what you had before,
> But true to Change, right English Men all o'er

and implicitly derided William's Irish campaign for its unprofitable outcome:

> And the fat Spoils of Teague in Triumph draw,
> His Firkin-Butter and his Usquebaugh.

Even the apparently harmless reference to 'a Female Regency', thrown in alongside sneers at the modish *fontange* head-dresses worn at court and the vogue for keeping negro pages, must have unsettled some of the more loyal spectators at the first performance.

The foreseeable result was that at the command of the Lord Chamberlain, Charles Sackville, Earl of Dorset (described by one of William's modern biographers as 'a rotund and opulent Maecenas'), the prologue was instantly suppressed. 'This happen'd', says Colley Cibber, 'when King William was prosecuting the War in Ireland. It must be confess'd that this Prologue had some familiar Metaphorical sneers at the Revolution itself; and as the Poetry of it was good, the Offence of it was less Pardonable.' An unnamed writer in 1707 tells us, on the other hand, that an old enemy of Dryden's was behind this act of censorship:

Mr Shadwell was the occasion of its being taken notice of by the Ministry in the last Reign: He happen'd to be at the House on the first Night, and taking the beginning of the Prologue to have a double Meaning, and that Meaning to reflect on the Revolution, he told a Gentleman, He would immediately put a stop to it. When that Gentleman ask'd, Why he would do the Author such a disservice? He said, Because while Mr Dryden was Poet Laureat, he wou'd never let any Play of his be Acted.

Dryden's contribution to *Dioclesian* was perhaps a signal that he and Purcell were moving closer together, if not politically, then certainly from an artistic point of view. The failure of *Albion and Albanius* had not hardened the poet's resolve against further experiments with opera, and he would have been well aware of Purcell's increasing success as a composer. Though for the time being they were not involved in any major collaboration, Purcell contributed significantly to the success, in October 1690, of a fine new comedy by Dryden: an adaptation, loosely based on earlier plays by Plautus and Molière, of the Greek myth of the wooing of Amphitryon's wife Alcmena by the god Zeus – Jupiter in Dryden's version – resulting in the birth of Hercules.

When Cibber first heard Dryden reading *Amphitryon or The Two Sosias* to the assembled players, he marvelled at what a boring reader the old poet was, 'so cold, so flat and unaffecting'. Nobody could have predicted from this the play's success with the public, despite some of its speeches sailing rather too close to the wind when it came to politics. *Amphitryon* is a delightful work, witty, irreverent, bawdy and full of rewards for the cast. Betterton's role as Jupiter was tailor-made for the great actor-manager, while the well-loved comedian Anthony Leigh enjoyed a show-stealing part as Mercury, who disguises himself as Amphitryon's servant Sosia, and Susanna Mountfort, a popular light-comedy actress, was given some hilarious situations as the maid Phaedra. Dryden, having worked with most of these stars before, had provided a comedy which, besides mingling farce and satire, subtly called upon his actors to guy themselves, with Betterton playing the boss, Mrs Barry going over the top as the blooming Alcmena and Mrs Mountfort attempting to upstage her. Reading *Amphitryon* today (it cries out for a modern revival), we must wish we had been present at its Drury Lane first night.

In an epistle dedicatory addressed to Sir William Leveson Gower, Dryden bravely acknowledged his own political misfortune, thanking his friend for being among 'such as have been pleas'd to own me in this Ruin of my small Fortune; who, tho' they are of a contrary Opinion themselves, yet blame me not for adhering to a lost Cause'. Admitting he was not exactly an Ovid exiled to Pontus, he conceded that 'I suffer no more than I can easily undergo; and so long as I enjoy my Liberty, which is the Birth-Right of an *English*-Man, the rest shall never go near my Heart.' If his play was at all successful, it owed something to the music:

> What has been wanting on my Part has been abundantly supplied by the excellent Composition of Mr *Purcell*; in whose Person we have at length found an *Englishman*, equal with the best abroad. At least my Opinion of him has been such, since his happy and judicious Performances in the late *Opera*; and the Experience I have had of him, in the setting my three songs for this *Amphitryon*: To all which, and particularly to the Composition of the *Pastoral Dialogue*, the numerous Choir of fair Ladies gave so just an Applause on the third Day.

The 'excellent Composition of Mr *Purcell*' (that 'third Day' was presumably his benefit night) perfectly encapsulated the play's distinctive wit in an overture, act music (including a characteristic Scottish tune), dances and three songs, probably late additions to the comedy inserted during rehearsal. One of them, 'Celia, that I once was blest', features a string ritornello at the end of each verse. Purcell had used this form of air, with the voice accompanied only by a continuo and the instruments bringing in new material to round it off, in the court odes, but its presence in his theatre music irresistibly recalls the Italian aria style of the period which he had favoured in a piece such as 'Oft she visits this lov'd mountain' in *Dido and Aeneas*. Most skilfully handled of all the *Amphitryon* songs is the pastoral dialogue 'fair Iris and her swain' which Dryden mentions in his introduction. Here the typical exchange between an ardent shepherd and a coy mistress is given further edge by not allowing the voices to blend too early in the piece. Even when they do, in a so-called rondeau:

> Thus at the height we love and live,
> And fear not to be poor:

We give, and give, and give, and give,
'Till we can give no more

the effect is comically acerbic rather than straightforwardly triumphant.

Taking part in this duet were the bass John Bowman, for whom
various solos in the odes were written, and the soprano Charlotte
Butler. Both were essentially actors rather than singers, but their
voices were evidently good enough to be treated to some of Purcell's best stage songs during the early 1690s. Butler, however
much admired for her professional brilliance, was continually
attacked for loose morals behind the scenes. An anonymous *Satyr
on the Players* proclaimed that

> Fam'd Butler's Wiles are now so common grown
> That by each Feather'd Cully* she is known,
> So that at last to save her Tottering Fame
> At Musick Club she strives to get a Name,
> But mony is the Syren's chiefest Aim.

while another nameless detractor starchily addressed her as

> Butler, oh thou Strumpet Termagant,
> Durst thou pretend to husband or gallant?
> Ev'n to thy owne Profession a disgrace

Purcell, on the other hand, seems to have been well pleased with
Charlotte Butler, and the music he presented her with was calculated to exploit her talents in soubrette roles or else in the type of
'breeches' part with which dramatists delighted to tease the men
in the audience, several of whom must in any case have come to
the theatre expressly to watch and listen to her.

It was just such a *travesti* heroine, though on this occasion
played by Susanna Mountfort, around whom the young Irish
dramatist Thomas Southerne had constructed his first essay in
comedy, *Sir Anthony Love or The Rambling Lady*, which had
immediately preceded *Amphitryon* on the Drury Lane stage that
autumn. Although the plot is a trifle overcrowded, with more

---

*'Cully' was a Restoration word for a dupe or gull, and could also mean
simply 'bloke' or 'chap'.

characters and situations than the play will easily bear, the originality and mature intelligence which mark Southerne out as one of the more distinctive talents of late Restoration drama are already present, whether in the figure of the feisty heroine Lucia, disguised as Sir Anthony Love, or in the playwright's scorn for the convention ordaining sex and marriage as the only bases for male–female relationship. Purcell contributed a boisterous overture and three carefully diversified songs, one of them a dialogue for Bowman and Butler, another set by the Lord Chamberlain's brother Major-General Edward Sackville of the Coldstream Guards, and the most captivating of all, 'Pursuing Beauty', written probably for the scene in Act IV where 'Sir Anthony' reveals her true sex to her male companion Valentine by putting on women's clothes. Southerne's five stanzas, from which Purcell chose three, are typically sympathetic to the heroine's predicament:

> We Women, like weak *Indians*, stand
> Inviting, from our Golden Coast,
> The wandering Rovers to our Land:
> But she who trades with 'em is lost.

Heralded by a short string prelude, the song is not set strophically, the composer preferring instead to handle it with a freedom offering as eloquent an expressive range as possible to the nuance of individual words in successive verses. 'Acted with extraordinary Applause, the Part of Sir Anthony Love being most Masterly play'd by Mrs Mountfort', the play clinched Southerne's success, establishing him as one of the most commercially flourishing dramatists in the century's final years. He and Purcell, patently kindred spirits, were destined to work together on four more plays in coming Drury Lane seasons.

For one at least of the comedies performed by the United Company during the autumn of 1690 we have no record either of its author or of the actual play. *The Gordian Knot Untied* seems never to have been printed and the name of its writer was kept secret, though a contemporary source hints at the Worcestershire squire William Walsh, an early mentor of the young Alexander Pope, as a possible candidate. The overture and incidental music Purcell furnished for the performances that November are spirited and tuneful enough to make us regret that no trace of the work they embellished has yet come to light.

Early the following year King William returned to The Hague for a grand congress of the allied powers in the war against France. The Spanish, Austrian and Savoyard envoys arrived, together with the electors of Brandenburg, Saxony and Bavaria, but the King himself only got to his Dutch capital after a hazardous voyage in an open boat through thick fog, in which he had at last to be put ashore on a desolate beach, accompanied by three courtiers on whose drenched clothes icicles were starting to form. A misreading of some rather confused rosters drawn up by Lord Dorset, detailing the court musicians who were to follow the royal progress to Holland, has led some writers to conclude that Purcell and Blow formed part of the King's suite, but we now know that they were both left at home, with only the trumpeters, the members of the royal hautboy band and a drummer going on the journey, under the supervision of Nicholas Staggins as Master of the Musick.

William came back to London briefly during April to face controversy over the appointment of new bishops to replace those, afterwards known as Nonjurors, who refused to take oaths of loyalty to him as head of the Church of England. To increase his domestic worries and those of Mary, who was growing tired of the perpetual backbiting and contentiousness among her courtiers, a fire had ravaged the riverside frontage of Whitehall Palace, 'beginning' as Evelyn sardonically notes 'at the apartment of the late Duchess of Portsmouth (which had been pulled down and rebuilt no less than three times to please her) and consuming other lodgings of such lewd creatures, who debauched both King Charles and others, and were his destruction'.

The Queen's birthday celebrations went ahead all the same, two weeks after the Whitehall fire, and once again Purcell assumed his station as official composer. The poet who supplied him with *Welcome, Glorious Morn* has preserved his or her anonymity, though perhaps Shadwell was again involved, since the poetry rarely transcends the typical mediocrity of laureate verse, and there are strong suggestions of padding and waffle by an inexpert muse armed with a fistful of clichés. Mary's birthday is welcomed as that of 'Nature's richest Pride', 'the noblest Theme, the loudest song of Fame'; Britannia, 'with an awful smile', is seized by poetic fury and thanks the gods for blessing 'sad Albion' with such a gift; there is the usual rather belated allusion to the absent William on the battlefield; and peace and happiness are forecast for Britain under its joint sovereigns.

Around this stodgy and unpromising text Purcell devised one of his handsomest, most glittering royal birthday tributes. Lacking something of the composer's softer, more introspective vein – it is one of the few odes without a minor-key countertenor solo – *Welcome, Glorious Morn* compensates us with the extraordinary verve and brilliance of the instrumental writing, shown in the answering trumpet calls of the opening symphony or in the ritornello linking the duet 'At thy return the joyful earth' to the choral reprise of 'Welcome, welcome'. Among the soloists, it is the tenor who receives two of the richest rewards, a thrilling air over a repeated two-note pattern for the string accompaniment which hurls the vocal line resistlessly along, and an equally exciting fusion of recitative and ground bass aria in 'And lo! a sacred fury', which then converts, under the heat of Purcell's inventiveness, into a grand chorus. Nothing in the ode appears wasted, bathetic or jejune, and the triumph is less that of a monarch's birthday than of a divinely gifted musician's display of an absolute mastery of artistic resource.

Some of the flavour of the major work in which Purcell was deeply involved during the spring of 1691 colours the mood and style of *Welcome, Glorious Morn*, for it is impossible to hear the ode without being reminded of the music for *King Arthur*, so soon to be offered to the Dorset Garden audience in the wake of the triumphant *Dioclesian*. Dryden's appreciation of the composer's gifts, so warmly expressed in the dedication of *Amphitryon*, must have encouraged him to consult his own interests, those of a writer badly in need of money, keen to capitalize on his position as a revered figure in the London literary world, and ready to make the best possible use of his inveterate gift for channelling current popular enthusiasms into his poetry and plays. Some seven or eight years earlier, in high favour under Charles II, he had started work on an English opera – that is to say, a spoken verse drama 'adorn'd with Scenes, Machines, Songs and Dances' – based on the half-legendary figure of King Arthur. This was to have been preceded by an allegorical prologue, sung throughout, which, in deference to Charles's desire for a French opera, was then separated from the work in progress and expanded into *Albion and Albanius*, though the first performance of the new piece was not actually given until June 1685, four months after the King's death. *King Arthur* was then shelved, only to be dusted off and carefully altered by Dryden in 1691 to render it more acceptable to the prevailing post-Revolutionary political orthodoxy.

The earlier version of *King Arthur* has not survived, but scholars are probably correct in assuming that it was intended to celebrate the Tory ascendancy of Charles II's closing years and his survival of the Popish Plot hysteria, together with the public reinstatement of his brother the Duke of York. Some commemoration of the twenty-fifth anniversary of his accession as restored King of England may also have been designed. As it stood, the opera would scarcely have been appropriate as propaganda on behalf of the new regime, but the warlike subject, the presence of a military hero and the concluding paean to British virtues were none of them out of place, even if the last element was probably part of Dryden's revision.

As his dedicatee the poet chose the former Earl of Halifax, who had been rewarded with a marquisate for his loyalty to William but had newly moved over to the opposition in the House of Lords; a shift some might have seen as consistent with the political attitudes espoused in his pamphlet *The Character of a Trimmer*, published in 1684, but which seems in fact to have been motivated by perfectly valid scruples. Dryden's epistle, elegantly phrased as ever, commends Halifax's share in rescuing the country from anarchy during his period of high office under Charles II, upon whom the writer heaps praise fulsome enough to suggest an oblique criticism of William through sheer force of comparison.

Purcell too comes in for his share of plaudits. 'There is nothing better than what I intended', says Dryden, 'but the Musick, which has since arriv'd to a greater Perfection in England, than ever formerly; especially passing through the Artful Hands of Mr Purcel, who has Compos'd it with so great a Genius that he has nothing to fear but an ignorant, ill-judging Audience.' He goes on to protest a little at having to adapt his verses to 'Vocal Musick . . . and make them rugged to the Reader that they may be harmonious to the Hearer', even if 'I have no Reason to repent me, because these sorts of Entertainment are principally design'd for the Ear and Eye; and therefore in Reason my Art, on this occasion, ought to be subservient to his.' The age-old librettist's complaint as to *prima la musica, poi le parole* is suppressed underneath the handsomely expansive folds of Dryden's amiable magnanimity. He could afford, after all, to be generous. Had not the Duchess of Monmouth – a rather unlikely enthusiast, it must be said, since she was the widow of his headstrong (and now, alas, headless) Achitophel – recommended the work to Queen Mary? And had not Her Majesty 'Graciously been pleas'd to peruse the Manuscript of this *Opera* and given it her Royal Approbation'? Dryden piqued himself on presuming 'to guess that Her Majesty was not displeas'd to find in this Poem the Praises of Her Native Country; and the Heroick Actions of so famous a Predecessor in the Government of *Great Britain* as King *Arthur*'.

Those unfamiliar with this bizarre but by no means ineffective creation, much more strongly operatic in character than *Dioclesian* (which, as one recent writer on Purcell observes, is really a play with music), should not expect Malory, Tennyson or T. H. White. Not a single Knight of the Round Table figures in the cast list, and the princess Arthur marries is not called Guinevere but Emmeline. The story, as conceived by Dryden, is closer to the historical King Arthur (whatever is known about him) in presenting the paladin as leader of the British resistance to the invading Saxons. Making use of sources such as Bede and Geoffrey of Monmouth, the drama reflects the growing interest in Britain's remoter past and the beginnings of a closer study of Anglo-Saxon among scholars and antiquarians.

The central plot, involving Arthur's love for the blind Emmeline, daughter of Conon, Duke of Cornwall, and the machinations of the Saxon King Oswald and his attendant spirit Grimbald, who contrive to abduct her, touches only here and there on the episodes Purcell was required to clothe in appropriate music. After a solemn sacrifice of horses to Woden and Thor, the Saxons are summoned to the mead hall to get drunk (Dryden had done his historical research very thoroughly here), but the Britons defeat them in battle. Subsequent acts include a pastoral interlude, a song for two sirens, a passacaglia on the theme of a lover's infinite happiness, and the celebrated 'Frost Scene' in which Cupid challenges the Genius of Cold Weather with the declared aim of raising an entire population 'of kind embracing lovers and embrac'd' to sing his praises.

Operatic much of this undoubtedly is, despite the marked difference in character and intention distinguishing the various moments in the score; and the zest, pace and concentration in Purcell's writing are substantially assisted by Dryden's gift for writing singable, swift-moving text. We can only regret that the pair of them never sat down with the serious project of a through-composed opera in front of them along the lines of *Dido and Aeneas*. The Frost Scene, in this as in other respects, was a success from the outset: the Dorset Garden audience watched entranced as Cupid came down in a machine to a little French symphony and roused the Genius, who rose from the earth to the accompaniment of a sinister sequence of quaver chords played tremolando by the string band. Cast as a bass, he sang an air of tortured mock gravity, lamenting the peremptory summons which called him to 'Rise unwillingly and slow/ From beds of everlasting Snow' before Cupid impatiently snapped back at him in a frisky rondeau, and the aged or ageless frost spirit was forced to acknowledge the presence of 'Great Love . . . Eldest of the Gods'.

Cupid was played by Charlotte Butler, whom Roger North recalled with delight many years later:

> I remember in Purcell's excellent opera of *King Arthur*, when Mrs Butler, in the person of Cupid, was to call up Genius, she had the liberty to turne her face to the scean, and her back to the theater. She was in no concerne for her face, but sang a recitativo of calling towards the place where Genius was to rise, and performed it admirably, even beyond anything I ever heard upon the English stage. And I could ascribe it to nothing so much as the liberty she had of concealing her face, which she could not endure should be so contorted as is necessary to sound well, before her gallants, or at least her envious sex.

Butler must also have sung in the masque rounding off Act V, a far livelier, more genuinely entertaining affair than its counterpart in *Dioclesian*, to a large extent because its form – that of a patriotic pageant with classical deities assisting – allows Purcell to romp exultantly through a whole gallery of different forms and styles with the aid of Dryden's protean versification.

A brisk trumpet tune welcomes Aeolus, god of the winds, who tells his 'Blust'ring Brethren of the Skies' to retire and allow Britannia to 'Rise in Triumph o'er the Main'. The sense of gradually descending calm after a storm is memorably conjured up by the use of two recorders to subdue the initial gales of semiquavers for the strings, before Britannia herself (perhaps the earliest stage appearance of a national icon whose monetary incarnation had been based on the abundant charms of one of Charles II's mistresses) arises in a machine, seated on an island. The 'soft Tune' for which Dryden's direction called was interpreted by Purcell as the most ravishingly beautiful slow symphony, in which a trumpet and two violins blossom into a garland of florid Baroque passagework, its serene enchantments the musical equivalent of those ornate sprays of flowers and leaves being carved for William and Mary's new apartments at Hampton Court.

True to the new commercial ethos of the 1690s, Pan and a Nereid, followed by a trio of shepherds, sing the praises of Britain's chief exports, fish and wool. We can feel Dryden's inexhaustible wit stretched to its fullest in lines like:

> Other Lands thy Fishes tasting,
> Learn from thee Luxurious Fasting

or

> Though Jason's Fleece was Fam'd of Old,
> The British Wool is growing Gold.

He and Purcell have less oblique fun with the ensuing knees-up celebration of harvest home. 'Your hay it is mow'd', set by the composer as a pseudo-folksong, realistic right down to the doggerel rhyme in the last verse:

We'll toss off our Ale till we cannot stand,
And Heigh for the Honour Old Eng*land*.

Nothing in *King Arthur* is more effectively managed than the contrast presented by the next air, 'Fairest isle, all isles excelling', sung by the goddess Venus. With the utmost simplicity Purcell yet again validates his claim, through this most artless of melodies, to be one of the greatest song-writers in the history of music. The aria heralds a representative dialogue between two lovers, divided into clearly delineated musical episodes and moving from initial uncertainty on the part of the woman to the man's plea for 'kindness' (sexual compliance) and culminating in a truculent celebration of mutual enjoyment:

Let us love, let us love, and to Happiness haste:
Age and Wisdom come too fast:
Youth for Loving was design'd.
You be constant, I'll be kind,
Heav'n can give no greater Blessing,
Than faithful Love and kind Possessing.

The masque, and indeed the entire opera, end with a grand chorus of homage to King William – not, as one modern Purcellian would have us believe, turning *King Arthur* into 'an audacious study in irony', merely an example of Dryden's supreme adaptability. While he could, and did, give political offence in plays such as *Cleomenes* or in the spoken prologue to *The Prophetess*, he was unlikely to want to involve Purcell too deeply in his own alienated stand against the new *status quo*.

Produced at Dorset Garden in May 1691, *King Arthur* may well have been intended as the kind of lavish crowd-pleaser which would help to recoup some of the United Company's box-office deficit. Nobody seems to have bothered to keep the musical score adequately together, and the result is a whole variety of sources and solutions, along with evidence of missing items. Roger North actually thought the whole thing had been lost for ever. 'There was so much of admirable musick in that opera, that it's no wonder it's lost; for the English have no care of what's good, and therefore deserve it not.'

Slowly the company started to fall back on revivals, old Dryden successes from the 1660s, pieces by Shakespeare and his fellow Jacobeans, but now and then new plays were commissioned from young dramatists, and one of these was Thomas Southerne's comedy *The Wives' Excuse or Cuckolds Make Themselves*, brought on at Drury Lane in December. The play has recently been revived by the Royal Shakespeare Company, in a production making an excellent case for its sophisticated development of the sex and marriage formula. Anticipating more modern techniques *à la* Pirandello, the dramatist introduces himself in the character of Wellvile, the author of the very play in which he appears, making significant interventions in the course of the drama. Though this was well received, Southerne evidently got into trouble for making fun of the fashionable music meeting with which the play opens. After an introduction in the form of a realistic dialogue among lounging footmen at a concert, we encounter the fashionable company itself, sharply divided as to the merits of English and Italian music. When one of them asks for an English song, Wellvile supports the request, demanding, 'Any song, which won't oblige a man to tell you he has seen an Opera at Venice to understand'.

Purcell obliges with the first of the play's four vocal numbers, 'Ingrateful love! thus ev'ry hour', another lyric from the pen of Major-General Sackville, an air whose musically rather sombre character hints at the comedy's darker touches. Each of the other three songs has its own well-defined personality. 'Corinna, I excuse thy face' in Act V is an agreeable Scotch tune, and for the same scene, a masquerade in which the egregiously repulsive Mr Friendall is set up in a discreditable amorous escapade by the procuress Mrs Wittwoud, the composer rewarded Charlotte Butler with a jaunty rondeau, 'Hang this whining way of wooing'. Most intriguing of all is 'Say, cruel Amoret, how long', sung by Friendall after a dinner in Act IV. Having earlier been told by a music master at the concert that the lyrics he has written are 'so abominably out of the way of music, I don't know how to humour 'em', he now provides his own setting, and a dismal affair, both in words and notes, it proves to be. Purcell deliberately emphasizes the threadbare poetic invention by providing the sort of music an amateur might have written, formless, going nowhere and full of pointless rhetorical gesticulation.

The Wives' Excuse was a great success, its triumph owing partly to fine performances by Elizabeth Barry and the increasingly popular Anne Bracegirdle. Though no beauty, Mrs Bracegirdle – actresses were never called by their Christian names – had an astonishing gift for holding audiences in the palm of her hand. Writing in the 1730s, Colley Cibber, one of her most fervent professional admirers, nostalgically recalled her impact:

> Her youth and lively aspect threw out such a glow of health and chearfulness that, on the stage, few spectators that were not past it could behold her without desire. It was even a fashion among the gay and young to have a taste or *tendre* for Mrs Bracegirdle. She inspired the best authors to write for her, and two of them, when they gave her a lover in a play, seem'd palpably to plead their own passions and make their private court to her in fictitious characters.

She was, what is more, a tolerable singer. 'Her voice and action gave a pleasure, which good sense in those days was not asham'd to give praise to'. Though the part of Emmeline she had created in *King Arthur* was strictly a spoken role, Purcell was to write several theatre songs with Bracegirdle's talent and charms firmly in mind.

Not all the Drury Lane audience were content to be seduced by Anne Bracegirdle's Circean allure. At the end of December there occurred the most undignified row between the theatre door-keepers and various members of the aristocracy, apparently also involving members of the guard of soldiers whose job it was to ensure orderly conduct within the house. After this 'great disorder, where the Lord Grey of Ruthin and Viscount Longueville were knockt down, and 2 other lords puncht with the butt ends of muskets', the place was punitively closed; but though during a House of Lords debate 'one of the bishops moved to suppresse the playhouse, it being a nursery of lewdness', the temporal peers objected and performances began again soon after Christmas.

The fracas got into the papers, of which by now there was a wide variety, especially in the new and well-liked form of magazines. Purcell himself, during the early months of 1692, started publishing his songs in one of the latest periodicals, *The Gentleman's Journal: or The Monthly Miscellany. By way of a letter to a gentleman in the country. Consisting of news, history, philosophy, poetry, musick, translations &c.* The journal was the brainchild of Pierre Antoine Motteux – Peter Motteux, as he became known in England – an enterprising young Huguenot refugee from Rouen, who combined literary interests such as translating *Don Quixote* with selling 'China and Japan Wares, Tea and Fans'. His death in 1718 in a brothel off the Strand was the bizarre and horrifying result of 'a very odd experiment, highly injurious to his memory', in which he had arranged to have himself hanged in a noose in order to test the possibility of prolonging an erection. Now very much alive in 1692, he issued several of Purcell's best songs in his magazine, including 'If music be the food of love' in the earliest of its three versions. Only the opening line is Shakespeare's, the rest of the poem being the work of a Suffolk gentleman Colonel Heveningham (as with Major-General Sackville, we may wonder how many army officers nowadays amuse themselves with writing song lyrics). With its marked allusion to the kind of Scotch tunes Purcell could throw off at the flick of a lace cuff, the song's memorable qualities owe something to the fact that its melody sounds like a typical 'Jockey and Jeanie' Strathspey taken at half speed. He was to write a second version of this song with an entirely different setting, printed in 1695, which makes a more blatant appeal to a professional singer with some knowledge of the latest Italian vocal style.

At some point early in 1692 Henry and Frances Purcell, with their two small children Frances and Edward, moved out of the house they had occupied for eight years in Bowling Alley East in the parish of St Margaret's, Westminster. The Bowling Alley residence was probably the composer's property, since an entry in the parochial vestry book calls it 'Mr Purcell's', and there is no indication as to why exactly the family decided to pack up or where they went. In 1694 Henry's name figures in parish accounts as the tenant of a house in nearby Marsham Street, and he is said to have lived for a time in the Gate House of St James's Palace, but nothing certain has yet come to light regarding a fixed home for the Purcells during the last three years of his life.

The note about the house in Bowling Alley East turns up in an assessment made 'by virtue of an Act of Parliament for raising money by a Poll payable quarterly for one year for carrying on Vigorous War against France'. St Margaret's parish raised the sum of £919 15s (Dryden's cousin Erasmus was one of the official collectors). Though the struggle with the French was afterwards to make William extremely unpopular with his subjects, nobody at this stage seems to have begrudged paying a poll tax to fund the continuing enterprise. The King left for the spring campaigning season on 14 March, his frail constitution revealing itself in an ominous spitting of blood throughout the previous day, to the horror of Queen Mary, who in any case had her own troubles to add to a continual affectionate anxiety over her husband's health.

One of the principal defectors from James II to William of Orange at the time of the Revolution had been John Churchill, recently created Earl of Marlborough for his share in suppressing Monmouth's rebellion. It was Marlborough's wife, the strong-willed Sarah Jennings, who had gained successful ascendancy over the Queen's sister Princess Anne as her bedchamber woman, and now strove to alienate her from both William and Mary, while the Earl himself started to send ingratiating messages to the fugitive James at St-Germain. Sir Winston Churchill's laboriously white-washing biography of Marlborough has sought to exonerate his distinguished ancestor from all charges of treachery, but it seems clear that the King and Queen were perfectly justified in fearing this unscrupulous self-seeker and in making their suspicions known. By the end of January 1692, William, armed with proof of Marlborough's ambitious double game, had dismissed him from court and instructed Mary to prevail upon Anne to do the same with Sarah. Anne, with her father's unforgiving Stuart obstinacy, refused, leaving Whitehall with her husband Prince George for Syon House, where they set up a kind of court in exile, their seething resentment fuelled by the angry Marlboroughs.

The rift with Anne, never to be properly healed, added to the already considerable stress Mary had to endure as regent in William's absence, and it is hard not to feel that some awareness of these pressures must have dictated the intimate and pensive character of the 1692 birthday ode *Love's Goddess Sure Was Blind*, Purcell's setting of a more than passable text by Sir Charles Sedley. Born in 1639, Sedley had begun his career as one of the most outrageously dissolute rakehells of the early Restoration, but by now he was decidedly reformed and steady, far removed from the drunken hooray Henry who, after preaching a blasphemous mock sermon from a balcony to a crowd of onlookers, had shown them his bare arse and defecated into the street below. Sobered by an unhappy marriage to a mentally unstable wife, he had discovered a talent for playwriting and urbane love lyrics, becoming one of that 'mob of gentlemen who writ with ease' unfairly mocked by the malicious Alexander Pope in the next poetic generation.

He had, what is more, been helpful to William at the Revolution, whether in reaction to his daughter Catherine's role as King James's mistress is unclear, and it may have been at Mary's personal request that he was summoned to write this year's ode. Catherine, in any case, having briefly been embroiled in a Jacobite plot, had now come over to her father's side and was soon readmitted to court as an enjoyably caustic commentator on everyone, not excluding the Queen herself. Sedley's wit was a father's legacy, and his birthday tribute to Mary has all the slightly faded gallantry of the elderly beau recalling Restoration Whitehall, as well as carrying faint memories of the Cavalier court in which he had come to maturity. Mary must have smiled at a stanza such as

> Long may she reign over this Isle,
> Lov'd and ador'd in foreign parts;
> But gentler Pallas shield awhile
> From her bright charms our single hearts

but what would she have made of the remarkable, indeed quite unprecedented *memento mori* quality of Sedley's final lines?

> May she to Heaven late return
> And choirs of angels there rejoice
> As much as we below shall mourn
> Our short, but their eternal choice.

227

The answer is probably that with her continual pious introspection Mary would have appreciated this graceful reminder of her mortality. She was not to know how soon, in a mere matter of two or three years, the end would come.

Purcell too had supplied a remembrance, but of a rather less morbid kind. The eighteenth-century musical historian Sir John Hawkins tells the relevant story as follows:

> The Queen having a mind one afternoon to be entertained with music, sent to Mr Gostling, then one of the chapel... to Henry Purcell and Mrs Arabella Hunt, who had a very fine voice and an admirable hand on the lute... with a request to attend her: they obeyed her commands; Mr Gostling and Mrs Hunt sang several compositions of Purcell, who accompanied them on the harpsichord; at length the queen, beginning to grow tired, asked Mrs Hunt if she could not sing the old Scots ballad 'Cold and Raw', Mrs Hunt answered yes, and sang it to her lute.

According to Hawkins, Purcell was 'not a little nettled at the queen's preference of a vulgar ballad to his music' and took the opportunity to work it into 'the next birthday song, viz. that for the year 1692', where indeed we find it as the bass line of the soprano solo 'May her blest example chase'.

The melody of 'Cold and raw', one of those Scotch tunes which end hanging on the dominant rather than returning to the tonic, had started life as a dance called 'Stingo or the Oil of Barley' and its 'ballad', a faintly bawdy affair in which a traveller 'riding over a knough' propositions a farmer's daughter, was added later, probably by Thomas D'Urfey, in whose *Pills to Purge Melancholy* the words first appear. Mary's impatience with art-music and sudden longing for an old tune are perfectly understandable – a case of Noël Coward's 'How potent cheap music is!' – and should not be held against her as pure philistinism. Purcell, irrepressibly witty as ever, plays up to the rustic jog-trot of the original in the string reprise which follows his air.

There is anyway nothing incongruous in such deliberate plainness, since the ode so carefully eschews the flamboyant gestures of its predecessors. Trumpets and oboes are banished, and the only colour added to the strings is that of recorders, gorgeously adorning the duet 'Sweetness of nature', whose grave rhythmic insistence sweeps us inexorably from the initial G minor into the various stages of a related key sequence, while the alto and tenor hymn the Queen's 'high pow'r with equal goodness join'd . . . The joy and wonder of mankind'. This particular vocal combination gives the ode its special hue, since Purcell exploits it once more to exceptional effect in 'Many, many such days may she behold', where a little ground bass emboldens the two voice parts to move with sidelong sinuousness over its determined tread. The last number of all is surely one of the finest single movements in any of the odes. Mining a (for him) completely new choral style, whose patterns and harmonies anticipate Handel – himself heavily influenced, as we know, by the older composer's manner – Purcell introduces Sedley's last couplets with opulent flourishes entirely suited to the vision of rejoicing angels conjured up by the second line. What then follows is both surprising and entirely consonant with the solemnity of the poem's close: a quartet of soloists move meltingly into the minor, among heart-stabbing dissonances, before the chorus shuts the scene in a mood as elegiac as the last moments of *Dido and Aeneas* and as flawless in its beauty.

The Mrs Hunt who had sung 'Cold and raw' to her lute presumably took part in *Love's Goddess Sure*, since 'May her blest example' is written for a soprano. She had appeared with Charlotte Butler in *Calisto* at Whitehall in 1675, each of them dressed in 'an African habbit of Black sattin cut upon gold tinsell . . . a black lambskin Capp lined and stifned with pearle'. Her lute playing was immensely admired and elicited an ode from the young William Congreve and a portrait from Godfrey Kneller, as well as one of the songs in John Blow's *Amphion Anglicus*, entitled 'On the Excellency of Mrs Hunt's Voice and manner of Singing', though Gostling, whose son told Hawkins the 'Cold and raw' story, thought this same voice was 'like the pipe of a bullfinch'. In 1680 she had wedded a Mr James Howard but, so Hawkins says, 'she had the misfortune to be married to a man who, for reasons that may be guessed at, ought to have continued for the whole of his life in a state of celibacy'. Soon resuming her maiden name, she 'lived irreproachably and maintained the character of a modest and virtuous woman'.

Poor Charlotte Butler, on the other hand, continued to attract prudish censure. She was to leave England in 1693 to act in Dublin, disappointed by the measly forty-shilling weekly salary paid her by Betterton's patentees. Her place was taken by Mrs Ayliff, for whom Purcell the previous year had composed the song 'Ah me! to many deaths decreed' with its ornate melismatic excursions, published in the August number of *The Gentleman's Journal*, but premièred earlier in John Crowne's tragedy *Regulus* at Drury Lane. Motteux thought Ayliff's singing incomparable. 'There is no pleasure like that which good Notes, when so divinely sung, can create.' The number was intended to reflect the mingled fortunes of the Roman lady Fulvia, mistress of the hero Attilius Regulus, whose torture by the Carthaginians (he was rolled in a spike-lined barrel) became a famous example of stoic fortitude. Crowne's play is typical of its author, a not untalented playwright with strong political interests, whose fondness for topical satire found its way into *Regulus*. The picture of the shifty inhabitants of Carthage intriguing with the enemy bears an uncomfortable resemblance to the situation with which Queen Mary and her few genuinely loyal ministers were having to cope during the spring and summer of 1692.

Politics had also played its part in the notoriety of John Dryden's tragedy *Cleomenes, the Spartan Hero*, which was due to have been staged at the Theatre Royal in April. We can scarcely blame the discarded laureate, alert as ever to the fluctuations of contemporary political life, for taking yet another opportunity to make embarrassing observations on the government. Mary, alerted to the sensitive nature of the piece, involving a fugitive king seeking military aid from a foreign power, vetoed the production, but Dryden had enough credit among discerning members of the establishment, including the poetically inclined Lord Chamberlain, to gain a lifting of the ban after only a fortnight, and the play finally opened before an excited and appreciative audience on 18 April. Purcell's contribution, written for Charlotte Butler, was the song 'No, no, poor suff'ring heart', a piece whose perfunctory simplicity made it popular as a tune for a variety of street ballads.

The success of *Dioclesian* and *King Arthur* was a natural incentive to Betterton and his company to plan another Dorset Garden spectacular. Even though Cibber cynically observes that the box-office receipts were insufficient to clear the players of 'a large debt, which it was publickly known was about this time contracted, and which found work for the Court of Chancery for about twenty years following, till one side of the cause grew weary', the management was evidently committed to investing in semi-opera as a bankable resource. 'Every branch of the theatrical trade had been sacrific'd to the necessary fitting out those tall ships of burthen that were to bring home the Indies. Plays of course were neglected, actors held cheap, and slightly dress'd, while singers and dancers were better paid and embroider'd.'

Cibber, even though his wife Catherine, daughter of the trumpeter John Shore, was one of Purcell's singers, never saw the point of opera in any form; but we are at liberty to wonder whether the audience attending the run of performances of *The Fairy Queen* at Dorset Garden, in May 1692, was necessarily interested in the spoken text, as opposed to Purcell's magnificent heaps of song, dance and instrumental music. As it happened, the words were mostly by Shakespeare, a rendered-down version of *A Midsummer Night's Dream* whose adapter has never been identified. The plot and much of the dialogue was retained, but 'the Most Lamentable Comedy of Pyramus and Thisbe' performed by Peter Quince's team of 'rude mechanicals' at the close of the play was transferred to Act III, and – boldest stroke of all in an age when Shakespeare had not yet achieved inviolable divinity – Theseus, Hippolyta and the four lovers actually met Oberon and Titania in the wood. It hardly needs pointing out that this encounter provides an obvious opportunity for a grand musical entertainment.

The music Purcell wrote for *The Fairy Queen* is richly alert to occasions of this kind, however artificially thrust into the action they may appear. What his librettist took out of the play or re-ordered within the text finds the handsomest of compensations in the score, so that there are many moments when we can imagine the composer as the dramatist's intuitive collaborator. Whether Purcell knew the original comedy is impossible to say. It was not a favourite with Restoration audiences, and only one production is recorded, in 1662 when Samuel Pepys thought the work 'the most insipid, ridiculous play that ever I saw in my life.' The fact is, nevertheless, that much of the enchantment (an entirely appropriate word in this case) of *The Fairy Queen*, which modern performance reveals to work perfectly well in the theatre, derives from an almost ideal marriage between its music and the unique Shakespearian distillations of *A Midsummer Night's Dream*.

Only two of the musical episodes are through-composed operatic scenes, the first being the fairies' baiting of a drunken poet in Act I. Owing to his stammer – 'I am a scu-scu-scu-scu-scurvy poet' – this is always said to be based on Purcell's friend Tom D'Urfey. At the end of the first edition of *Sir Barnaby Whigg* (1681) though apparently not among the songs set by the composer, is a little mock-autobiography, a cheeky *envoi* from the dramatist himself:

> Farewell my Lov'd Science, my former delight,
> Molière is quite rifled, then how should I write?
> My fancy's grown sleepy, my quibbling is done;
> And design or invention alas! I have none.
> But still let the Town never doubt my condition;
> Though I fall a damn'd Poet, I'le mount a Musician.
>
> I got Fame by Filching from Poems and Plays,
> But my Fidling and Drinking has lost me the Bays;
> Like a Fury I rail'd, like a Satyr I writ,
> Thersites my Humour and Fleckno my Wit.
> But to make some amends for my snarling and lashing,
> I divert all the Town with my Thrumming and Thrashing.

Given the abundant evidence here of D'Urfey's amiable gift for self-mockery, could it be that he himself was the anonymous *Fairy Queen* librettist? Whatever the truth, the scene, with its roguish musical simulation of the bibulous hack lurching to and fro among different rhythms, is one of Purcell's liveliest essays in broad comedy.

Entirely different in mood is the masque in Act II, where Titania makes ready for sleep, with delicious evocations of forest birdsong, a trio 'May the god of wit inspire' where the voices assume the role of trumpets and hautboys, a gorgeous *nachtmusik* sequence ushered in by Night herself with muted strings and Secrecy as a countertenor accompanied by recorders, almost like a number in one of the court odes. The instrumental and vocal blending enhances the erotic promise of the lyric:

> One charming night
> Gives more delight
> Than a hundred lucky days.
>   Night and I improve the taste,
>   Make the pleasure longer last,
>   A thousand, thousand sev'ral ways.

After an air for Sleep himself, in which the spaces between the notes are as eloquent as the notes themselves, the 'Followers of Night' (one wonders what exactly their costumes looked like) dance to a learned double canon, evidently another of Purcell's admiring references to Matthew Locke's *Tempest* score, which had made such an impression on him as a young musician setting out on his career.

In Act III the drama is once again opened up to allow room for Titania's entertainment of the ass-headed Bottom, and here it is Purcell, as master of the individual number, who shines forth. The lovely minuet 'If love's a sweet passion' is enriched with a string symphony and one of those extended choral conclusions which are the glory of this lavishly adorned score. A little dance sequence, involving swans who turn into fairies, scared off in their turn by four savages, was originally followed by a comic duet, but for the revival of *The Fairy Queen* in 1693 Purcell inserted an elaborate Italian-style da capo air 'Ye gentle spirits of the air' between these two episodes. The duo, when it appears, is a hilarious mock-pastoral dialogue between Coridon and Mopsa, two rustics with plenty of musical straw in their hair and clearly first cousins of the harvest-homers in *King Arthur*. Originally this was sung by Mrs Ayliff and the bass John Reading, but for the revival somebody, probably Purcell, seems to have thought that it would work more effectively with Mopsa as a man in drag, and the part was given to John Pate (a noted Jacobite), who sang it in 'a woman's hat and waistbelt'.

The jubilation accompanying Oberon and Titania's reunion in Act IV was the cue for some spectacular scenery, including fountains, cypress trees, statues and columns, around a massive flight of steps. Purcell's use of trumpets in the bouncing 'Now the Night is chased away' shows an obvious desire to match this visual splendour, and the pageant of the four seasons, each little air given its individualizing obbligato (solo violins in 'Thus the ever-grateful Spring' and a pair of oboes in 'Here's the summer, sprightly, gay') is a perfect row of decorative vignettes.

To end the opera, a masque was provided, set in 'a transparent Prospect of a Chinese Garden, the Architecture, the Trees, the Plants, the Fruits, the Birds, the Beasts quite different to what we have in this part of the World'. Purcell had no more knowledge of China than he had of the North Pole, but with the increasing vogue for tea-drinking and the decorative passion for *chinoiserie* in everything from lacquered screens to blue and white porcelain, a trend encouraged by William and Mary themselves, anything even vaguely exotic in this line was bound to please, and when Hymen, god of marriage, arrived to kindle his torch from orange trees miraculously sprouting from china vases, the Dorset Garden audiences must have been in raptures. The music, in any case, did not disappoint them: a string of Purcellian show-stoppers included the trumpet air 'Thus the gloomy world', the filigree-textured 'Hark! the echoing air', the grand chaconne to be danced by 'The Chinese Man and Woman' and, last of all, 'They shall be as happy as they're fair', a triumphant jig for assembled singers and chorus. As elsewhere in the drama, the act is rounded off with spoken dialogue, in this case a remarkably apt episode in which Oberon and Titania relinquish make-believe for their real-life personae as actors, leading us into a typically witty epilogue. Here again it is difficult not to see D'Urfey's hand at work. Great dramatist he may not have been, but he was full of original theatrical ideas, and perhaps this was one of them.

The Fairy Queen was an immediate hit. 'The Court and the Town', says a contemporary source, 'were wonderfully satisfy'd with it; but the Expences in setting it out being so great, the Company got very little by it.' Doubtless this was why the management was so keen to revive it the following year, when several changes were made to the score, not necessarily all of them by Purcell. The published text for this 1693 revival includes the jejune aria over a ground bass with obbligato violin known as 'The Plaint', which Oberon in Act V asks to hear. The music does not appear in any of the composer's manuscripts and the earliest source is in *Orpheus Britannicus*, issued by Henry Playford in 1698, but it goes on being performed as authentic Purcell today. It probably is, but by Daniel rather than Henry. The younger brother had been appointed organist of Magdalen College, Oxford, in 1688, during the controversial intrusion of the Papist fellows, and was starting to make a name for himself in various spheres already touched so brilliantly by the elder. What may have happened was that the good-natured Henry, ready to advance Daniel's career, had been content to insert this laborious imitation of his own style into the new score, where indeed it has proved obstinately resistant to any attempt to purge it in the name of authenticity.

Purcell was now a valued asset to the United Company, and during the autumn of 1692 further songs from his pen continued to figure in the season's new productions. Nobody has yet determined the authorship of *Henry the Second, King of England*, given early in November, though the play has been generally admired for its skilful mixture of topical satire and tragic love, dealing as it does with the famous, half-legendary, amour of King Henry and Rosamond Clifford, who was supposedly forced to drink poison by the jealous Queen Eleanor. The part of Rosamond was well designed for Anne Bracegirdle, but Purcell's song 'In vain 'gainst Love I strove', divided into two markedly distinct sections, was sung to her by an attendant, played by Mrs Dyer, who had taken various singing roles in *The Fairy Queen*.

A more important commission arrived with the tragedy of *Oedipus*, a joint work by Dryden and Nathaniel Lee, originally brought on at Dorset Garden in 1678. 'Sophocles is admirable every where', says Dryden in his preface to the play, 'and therefore we have followed him as close as possibly we could.' This is not necessarily true, and it is pointless to start matching the great Greek drama against Lee's more hysterically high-flown lines or the amatory sub-plot introduced by the dramatists to satisfy Restoration taste and provide extra roles for the company. 'Custom likewise has obtain'd, that we must form an Under-Plot of second Persons which must be depending on the first; and their By-Walks must be like those in a Labyrinth, which all of them lead into the great *Parterre*, or like so many several Lodging-Chambers, which have their Out-lets into the same Gallery.' On its own terms, in the context of late seventeenth-century tragedy and as the work of two outstanding theatrical talents, *Oedipus* is an excellent play, grand, thrilling, consistently dramatic and well deserving the admiration it received from contemporary spectators and readers.

It was for one of Dryden's portions of the text that Purcell wrote his music. The setting for Act III is 'a dark Grove' in which Tiresias and his priests, 'all clothed in long black Habits', conjure up the spirit of the dead King Laius, to the accompaniment of thunder and lightning 'then groaning below the Stage'. Once Tiresias has bidden his assistants to

> tune your Voices
> And let 'em have such Sounds as Hell ne'er heard,
> Since Orpheus brib'd the Shades

the priests begin the solemn trio 'Hear, ye sullen Pow'rs below', which introduces one of the most famous of all Purcell's airs, 'Music for a while'. The design, a vividly descriptive vocal line over a double ground created by interweaving a simple ascending six-note bass with a markedly chromatic upper part, is a perfectly calculated synthesis of the different elements in Dryden's text, intended as these are to reflect music's dual gift for soothing and infuriating. This was a hugely popular song among Purcell's contemporaries, though they evidently wanted more accidentals than the composer actually wrote, which is why the notorious $C^\flat$ in the melisma at the word 'eternal' has fetched up in modern performances without any canonical authority.

In this busy autumn of 1692 the London stage was convulsed by a series of disasters involving several of its principal performers. In one performance of *Oedipus* Samuel Sandford, 'an excellent actor in disagreeable characters' and much applauded on this occasion in the role of the villainous Creon, seriously wounded George Powell, playing Prince Adrastus, with what both of them had been given to understand was a retractable stage dagger. Not long after this died the well-loved comedian Anthony Leigh, the original Mercury in *Amphitryon*, who had made his name in the title role of an earlier Dryden play, *The Spanish Friar*, first produced in 1680. Saddest loss of all, however, was William Mountfort, a friend, we may presume, of Purcell's and one of the most versatile stage performers of his day. On a December night in 1692 he was stabbed and murdered by an officer, Captain Hill, newly returned from King William's current campaign in Flanders.

The cause of the attack was jealousy over Mountfort's supposed attachment to Anne Bracegirdle, with whom Hill, like so many others, had fallen in love and whom he had even tried to kidnap, rounding up a party of fellow soldiers to help him. Mountfort, happily married as far as his friends knew, was met in the street by Hill and a mutual friend Lord Mohun, who embraced him while the enraged Captain, seizing his chance, stabbed the imagined rival through the heart and ran off. Mountfort died of his wounds the following afternoon, but any hopes his fellow actors might have had of securing justice against the murderers were dashed when Hill managed to flee to the Channel Islands, though he was later brought back. Mohun, largely, we may presume, because he was a viscount and Mountfort but a common player, was acquitted after trial by his peers, apparently because he was only fifteen years old. The funeral, on the night of 13 December at the church of St Clement Danes, was a notable event, attended by nearly a thousand mourners, with several members of the nobility sending empty coaches, as the custom was, to show their respect for the great actor. Perhaps it was Queen Mary herself, an admirer of his various roles, who authorized the attendance of the Chapel Royal choristers with Purcell as organist, though we do not know which of his anthems they sang as a tribute. While the great bell of St Clement's was ringing Mountfort's knell it was heard to crack, something 'taken much notice of by the criticks'. Purcell too might have detected something ominous in the sound.

7

The Last Song

The deaths of Mountfort and Leigh cast shadows over what, in other respects, had been a highly successful year for Henry Purcell. 1692 culminated in the performance on 22 November of the ode *Hail, Bright Cecilia* as the principal item in the St Cecilia's Day celebrations, which, as noted earlier, were an established part of the London musical calendar. No less than a dozen soloists were engaged for the occasion, including experienced theatre singers such as Mrs Ayliff and the countertenor John Pate, for whom Purcell wrote an elaborately ornamented solo ''Tis Nature's voice'. Peter Motteux, in *The Gentleman's Journal*, has confused many writers on Purcell, since he told his readers that the ode was 'admirably set to Music by Mr Henry Purcell, and perform'd twice with universal applause, particularly the second Stanza, which was sung with incredible Graces by Mr Purcell himself'. Since the composer was a bass and Pate's name is attached to ''Tis Nature's voice' in the autograph score, Motteux's ambiguous phrasing surely refers to Purcell as composer rather than singer, and indeed the written-out ornament here is distinctive enough to deserve remark in an age when singers were encouraged to make their own 'incredible Graces'.

The poet on this occasion was Nicholas Brady, known to Purcell as the vicar of St Katherine Cree, where he had helped to appoint the new organist several years earlier. Even if the inspiration for his verses obviously comes from Dryden's fine 1687 St Cecilia ode 'From Harmony, from Heav'nly Harmony', which in its setting by Giovanni Battista Draghi made such a crucial impact on Purcell's style, Brady's lines are some of the best the English composer ever set, elegant, dignified, fully consonant with the classicizing genius of the Augustan age and continuously sensitive to the needs

238

of the occasion itself, a moment when the cream of London's professional musicianship could flourish its talents before a discerning audience.

Thus in *Hail, Bright Cecilia*, Purcell was not just concerned to establish his authority as the most versatile composer of his generation, in command of all the humours and moods, swagger, lyricism, tenderness, meditation and panegyric, from the massive trumpet sinfonia (effectively a small 'symphony' in the classic sense) to the tremendous closing invocation to Cecilia as 'Great Patroness of Us and Harmony!' He was also celebrating, with the help of Brady's well-wrought poem, the all-encompassing magnificence of music itself, an art of which several poets and philosophers in this rational age were growing wary because of its incalculable power over the emotions. Within this complex work, one of the greatest achievements in the entire musical history of England and a proof, if we needed any, that Purcell really was, as Dryden called him, 'a composer equal with the best abroad', he devised the most fully rounded portrait of himself as a creative personality.

Though an overall unity is created through the use of a carefully plotted key sequence, the positioning of the three choral numbers in such a way that their dramatic and structural effect can make its due impact and through the contribution made by the various ground bass airs, enormous care is devoted to giving each item its own individual profile. Instrumentation, as we might expect in a festive homage to music, is a special priority, with recorders and violins featuring in 'Hark, each tree its silence breaks', a pair of oboes in 'Thou tun'st this World', trumpets and drums in 'The Fife and all the Harmony of War' and the full string band to accompany the choruses. Mood and vocal colour are equally varied, and in this respect we need to remember that the impact of the original performance would undoubtedly have been heightened by the distribution of so many solo voices throughout the work. Thus, in the commemoration of Cecilia's supposed invention of the organ, which forms the core of Brady's ode, Purcell is continuously attentive to shifting nuance and the need to balance grandeur and spirituality against something more emphatically of this world. After the ethereal trio 'With that sublime Celestial Lay' comes a nudgingly humorous ground, 'Wondrous machine', for bass soloist with a pair of chattering oboes, followed by a sprightly air ironically dismissing the violin's claims to rival 'all thy consecrated lays' even while a brace of fiddlers discourses a seductive accompaniment. We may wonder, indeed, whether Brady, setting at naught the other instruments in successive verses, and concluding

> Thou summ'st their diff'ring Graces up in One
> And art a Consort of them All within thy Self alone

was not recalling that day at St Katherine Cree when Purcell, Francis Forcer and the others had listened so assiduously to performers on the 'wondrous machine'.

The St Cecilia ode was instantly popular, and its radical influence can be felt on English musicians from William Croft, who made a copy for a performance in 1695, to Handel, who obviously looked at it before writing his setting of Dryden's 'From Harmony, from Heav'nly Harmony' in 1737. Its energy, gusto and brilliance of invention must owe something to the simple fact that the occasion for the work offered Purcell a break from writing theatre music, although there is no evidence that he was losing interest in the stage, providing him as it did with such a steady source of income. In February 1693 Thomas Southerne brought out another successful comedy, *The Maid's Last Prayer, or Any Rather than Fail*. 'It discovers much knowledge of the Town by its Author; and its Wit and purity of Diction are particularly commended.' Written in the same vein as *The Wives' Excuse*, the play discloses even more strongly Southerne's real interest in music and his contempt for those who saw it either as a mere adjunct to socializing, the 'musical wallpaper' of our own day, or for amateurs keen to show off their *savoir-faire* as critics and performers. In the midst of an anarchic concert presided over by the know-all Sir Symphony – 'Now the Fuga, basses! again, again! Lord! Mr Humdrum, you come in three bars too soon' – two of Purcell's songs are skilfully inserted for maximum effect. While the first, 'Though you make no return to my passion', with its playful endorsement of marital infidelity, obviously relates to the comedy itself, the second, a duet for Mrs Ayliff and Mrs Dyer, 'No, no, resistance is but vain', is doubtless intended as a reproof to the music-makers on stage, since it has no other evident link with the action. This, Southerne and Purcell imply, is what good music ought to sound like, and the song is among the composer's most artful fusions of pure science and aural pleasure, changing its shape with protean aptness according to the associative weight of individual words and phrases, to the point at which the enraptured listener wishes it might last for ever.

The words of 'No, no, resistance is but vain' were written by the noted wit Anthony Henley, a friend of Lord Dorset, who later became MP for Andover. Well known to Swift and Steele, to whose *Tatler* he contributed some papers, he was also a keen musician with a good voice, who took Daniel Purcell under his wing in the years after Henry's death. A third song for *The Maid's Last Prayer* had words by William Congreve, a young poet and dramatist about to make his name as a worthy rival to Southerne among the rising generation of new playwrights during the 1690s. Congreve's theatrical début took place at Drury Lane in March 1693, with *The Old Bachelor*, a comedy which, for all its recourse to well-tried stereotypes, already shows that inimitable brio and elegance in the dialogue which was soon to give the author classic status in *The Way of the World*. Southerne, with his usual amiability towards fellow writers, had been instrumental in bringing the play to Dryden's attention, and both eagerly recommended it to Betterton's company, for whom several of the leading roles had been clearly fitted. With a launch as auspicious as this, it was hardly likely that *The Old Bachelor* could fail, and indeed so successful did it prove that the run was extended for an unprecedented fourteen nights in a row.

It has been pointed out that an early manuscript of Purcell's incidental music to the play assigns the various pieces to D'Urfey's adaptation of Chapman's *Bussy d'Ambois*, produced in 1691, and the overture's gloomy colouring relates it more directly to a tragedy than one of the last of those characteristic Restoration imbroglios of cuckoldry, scheming and seduction. What may have happened is that the other numbers, including a minuet, a sturdy 'boree', one of Purcell's catchiest hornpipes and – for the multitude of seasoned campaigners in the audience – a spirit-stirring march, were tacked on by the composer for the later play. Whatever the exact circumstances, Congreve, with Purcell's help, made a magnificent start, and the pair were to work together again when *The Double Dealer* was produced at the end of the year.

A very different type of comedy altogether was Tom D'Urfey's latest farce *The Richmond Heiress or A Woman Once In The Right*, capitalizing on the talents of the up-and-coming Thomas Doggett, who had tickled the audience in the same dramatist's *The Marriage-Hater Match'd* produced the previous year, to which Purcell had contributed a song. *The Richmond Heiress* is a typical D'Urfey mishmash, overstuffed with character parts and plotlines, but full of crude life, especially in the scene where the composer was concerned, which takes place at an early form of 'therapy session' run by the irresponsible quack Dr Guiacum. Fulvia, the eponymous heiress, feigning madness, is entertained by a lunatic dialogue between a soldier who has lost his wits during a battle and a woman driven mad from jealousy of a rival. As it happens, Purcell's dialogue 'Behold the man', intended as a vehicle for Mrs Ayliff and John Reading, comes in somewhat inopportunely here and rather outstays its welcome.

More successful than 'Behold the man' was a second mad duet, the work of the young John Eccles, a composer who was to come into his own during the next two decades as a popular writer of theatre songs and music for court odes. Dryden, present at one of the handful of performances *The Richmond Heiress* received, thought this more effective in the hands of Doggett and Brace-girdle than Purcell's mad scene, entrusted as the latter was to professional singers. As he told the critic and patron William Walsh:

Durfey has brought another farce upon the Stage: but his luck has left him: it was suffered but foure dayes; and then kick'd off for ever. Yet his Second Act was wonderfully diverting; where the scene was in Bedlam ... The rest was woefull stuff, & concluded with Catcalls; for which the noble Dukes of Richmond and St Albans were chief managers.

Both noblemen were bastard sons of Charles II who appear,

like their half-brother the Duke of Grafton, to have made their peace with William and Mary rather than follow James II to France. Just who was or was not corresponding with the court of St-Germain had become a continuous source of anxiety for Mary. Those in authority, whether at court or in government, displayed, as she confided anxiously to her journal, 'a kind of affectation to do all that was insolent to the King without fear of punishment, so that he could not govern his own servants, nay, that he durst not punish them, but was obliged to keep those in his service who least deserved it and who he might be pretty sure would not really serve him'. The campaigning season would lead to a serious setback for William, who was forced to withdraw at the hard-fought Battle of Landen, while a further blow arrived with the French capture of England's Levant merchant fleet bringing home Oriental treasures from the markets of Smyrna. Though the King, among both his allies and his enemies on the Continent, gained enormous credit for his bravery and resourceful generalship even in retreat, the English in their surly insularity were still unable to see the point of the strange little hook-nosed Dutchman they had taken for their sovereign.

'Will should have knotted and Moll gone to Flanders' ran an anonymous broadsheet libel, referring to the craze for macramé or 'knotting' which Mary had begun, and which Sir Charles Sedley made the subject of a little poem 'The Knotting Song', set to music by Purcell and published in *The Gentleman's Journal* that summer. As it was, Mary stayed at home, putting on a brave face as now she so often needed to, while her thirty-first birthday came round and with it another congratulatory ode. Shadwell, the Laureate who might have received the commission, had died the previous year, in the midst of writing a comedy on the topical theme of stocks and shares, and now Nahum Tate had succeeded him. Whatever flashes of grace and ingenuity he had shown in *Dido and Aeneas* were scarcely in evidence for the new ode *Celebrate This Festival*. Yet, pedestrian as Tate's muse undoubtedly was, he could hardly be accused of triviality. Sensitive to the Queen's feelings, he symbolically banished warlike associations and ordered the day to be devoted to peace and harmony. Britain was enjoined, reasonably enough, to stop grumbling and plotting and count its blessings instead. Much may be forgiven Tate for his final wish, shared wholeheartedly by Mary herself:

> Kindly treat Maria's day
> And your homage 'twill repay,
> Bequeathing blessings on our isle,
> The tedious minutes to beguile,
> Till conquests to Maria's arms restore
> Peace and her hero, to depart no more.

Even if the soprano soloist sings 'Cease, trumpet, cease', that instrument, as played by the versatile John Shore, is summoned back in the penultimate number 'While for a righteous cause' to perform a florid exhibition piece in which – rather as in the operas and cantatas Alessandro Scarlatti was writing in Italy at the same period – vocalist and trumpeter enter into elaborate emulation with one another. To offset the extrovert glitter of numbers such as this, Purcell was always ready with something softer, more delicate in texture, and in 'Crown the altar, deck the shrine' he gave the countertenor an air above another of those double-layered grounds so memorably exemplified in 'Music for a while', subsequently arranging the whole thing as a most effective keyboard solo.

Celebrate This Festival is a thoroughly accomplished exemplar of a genre in which Purcell had now grown nonchalantly self-assured. It was in another guise altogether that he appeared that summer of 1693, when, on 1 July, an imprimatur was given by the Bishop of London's chaplain William Lancaster to a second volume of *Harmonia Sacra*, published by Henry Playford in a similar format to the 1688 instalment, with the same musical angels engraved by Simon Gribelin and a dedication to Henry Aldrich, Dean of Christ Church and Vice-Chancellor of Oxford University. Aldrich was what the seventeenth century liked to call a man of parts: he was editor of Clarendon's *History of the Rebellion*, author of a classic treatise on logic, an amateur architect said to have designed the fine Baroque chapel of Trinity College, Oxford and passionately devoted to music, to the extent of composing himself in the liturgical line. Like Purcell, he had been educated at Westminster, and the two were almost certainly friends, as the musical Henry's setting of the academic Henry's catch in praise of drinking, 'If all be true that I do think', suggests.

As for Henry the publisher, he too knew his man. 'In addresses of this kind', Playford tells Aldrich in the dedicatory epistle:

> men are usually so far from suiting the subjects of their treatises to the qualifications of the persons they apply to, that we may shortly expect to see musick dedicated to the deaf, as well as poetry to aldermen and prayer-books to atheists: and though generally it is a difficult matter to find a worthy patron for any one of these excellencies, yet we may happily find them lodg'd in yourself.

To please the Dean still further, he had added to this largely English collection of motets and dialogues a number of pieces by Bonifazio Graziani, *maestro di cappella* at the church of the Gesu in Rome and a much-esteemed sacred composer of the mid-century, as well as works by Giacomo Carissimi, one of the most influential of all Italian Baroque masters, especially in the fields of oratorio and cantata writing.

Three commendatory poems adorned the opening pages, one of them by Thomas Sacheverell, who would achieve notoriety in Queen Anne's reign as an apostle of High Tory clerico-politics, but who for now was content to hymn Blow and Purcell as unmatched masters of sacred music:

> The Church as yet could never boast but two
> Of all the tuneful race from Jubal down to you.

Another, addressed 'to his unknown friend Mr Henry Purcell', was by the witty miscellanist Tom Brown, concluding, not without a tang of irony

> This tribute from each British muse is due,
> Our whole poetic tribe's oblig'd to you.
> For where the author's scanty words have failed,
> Your happier graces, Purcell, have prevail'd.
> And surely none with equal ease
> Could add to David and make D'Urfey please.

Purcell's celebrity meant that his presence dominated the 1693 *Harmonia Sacra*, important though this volume was for intro-

ducing another of his brother Daniel's compositions to the public
and for the presence of Jeremiah Clarke, one of the most promising
younger musicians in the composer's orbit. Five very different
works demonstrated to anyone who might have been tempted to
complain that Henry was frittering away his talent on act tunes,
mock mad-scenes and Scotch songs that none of his old inspiration
in the handling of spiritual texts had been quenched, and that the
same vein of Anglican Baroque piety which had so potently exer-
cised his fancy and intelligence in the works Playford had gathered
together in 1688 could be mined once more, to yet richer effect.

Again he turned to the poetry of Abraham Cowley and William
Fuller: the former in the shape of an ode on the Resurrection,
Begin the Song, which in Purcell's hands assumes all the colourful
plasticity of a contemporary religious fresco; the latter in the
unsettled, ever-questioning psalm paraphrase *Lord What Is Man*,
whose rhetorical zigzags enable him to embrace once more that
loose-bodied declamatory form in which he had never lost interest
since the elegy on Matthew Locke first appeared some fifteen
years earlier. Nothing could have supplied a sharper contrast to
this elaboration of a well-tried English compositional style than
the rumbustiously Italianate setting of Nahum Tate's 'Hymn
upon the Last Day', *Awake Ye Dead*, which is a companion piece
to the Cowley poem, arranged as a duet for two basses and a
superb example of Purcell's *multum in parvo* technique, cramming
the whole apocalypse into under four minutes of music. Every
nuanced word, 'sleep', 'aloft', 'fall', 'loud', 'roar', is individualized
by the composer's thrilling exploration of its associative potential
in music. Verses like:

> Alarm'd, amaz'd, the clatt'ring orbs come down.
> The virtuous soul alone appears
> Unmov'd while earth's foundations shake,
> Ascends and mocks the universal wreck

show us why he continued to favour Tate's texts, for all their
periodic slithers into banality, and the piece constitutes an extraordinary little Purcellian hand-grenade packed full of explosive
energy and divine wit.

Tate was once more the poet in *The Blessed Virgin's Expostu-*

lation, also known by its first line, 'Tell me, some pitying angel', which bears the subtitle 'When our Saviour (at Twelve Years of Age) had withdrawn himself, &c. Luke 2. v. 42' and dramatizes to maximum effect Mary's horror at losing her son when he wandered off into the Temple to dispute with the doctors of the law. Here again the verse shows a remarkable aptness for musical setting. The distraught mother's confusion and anguish are displayed by her muddled assemblage of cries, demands, rhetorical outbursts and frantic imprecations. It is essentially a dramatic monologue to which Purcell responded by arranging it in the form of a cantata, though it is more markedly Italian in its division of recitative and aria episodes than several similar structures which he had created earlier among his solo songs and elegies. The entire piece, with its increasingly frantic use of melisma, its startling repetitions, especially the four fruitless invocations of the archangel Gabriel, sounding his name on an exposed high G, and its bitter acknowledgment, through heart-wrenching discord and suspension, of the divide between the earthly mother and her heaven-sent son, is one of those strokes of genius which establishes Purcell's position in the field of solo art song as an heir to Dowland and an outstanding forerunner of Schubert.

Unquestionably the finest work in *Harmonia Sacra II*, and one of those compositions which admirers of Purcell would select without reservation as touchstones of his genius, is the miniature oratorio – or, if we are ploddingly pedantic, the musical dialogue – *Saul and the Witch at Endor*, also called *In Guilty Night*. In the years before the Civil War, young composers eagerly embracing the Italian *seconda prattica* style had written dialogue songs, involving small dramatic scenes between pastoral, mythological and occasionally between biblical characters. One such musician had been John Hilton the younger, organist of St Margaret's Westminster, whose little oratorio-like episodes based on such moments as the judgment of Solomon were probably inspired by a glance at some of the many Italian essays in the form by composers like Francesco Anerio and Alessandro Grandi. Another, who may have been Hilton's teacher at Cambridge, was Robert Ramsey, organist of Trinity College from 1628 to 1644. It may have been his friend the poet Robert Herrick who wrote the words of *Saul and the Witch at Endor* which, in Ramsey's setting, was extremely popular with musicians well into Henry Purcell's maturity. For the brightest hope of English music in the 1690s to produce his own version of the scene, far from showing any disrespect towards the older work, would surely have been seen as an act of noble emulation.

The moment as described in the First Book of Samuel is one of the most poignant in the Old Testament, and was to inspire Handel to similarly happy creative effect in his *Saul*, written forty years after Purcell's treatment of the scene. Saul, King of Israel, plunged in manic depression and paranoia regarding his son-in-law and former protégé David, and facing a decisive engagement with the Philistine army, prepares to break Jewish law by consulting a witch who will summon up the ghost of the prophet Samuel. The disturbed spirit, angry at confronting the man who so wilfully ignored his holy counsel, tells Saul that he and his sons will be slain in battle and that his kingdom will fall into Philistine hands.

Purcell's eerie, heart-rending and tautly dramatic handling of the anonymous playlet is for three solo voices, soprano (the Witch) countertenor (Saul) and bass (Samuel) combining at either end of the work as a chorus. The whole Caravaggesque chiaroscuro of the action is established at once through the furtive entries of the opening trio on the words 'In guilty night', and a depth of pathos unbearable, we may feel, to the composer, let alone to us for whom he evokes it, is mined from the outset by descending chromatic sequences on the words 'forsaken Saul'. Florid melisma plays its part as eloquently here as in *The Blessed Virgin's Expostulation*, sharpening the edge of Saul's near-hysterical despair as he calls upon the Witch to 'arise, call pow'rful arts together/ And raise the ghost, whom I shall name, up hither', yet it is her own terrified cries of 'Alas!' as she acknowledges the King's presence which intensify the macabre urgency at the heart of the encounter between these two outcasts. Samuel, when his shade arises, brings no mitigation for Saul's sufferings, given stronger definition by the way in which Purcell enables him to repeat the words 'for pity's sake'. The prophet remains utterly pitiless, his final couplet charged with something almost akin to scorn:

Tomorrow then, till then farewell, and breathe:
Thou and thy son tomorrow shall be with me beneath.

It is in the coda to the piece, however, that Purcell traces the signature of a sublime inspiration. Taking the word 'farewell' from the penultimate line, he creates a chorus which, in its ten-bar span, encapsulates the unredeemed hopelessness pervading the moment and foreshadows the tragedy awaiting the King. To the accompaniment of Saul's anguished gasps on falling semitones, Samuel and the Witch, inexorably intoning their farewells, invoke a harmonic world not unlike that of Dido's 'When I am laid in earth', but without any salving dimension of mercy. All the darker moods of the Baroque, setting at nought our sneering notions of its art as mere froth, posture and decoration, coalesce in this stupendous miniature, and anybody whose responsive imagination has been stirred by contact with Purcell's music elsewhere should find some means of listening to it.

In December 1693 a distinguished guest arrived in London from the Continent, in the person of Prince Ludwig, son of the Margrave of Baden. An extremely able soldier, after fighting the Turks in the ongoing war along the Hapsburg Empire's Hungarian frontier, Ludwig had thrown in his lot with William of Orange against the French. Handsomely welcomed by the King and Queen, 'Prince Lewis' spent six weeks in London, and among the programme of entertainments provided for him was an ode, *Light of the World*, with words by the young diplomat Matthew Prior. This elegant and substantial poem was apparently 'set to music by Dr Purcell', whom we might suppose to be Daniel, a Mus.D. at Oxford since 1688, but experts concur in thinking that Henry is meant here, even though he was never given a doctorate by either university. The music in any case is lost, and was not, besides, Prince Lewis's only encounter with Purcell's genius, since on 11 January he attended a revival of *Dioclesian* at Dorset Garden, and on the 25th a concert was given in his honour at York Buildings off the Strand, where *Hail, Bright Cecilia* was performed.

One of the Prince's fellow commanders in the French war was James, 2nd Duke of Ormonde, the valiant son of an equally brave father and one of the premier magnates of Ireland. The Duke had apparently been active in promoting the military career of Purcell's brother Edward, and it may have been through this connection that Henry secured his next major commission, to write the music for an ode celebrating the centenary of the founding of Trinity College, Dublin, by Elizabeth I in 1594. After a somewhat stormy interlude when James II, in attempting to regain Ireland in 1689, had quartered troops in its various buildings and threatened to disperse the library, Trinity had regained its status as the Irish Protestant university to which the newly empowered 'Ascendancy' sent its sons, and in front of whose gates the statue of King William was raised triumphantly, not to be removed until full nationhood arrived in our own century.

The poet for the ode was Nahum Tate, who enjoyed the status of a distinguished Trinity alumnus. Though there was no question of Purcell crossing over to Dublin to superintend the performance of the ode, *Great Parent, Hail to Thee*, the piece seems to have been presented without a hitch as part of an extremely crowded day's programme on 9 January 1694. A service at Christ Church featured one of John Blow's most majestic Chapel Royal anthems, *I Beheld and Lo, a Great Multitude*, and a sermon by the college's provost Dr George Ashe, who had taught the young Jonathan Swift and who now chose as his text Christ's words on the woman with the box of ointment, 'Verily I say unto you wheresoever this Gospel shall be preached in the whole world, there shall also this, that this woman hath done, be told for a memorial of her.' Nobody was especially offended that words originally bestowed on a prostitute were now spoken in praise of the august royal foundress.

Further praise for Queen Elizabeth came in the Latin speeches made that afternoon, followed as they were by panegyrics, poems, a debate on the currently fashionable issue of Ancient versus Modern Learning, a comic discourse and the ode itself, 'sung by the principal gentlemen of the kingdom', according to one member of the audience. Afterwards the whole company, including nobility and gentry, several Anglican bishops and the Mayor of Dublin, left the college in solemn musical procession while all the windows of Trinity blazed forth in festive candlelight.

'Oda Eucharistica, vocum et instrumentorum Symphonia,

decantatur' says the Latin account of the proceedings. Purcell's ode was carefully tailored to available resources: no trumpets or oboes; a pair of recorders used to give some colour to at least one of the numbers; otherwise a string band and continuo, with vocal solos unlikely to put too much of a strain on the singers mustered for the occasion, who were perhaps members of the choirs at Christ Church and St Patrick's – the 'principal gentlemen of the kingdom' presumably formed part of the chorus. The work itself, not the most inspired of its kind, bears out the suggestion that the composer was writing purely to earn money. Two or three of the numbers, nevertheless, catch fire, most notably the bass air 'Awful Matron take thy Seat', imbued with appropriately donnish grandeur in both the vocal line and its underlying orchestral textures, and the skilfully managed 'Thy Royal Patron sung' in which praise of dead and living dukes of Ormonde is divided by the soprano between a wistful opening section with attendant recorders and a catchy tune to round off the movement, which sounds oddly Irish but is more probably a recycled idea for a Chapel Royal 'alleluia' which Purcell had put aside while composing an anthem.*

A more enticing commission was of course the ode for Queen Mary's thirty-second birthday, which she spent in her husband's company at the new palace of Kensington. The last such piece Purcell was to write for her, *Come, Ye Sons of Art, Away*, to another and altogether better Nahum Tate text, has become one of his most popular works, and the reasons for its success are not hard to seek. Praising the Irish ode, Peter Motteux had told readers of *The Gentleman's Journal*: 'Mr Tate who was desired to make it has given Mr Purcell an opportunity by the easiness of the words to set them to musick with his usual success.' This was in fact much more obviously true of *Come, Ye Sons of Art, Away*, in whose verses the multiple references to music warmed the composer's invention in ways which some of the earlier court

---

*When Trinity celebrated its three hundredth birthday in 1894, a possible revival of the ode was abandoned. As the great Dublin polymath J. P. Mahaffy observed: 'The music, which is extant, was written by the famous Purcell, but is as bad as the words.'

poets, concentrating too sycophantically on Mary herself and her warlike William, had been unable to discover.

The genuine impact here is contrived as much through a mastery of structure as through the nonchalant grace with which Purcell shifts positions in his assault on our sensibilities. After the trumpet overture, with its arrestingly poignant slow section, the disposition of the vocal numbers neatly divides into an alternating sequence of four minuets and three grounds. To break too tight a symmetry Purcell throws in a slow, free-flowing, 'plaint'-like solo with obbligato oboe, 'Bid the Virtues, bid the Graces', creating a contemplative core within a work whose mood is otherwise one of exuberant festivity.

It seems like another stroke of genius that in the justly famous alto duet 'Sound the trumpet' it is the singers, rather than the eponymous instrument, who do the trumpeting. Here, as in the ensuing 'Strike the viol', with its ethereally blended alto and recorders, the busy motion of the quaver pattern in the ground bass whirls the voice on high like the well-oiled machinery of some Baroque theatrical apotheosis. To the bass falls the task of celebrating both the day's particular merit – 'let it have the honour of a jubilee' – and 'the sacred charms that shield/ Her daring hero in the field'. By the time the final duet and chorus, 'See Nature, rejoicing, has shown us the way', begin their progress through the various phases of a rondeau with interludes in the minor for the soprano and bass soloists and a grand choral reprise (which may or may not have been accompanied by a kettle-drummer), we may well feel that the whole of what music can do to the emotion and the intellect has been realized in this superfine panegyric.

There had been no let up, meanwhile, in demands for Purcell's music at Drury Lane. In January he had set a song written by Congreve for Dryden's not very distinguished farewell to the stage, the tragi-comedy *Love Triumphant or Nature Will Prevail*, and a month later Southerne's hugely successful *The Fatal Marriage or The Innocent Adultery* offered one of his musical collaborator's most expressive airs, 'I sigh'd and own'd my love', the perfect case history, for voice and continuo, of an ultimately unsatisfied passion. Had Purcell read Aphra Behn's novel on which this tragedy of an ex-nun compelled to marry a man she does not love in order to satisfy her first husband's greedy family is based? 'The town' judged the play 'one of the greatest ornaments of the stage, and the most entertaining play that has appeared upon it these 7 years ... This kind usage will encourage desponding poets and vex huffing Dryden and Congreve to madness.' Southerne was far too amiable a man to want to annoy either of his two friends, but it must have seemed that with audiences in the 1690s he could do no wrong. Purcell's instinctively sympathetic contributions to sustaining the mood of the play added their share to his triumph.

The United Company, as both dramatist and composer might probably have suspected, was poised on the brink of collapse, but Betterton and his troupe were determined on yet another attempt at staging a play with a substantial musical component, in this case a work very different from the handsome excursions into legend and antiquity proposed by *Dioclesian, King Arthur* and *The Fairy Queen.* Indefatigable playmaker that he was, Thomas D'Urfey now devised a trilogy based on the perennially popular *Don Quixote*, the novel by Miguel Cervantes originally published in 1604 and first translated into English some thirty years later. The three comedies were designed to include most of the story's better-known episodes, including the fight with the windmills, Sancho Panza in Barataria, the Don's fantasy passion for Dulcinea del Toboso, the tale of Cardenio and the episode of Master Pedro's puppet show (used in our own century as operatic material by Manuel de Falla). All the narrative's myriad subtleties evaporate into crude farce, and D'Urfey's old vice of trying to please everybody at once is given free rein. The music for the shows was entrusted mostly to Henry Purcell and John Eccles, each of whom appears to have thrown himself wholeheartedly into the spirit of the enterprise, however dubious it may have appeared to 'the graver sort'.

Including several of his best theatrical numbers, Purcell's songs for *The Comical History of Don Quixote* nearly all arise directly from different dramatic occasions in the various parts of the trilogy. True to the age's bellicose temper, two at least are military in inspiration – the duet for countertenor and bass 'Sing all ye muses' which springs from the mock investiture of Don Quixote as a knight, and the patriotic trumpet air 'Genius of England, from thy pleasant bower of bliss', given during the entertainment which concludes Part II. The first of these is in essence a piece of programme music, one of the innumerable *battaglie* which stretch from Renaissance madrigals and keyboard pieces down to Beethoven's *Die Schlag bei Vittoria* and Tchaikovsky's *1812* overture. D'Urfey's text graphically evokes the arts of warfare in the age of Vauban and Marlborough, with besiegers 'storming a town/ Through blood and through fire to take the half moon', scaling ladders, the roar of cannon and the explosion of mines, all of them nudging Purcell towards a meticulous musical portrait of the soldier's varying fortunes in love and war. 'Genius of England', with trumpet passages for John Shore recalling Purcell's earlier Lullian 'Cibell'*, is much simpler in outline, and is distributed between a tenor, who exhorts the Genius to 'guard from foes the British State', and a soprano, whose appeal to manly bravery and a kindly reception from 'Celia's eyes' for 'the noblest scars' is not much different in its evident recruiting intention from the First World War music-hall song whose refrain ended with the words:

> On Saturday I'm willing, if you'll only take the shilling,
> To make a man of any one of you.

Subtler than these, and surely the most memorable Purcellian items in *Don Quixote*, are the two solo songs 'Let the dreadful engines of the eternal will' and 'From rosy bow'rs, where sleeps the God of Love', each devised for a singing actor or actress whose specific talents were already well known to Purcell. The high bass John Bowman, working with the composer on stage and in the court odes, was rewarded, as the half lunatic Cardenio, with a ferociously elaborate mad scene in 'Let the dreadful engines', whose declamatory freedom of movement conceals an extremely firm grasp on those moments where air and recitative spill over into one another, and on the relationship of changing keys to the character's mood swings.

---

*The 'Cibell' or 'Cebell' was a trumpet march, whose form was suggested by a number in Lully's opera *Atys*: the name itself derives from a character in the same work.

'From rosy bow'rs', written for Part III, was sung by Letitia Cross, then a girl of about fourteen, whose presence in *Don Quixote III* is symptomatic of the unhealthy preoccupation with precocious infant sexuality displayed by 1690s audiences and earned D'Urfey a well-merited rebuke from Jeremy Collier in his devastatingly influential assault on the Restoration theatrical ethos, *A Short View of the Immorality and Profaneness of the English Stage* (1698). Whatever Letitia lacked in years she made up for in talent, and Purcell's swansong honoured her artistry with a small cantata, in which the soubrette-like Altisidora flirts with Don Quixote with the aim of diverting his thoughts from the inevitable Dulcinea. 'Come now', she declares, 'you shall see me sing and dance, and how far I excel dull Dulcinea.' Once more Purcell is happy extolling the powers of his own art, as the singer flits effortlessly between sections headed 'Love', 'Gayly', 'Melancholy', 'Passion', 'Frenzy', each joined by a bridging recitative and pushing individual exploration of specific emotional states to an imaginative limit which is hard, at first hearing, to equate with an atmosphere of disease and death drawing the curtain on a meteoric career.

The first two parts of *The Comical History of Don Quixote*, brought on at Dorset Garden during the summer of 1694, were surprisingly successful, owing partly to a brilliant cast, which included Thomas Doggett as Sancho Panza and Mrs Bracegirdle as Marcella, 'a young beautiful Shepherdess who hates Mankind', for whom D'Urfey and Eccles furnished a scene which effectively allowed her to comment on her relationship with the hapless William Mountfort. Ironically, it was Mountfort's widow Susannah, recently remarried as Mrs Verbruggen, who made the biggest hit of all in the role of 'Mary the Buxom, Sancho's Daughter, a rude laughing clownish Hoyden', a part she sustained throughout the trilogy.

All that season King William had been in Flanders vigorously pushing home his various advantages against the French, while his allies were generally heartened by the presence of Admiral Russell's Mediterranean fleet and the astonishing successes of King Victor Amadeus of Savoy at the head of his powerful army. Once autumn closed in and William eventually arrived in London after landing at Margate on 11 November, it fell to Purcell to produce a new anthem for the Chapel Royal and something more substantial besides, which should accord with 'their majesties' proclamation for a publick day of thanksgiving for preserving their majesties' persons and government, and giving successe to their arms by sea and land'. The anthem was a decidedly stilted setting of verses from Psalm 18, *The Way of God Is an Undefiled Way*, in which the singers (including, on this occasion, John Gostling) go through the motions of what might be considered a typically Purcellian sacred work, but without really conveying any impression of the artist's commitment to his material. William's unwillingness to countenance string symphonies in Chapel anthems was respected, but Purcell offered little beyond a series of sterile formulae in the way of compensation for whatever the piece might lack in ceremonial pomp. The glad confident morning of *My Beloved Spake* had dimmed to a mere twilight of gesture, token and parade.

Better by far were the two works supplied for the St Cecilia's Day commemoration on 22 November, an occasion whose spirit that year would anticipate that of the official thanksgiving ordered for a fortnight later. The great Te Deum and Jubilate for choir with soloists, accompanied by trumpets and strings, was performed at the church of St Bride's, Fleet Street, built by Sir Christopher Wren in 1678, as a dignified opening to the day's festivity. We should remember, in listening to these canticles in so sumptuously conceived a setting, that nothing like them had ever been heard before, and the sense that their composer was, to whatever degree, compensating for what he could no longer do in his capacity as a Chapel Royal composer is unavoidable.

The impact they made on at least one contemporary listener is captured for us in words which almost fall over each other in their eagerness to encapsulate the transfiguring splendour of the experience. Thomas Tudway, Purcell's friend and near-contemporary as a Chapel Royal chorister and afterwards organist of King's College, Cambridge, remembered the gorgeous sounds years later, as he had heard them at the consecration of St Paul's Cathedral in 1697, two years after the composer died. He recalled:

There is in this Te Deum such a glorious representation of the Heavenly Choirs, of Cherubins & Seraphins, falling down before the Throne & singing Holy, Holy, Holy &c As hath not been Equall'd by any Foreigner or Other . . . He brings in the treble voices, or Choristers, singing, To thee Cherubins & Seraphins continually do cry; and then the Great Organ, Trumpets, the Choirs, & at least thirty or forty instruments besides, all Joine, in most excellent Harmony & Accord . . . This most beautifull & sublime representation, I dare challenge all the Orators, Poets, Painters &c of any Age whatsoever, to form so lively an Idea of Choirs of Angels singing, & paying their Adorations.

Tudway was right up to a point, but the larger canticle's music never quite succeeds in transcending its potentially over-fragmented form. Where later composers such as Handel and Haydn take a more expansive view of the text, whether in English or in the original Latin, spanning the verses with a broader conceptual arch, Purcell tends to proceed piecemeal, dispensing passage after passage in small sections, and dwelling somewhat too heavily on the relative novelty of trumpets used to colour a religious composition. The result is that the episodes most listeners find genuinely moving are not so much the big public acclamations of the kind which excited Tudway, but more inward-looking moments, such as the setting of 'Vouchsafe, O Lord, to keep us this day without sin', where the composer's extraordinary gift of empathy expresses itself through the unsettling harmonies and lyrical intensity of vocal and instrumental lines. The same is true in the Jubilate, where, for all the brio of its opening, many of us feel more at home among the quieter reaches of 'Be ye sure that the Lord he is God', arranged as a treble and alto duet, or in the conscious intellectualism of the canon 'O go your way into his gates'. The two pieces nevertheless established a model for English choral composers, and their influence on cathedral and festival music can still be felt today.

Some of the musicians who heard the Te Deum and Jubilate at St Bride's would have drawn instruction from the score as well as experiencing the kind of ecstasy portrayed by Tudway. That year Henry Playford had produced a twelfth edition of his father's

Introduction to the Skill of Music, and called on Purcell to act as professional reviser. Since little enough is known of the composer's own views on his art, we should be grateful for the scraps of evidence offered here. Singers, for example, are told to 'let the Sound come clear from your Throat, and not through the Teeth by sucking in your Breath, for that is a great Obstruction to the clear Utterance of the Voice'. Those desiring to write canons are recommended to consult John Blow's setting of the *Gloria Patri,* generously praised by Purcell as 'enough to recommend him as one of the Greatest Masters in the world'. Typical of the composer's pragmatic approach to harmony, which has earned him much criticism from his own day to ours, was the assertion that 'imperfect Chords are more pleasant and less cloying to the Ear than many perfect Chords'.

Only the greatest master of the ground could declare that composing it was 'a very easy thing to do and requires but little Judgment'. As for sonatas, he aptly summed up, without mentioning it, his own achievement in the field by the phrase 'a great deal of Art mixed with good Air, which is the Perfection of a Master'. The sonata from which he chose to illustrate an example of what he called 'double descant' (triple invertible counterpoint) was attributed here to Lelio Colista, though in fact it is probably the work of Carlo Ambrogio Lonati. Purcell's observation elsewhere in the book, regarding contrapuntal movement in thirds – ''tis the constant Practise of the Italians in all their Musick, either Vocal or Instrumental, which I presume ought to be a Guide to us' – says much about his openness to the influence of Italian music, as marked now as it ever had been ten or fifteen years earlier when he was at work on his own sonatas.

As winter drew on, so the weekly bills of mortality published in London increased their numbers, swollen this year by an epidemic of smallpox, a killer disease from which only the luckiest recovered. On 19 December at Kensington Palace, Queen Mary, suffering from a heavy cold, noticed a rash over her arms and shoulders and recognized at once the warning signs. With remarkable coolness and a characteristic regard for those around her, she gave orders that only those who had already endured smallpox should stay in the palace and that the rest were to leave immediately. Then, shutting herself in her closet, she sifted carefully through her journals and the various letters written to her, destroying all she could find, including those from William, who was at Whitehall and by her command had not yet been informed of her illness. A last letter to the King spoke plainly of the unhappiness he had caused her through his longstanding liaison with Lady Betty Villiers, but when at length he was sent for, the pair of them broke down and wept together.

Rallying briefly, Mary now entered the last fatal stages of her illness. As William himself grew frantic with thoughts of losing her, sobbing hysterically and at one point falling into a faint, the Queen sank towards delirium, accusing one of her doctors of having 'put a Popish nurse about me', before returning to full consciousness to receive a message from her sister Anne, who was racked with guilt over their earlier rift, and to take the holy sacrament from the new Archbishop of Canterbury, Dr Tenison. On 28 December, Narcissus Luttrell noted laconically: 'Yesterday about one in the morning her majestie departed this life at Kensington; the king is mightily afflicted thereat, and the whole court, as also this citty, and 'tis impossible to express the general grief upon this occasion.'

Indeed it was. Mary had been more deeply loved than she, with all her Christian humility and self-doubt, could ever have suspected, and the news of her death shocked not just her own subjects, but those of courts throughout Europe. Only her father King James, implacable as ever, refused to allow mourning for her among his followers at St-Germain, and managed to persuade Louis XIV to dispense with it among his own courtiers. Irked by such unworthy vindictiveness, many French noble families honoured the memory of a queen they had never met and whose country was at war with theirs by withdrawing from social engagements for a decent interval.

Mary had never wanted a grand funeral. Having paid off her debts and left several touching bequests of money and clothing for two pauper children she had adopted, she asked to be buried without 'extraordinary expense' so as not to be a charge to an already heavily burdened public purse. Neither her husband nor the nation itself, let alone a general sense of what was fitting at a monarch's death, could tolerate such posthumous self-denial, and the result was some of the grandest royal obsequies of the entire seventeenth century, a ceremony which undoubtedly set a precedent for those great public occasions of mourning or rejoicing which the English court is always said to do so well, and one which was talked about and written up throughout Europe.

The embalmed corpse lay in state in the Banqueting House in Whitehall from 21 February, under black glass chandeliers and surrounded by ladies dressed in mourning who went off duty every half-hour. Thousands came to pay their respects to the dead Mary, lying on draperies of purple velvet fringed with gold, with the crown, sceptre and orb laid beside her, while William, almost suicidal with misery, watched from a curtained alcove under the royal coat of arms. On the cold, snowy morning of 5 March, the body, now laid in its coffin and placed upon a specially constructed 'chariot', was carried in slow procession from Whitehall to Westminster Abbey, through streets lined by horse and foot guards. In remembrance of her charity, the cortège was led by 300 poor old women, each wearing a black gown and escorted by a boy train-bearer. The heralds, the Queen's horse, the chief ministers of the crown, the two Houses of Lords and Commons arrayed in long black cloaks, the Lord Mayor of London with his aldermen, and the Duchess of Somerset as chief mourner, attended by the royal ladies-in-waiting, swelled the immense throng at a ceremony which, John Evelyn reckoned, cost £100,000, 'infinitely expensive, never so universal a mourning'.

All the Gentlemen and Children of the Chapel Royal were present at the funeral, and as Abbey organist Purcell would have been charged with overseeing the music for the service. The procession itself moved to the music of trumpets and drums, the latter divided between muffled side-drums and kettle-drums, probably carried by horses with drummers astride. Purcell composed a piece for the march which he was to use again, presumably on the assumption that it would not be immediately remembered by those present at the funeral, in a Drury Lane revival of Thomas Shadwell's play *The Libertine*. This *March for the Flatt Trumpets*, a brief, very simple, wholly effective C minor sequence for the reverse-slide trumpets, which had been brought into England by the versatile Moravian Gottfried Finger some ten years earlier, is now the subject of the most acrimonious controversy among Purcell scholars. For many years it was believed that the march had been accompanied by the drummers mentioned in various accounts of Queen Mary's funeral, and the great Cambridge musicologist Thurston Dart went so far as to reconstruct a drum part, four semiquavers followed by two crotchet beats, to fill in the rests between the flat-trumpet phrases. This became accepted practice until the conductor Robert King recently proposed an entirely different state of affairs, in which the trumpeters had not actually played while walking in the cortège and the drums were in any case silent during the piece, since their united rolling, together with the sound of horses' hooves, the 'chariot' wheels and the thumping of innumerable feet over the black-lined boards laid along the processional route, would have drowned out the march altogether.

The latest stage in the ongoing argument is the challenge to King's theories – put into practice during the course of his complete recording of Purcell's sacred works – by Bruce Wood, who has convincingly suggested that what the drummers actually played was a tattoo known as the Old English March, dispensed by infantry bands since before the Civil War. The trumpeters, he claims, did indeed perform the piece as the procession moved along, and what is more, the canzona Purcell wrote for them to play at the moment when the body was lowered into the grave was accompanied with drums.

That is not all as regards the current dispute. We know that while still in his teens Purcell wrote a setting of three of the Prayer Book's Funeral Sentences, 'Man that is Born of a Woman', 'In the Midst of Life' and 'Thou Knowest, Lord, the Secrets of Our Hearts', and that some years later he made two revised versions of them. They were probably written for a musician's funeral in Westminster Abbey (it may have been that of Henry's drunken teacher Christopher Gibbons). Each is marked by the stark, visceral eloquence of his early style, so memorably displayed in the motets he was writing for the Charterhouse around 1680, and the revisions enhance rather than diminish their noble melancholy.

It has often been assumed that these Funeral Sentences were

sung at the royal obsequies of 1695, but in fact there is no real evidence to substantiate this. Another setting of 'Thou Knowest, Lord' exists, simpler in design and layout and in a different key, and this was the one Purcell surely wrote for inclusion in a service where the Sentences sung were those composed a hundred years earlier by Thomas Morley, and equally appropriate in their grave beauty. As a further authentication Bruce Wood has adduced the presence in the Bodleian Library of a manuscript containing Purcell's new setting within this same context of the Morley Sentences, to which he obviously strove to match the style used here.

We know, what is more, that 'Thou Knowest, Lord' was accompanied by the flat trumpets: the heavily chordal structure seems to invite this in any case. Thomas Tudway, present on the occasion, is once more an invaluable witness to the effectiveness of Purcell's music. His manuscript note to a copy of the anthem says that it was 'accompanied with flat Mournfull Trumpets' and

compos'd by Mr Henry Purcell after ye old way; and sung at ye interrment of Queen Mary in Westminster Abbey; a great Queen, and extremely Lamented, being there to be interr'd, every body present was dispos'd and serious at so solemn a Service, as indeed they ought to be at all parts of divine Worship; I appeal to all yt were present, as well as such as understood Music, as those yt did not, whither they heard heard anything so rapturously fine, so solemn and so Heavenly in ye Operation, wch drew tears from all; and yet a plain Naturall Composition, which shews ye pow'r of Music, when 'tis rightly fitted and Adapted to devotional purposes.

The single feature of the service which failed to impress the assembled mourners – William himself, despising the pomp which the English always expected to surround royalty, had wanted a private funeral and retired to Kensington to nurse his misery – was the banal eulogy of Mary's virtues by Archbishop Tenison, for which he later received a pedantic rebuke from Bishop Ken, ejected at the Revolution from his see of Bath and Wells. Across London more able preachers such as the Huguenot Pierre Jurieu, whose sermons the Queen had especially admired while living in Holland, and her closest spiritual guide, Gilbert Burnet, Bishop of Salisbury, extolled her piety and goodness. Only one audacious Jacobite dared to take as his text Jehu's terrible words on the dead Jezebel, 'Go now; see this cursed woman, and bury her; for she is a king's daughter.'

It can scarcely have been pure opportunism which encouraged John Blow and Henry Purcell to compose their *Three Elegies upon the Much-Lamented Loss of Our Late Most Gracious Queen Mary*, which Playford published that same year of 1695. Though Blow's setting of the English poem *No, No, Lesbia* by a Mr Herbert seems a trifle pallid beside its companion pieces, it is no less sincere, and there can be no doubting the integrity of Purcell's contributions, a solo motet *Incassum, Lesbia, Rogas*, based on a Latin version of Herbert's lines, subtitled 'The Queen's Epicedium' (the word means a funeral lament) and a duet *O Dive Custos, Auriacae Domus*, to hendecasyllabic verses by an Oxford don named Henry Parker. Both works emphasize the shift he was able to make when it suited him, in his more intimate vocal compositions, from the English declamatory idiom to a more self-consciously modern, architecturally Italianate manner, surely proposed to him here by the Latin texts. The international language of learning and science, though no longer of diplomacy (where French had taken its place), invoked a cosmopolitan musical discourse whose rhetoric of ornament and symmetry he assumed with supple ease. Nobody hearing the pastoral elegy *Incassum, Lesbia*, a tragic scena for high voice, making potent use of melancholy repetition in lines like 'O! Damnum non exprimendum', could set down its composer as some remote provincial, out of touch with, or uninterested by, newer European music. Still less might this be said of the exquisitely poignant duet *O Dive Custos, Auriacae Domus*, in which God, as guardian of the House of Orange, is called upon to witness the grief of the royal household and to hear the prayers of 'Oxonidum chorus', the chorus of Oxonians, or of 'those more distant who live by the swift waves of Cam'. Few of Purcell's closes are more tearfully affecting than the layered chromaticisms of the final verse:

> Maria Musis flebilis occidit,
> Maria gentis deliciae breves,

O flete Mariam Camoenae;
O flete Divae! Flete Dea moriente!

From mourning for Queen Mary, Purcell was forced to turn swiftly back to the business of stabilizing his fortunes in the theatre, as the United Company staggered towards final dissolution. At the end of 1694, disgusted with the financial management of Drury Lane under the nefarious ex-lawyer Christopher Rich, who had bought the concern four years earlier, Thomas Betterton had petitioned the Lord Chamberlain against 'the unjust oppressions & Violations of almost all the By lawes Customes & usage that has been established among us from ye beginning', a remonstrance countered at once by Rich and his fellow patentees, who secured a government assurance that nobody should be licensed to open a playhouse without prior notice being given to the Drury Lane management. A series of resignations was the inevitable consequence, and Betterton found a sympathetic ear in King William, who immediately gave the renegade actors, including stars like Elizabeth Barry, Anne Bracegirdle and Thomas Doggett, permission to perform where they chose. When Betterton had scraped together sufficient funds, a new theatre was opened in the converted tennis court on the south side of Lincoln's Inn Fields, to the not altogether undivided joy of the local residents.

Nobody is quite certain why Purcell chose to remain at the Theatre Royal, rather than following the illustrious thespian rebels to their makeshift playhouse, especially since the singers left to him, though they included Letitia Cross and the gifted boy Jemmy Bowen, must have seemed a decidedly omnium-gatherum lot. John Bowman left with Betterton, so did Pate and Reading, the comic Coridon and Mopsa from *The Fairy Queen*, and with them the captivating soprano Mrs Ayliff. Purcell was nevertheless to stay firmly loyal to Drury Lane, where the change of management and personnel seems ironically to have spurred him to produce some of his most powerful music for the stage.

As their opening production in April 1695, the company staged a revival of Aphra Behn's shamelessly melodramatic *Abdelazer or The Moor's Revenge*. As well as an elegantly written song 'Lucinda is bewitching fair', Purcell produced an overture and a set of eight act tunes, including the D minor rondeau which later provided Benjamin Britten with the theme for his *Young Person's Guide to the Orchestra*. 'The house was very full,' says Colley Cibber of the first night, 'but whether it was the play, or the actors, that were not approved, the next day's audience sunk to nothing.' Young Colley, who had newly joined the company, did well out of the occasion all the same, having written a new prologue to the play, though he was disappointed to be told that even if the management was prepared to pay him ten guineas for his pains, he was not important enough to be allowed to speak his own lines.

While 'the enemy', as Cibber calls Betterton's troupe, gained a mighty advantage in signing up William Congreve to write for them, the Theatre Royal company undertook another revival in the form of Shadwell's *The Libertine*, an extremely crude treatment of the Don Juan story earlier handled by Tirso de Molina and Molière. Originally produced in 1675, it was reprinted in 1692, but Purcell's contributions probably belong to later performances, since one of Henry Playford's song anthologies, *Deliciae Musae*, issued in its second volume in 1695, includes 'To arms, heroic prince', a trumpet song apparently written for Jemmy Bowen to sing between the acts in '*The Libertine destroy'd*'. While the play was yet in rehearsal, Jemmy, or 'the boy' as he is called in contemporary sources, was enjoined by one of the musicians 'to grace and run a Division in such a place'. Purcell himself intervened, saying, 'O let him alone, he will grace it more naturally than you or I can teach him.' Since this is almost the only moment at which the scanty life records allow us to hear the composer speak, his biographers inevitably make much of these words, but they certainly bear witness to a mixture of humanity, professionalism, true aesthetic judgment and pure common sense which were surely typical of both man and artist.

'To arms, heroic prince' is the most tedious of Purcell's trumpet songs, its melismatic fancywork and predictable voice-and-instrument imitations quickly outstaying their welcome. Much better are the doomed pastoral festivities of 'Nymphs and shepherds, come away' with its pendant chorus, in Act IV. The song, in a garbled form, became a girls'-school favourite earlier in our own century, though the shepherds themselves, it should have been born in mind, are destined to be murdered by Don John and his fellow libertines. As for the flat-trumpet prelude heard at Queen Mary's funeral, this turns up in the last act as an ominous 'Flourish' to herald the Don's final whisking down to hell. This process is enacted partly in a fine diabolical trio, 'Prepare, prepare, new guests draw near', whose menace is enhanced by Purcell's distribution of the text between solo episodes and choral repetitions of the opening 'Prepare' as an ominous harbinger of the fate in store for the hero – if such indeed he is in Shadwell's not especially glamorous presentation of him.

Another Shadwell revival at Drury Lane took place during the early summer of 1695, when the company presented his adaptation of Shakespeare's *Timon of Athens*. As with so many Restoration remodellings of Shakespearean texts, an element of sexual intrigue was grafted on to the play in the form of Timon's choice between two very different mistresses: the gold-digging Melissa, a sophisticated metropolitan adventuress, and the more passively virtuous Evandra, whose jealousy of her rival reaches crisis point following a masque at which she has watched Melissa dancing with Timon.

The masque episode, rewritten for the 1695 production, gave Purcell the chance to compose one of his more winningly light-hearted scores, a set of little airs, ensembles and choruses which, though ostensibly nothing more than the frothiest of entertainments, avoids cloying sugariness through its sensitivity to formal contrast. A merry war between Cupid and Bacchus, the battles are fought out in delightful numbers like the brisk 'Hark how the songsters' for two sopranos with recorders over a busy ostinato, the more self-consciously reflective trio 'But ah! how much are our delights' and Bacchus's two defiant airs coloured by scoring for a beefy brace of oboes. Grandest of all the vocal items in design is the chorus 'Who can resist such mighty charms', in which we can perhaps detect a certain nostalgia on the composer's part for the brave old Chapel Royal days when his choral invention was adequately stretched. Though written in the minuet rondeau form associated with secular entertainment, the piece reaches out towards something more complex, both in its various key changes and in the frankly pictorial way in which it evokes the conquering power of love. Regarding one other piece, a harmonically free-ranging G minor curtain tune which keeps us on the edge of our seats with its grimacing dissonances over a fretful ground, it is not hard to accept the Purcell scholar Curtis Price's view that it wasn't actually a curtain tune as such, but a morsel of background music crucial to the atmosphere of Act IV, when Timon has retired to brood in the misanthropic solitude of his cave.

Most of the remaining *Timon of Athens* music was composed by James Paisible, a Frenchman who had formerly been among the instrumentalists attached to King James's Catholic chapel, and was now making a name for himself as an oboist and recorder player. Purcell had contributed a trumpet overture to the play, and the piece was to appear again, perhaps in response to an official request, as the introduction to his latest court ode, *Who Can from Joy Refrain*, written to celebrate the sixth birthday of Prince William, Duke of Gloucester, only surviving child of Princess Anne and George of Denmark, on 24 July 1695. The venue chosen for this has been variously assigned to Richmond House, Kew, Camden House, Kensington and Windsor Castle. Wherever it was, Purcell had gathered together a small instrumental ensemble, including a band of three oboes and bassoon (the latter a comparatively recent French import) together with the trumpeter John Shore, for whom he provided some expressive passages in the score. The wind players were probably members of a martial oboe band specially attached to the Princess's household, to which Shore also belonged, and it has been suggested that the ode, whose text remains anonymous, was intended to convey subversive implications connected with Anne's ill-treatment by her brother-in-law the King.

This is probably true if we read lines like 'She's great, let Fortune smile or frown' with due care, but it needs remembering that by now William had made a conspicuous effort at reconciliation with his sister-in-law, giving her all his late wife's jewels, a residence at St James's Palace and an extra allowance of £20,000 a year. He and Mary had, what is more, been deeply attached to the little Duke of Gloucester, who had the misfortune to be hydrocephalous, his head being far too big for his body, making him continually fall over, for which his unregenerately stupid father used to beat him on the backs of his legs. It was no wonder that the boy preferred running about after his Aunt Mary – the pair must have made a bizarre sight, since the Queen was over six feet tall – or showing off his private regiment of ninety red-capped schoolboys, carrying wooden swords and firing salutes from toy cannon mounted on a cardboard fort. When William, who adored children, solemnly reviewed the infant troop, Gloucester assured him, 'My dear King, you shall have all my companies with you to Flanders.'

William was off besieging the key fortress of Namur when *Who Can from Joy Refrain* was performed on a royal birthday observed in London 'by ringing of Bells, and other Demonstrations of Joy suitable to the occasion'. The singers included the Chapel Royal bass Leonard Woodeson, to whom Purcell assigned a solo in praise of Prince George of Denmark, and the countertenor John Howell, whom a contemporary wit describes as 'a-stretching his lungs in order to maintain a long white wig and a Hackney coach'. Three high tenors also took part, the Huguenot Alexander Damascene, who had been naturalized in 1682 and entered the King's Private Music, the Catholic Anthony Robart, whose father had come over from France as a musician with Queen Henrietta Maria, and John Freeman, who had sung in *The Fairy Queen*.

With its emphasis on war and conquest (little Gloucester's words of command were later set to music by the Chapel Royal singer John Church), the ode could well have become a mere one-dimensional essay in periwigged militarism, but Purcell does his best to prevent that happening, not always, alas, very successfully. Best of the various numbers are probably the tenor solo 'A Prince of glorious race descended', in which the strings take over in mid-course from the voice above its passacaglia-like ground, and the exceptional closing Chaconne, whose artful deployment of resources prevents its insistent C major from growing redundant.

London, with its soaring prosperity and acquisitive if often rather simple-minded cosmopolitanism, now became a veritable gold-mine for foreign musicians, and during the early months of 1695, several of their names had figured alongside Purcell's in a magazine entitled *A Collection for Improvement of Husbandry and Trade*, where an advertisement proposed 'The *Royal Academies*: Encourag'd by several of the Nobility, and many other very Eminent Persons'. According to this, 2,000 lucky winners from a sale of 40,000 lottery tickets could acquire 'liberty to chuse any of the following *Accomplishments* they shall have a mind to Learn . . .' These included languages, mathematics, writing, dancing, fencing and of course music, taught, it would seem, by the very best masters then available in the capital. Gottfried Finger, for example, was to give lessons on the viola da gamba, John Banister the younger on the violin and James Paisible on the recorder. Organ and harpsichord tuition was offered by 'Mr Baptist', that is to say Giovanni Battista Draghi, the German instrumental composer Gottfried Keller and a 'Mr Purcell', who might have been either Henry or Daniel, who had recently arrived in London from Oxford, whence he had brought a reputation for deep drinking, wenching and excruciating puns.

The 'two great *Academies*', one in the City near the Royal Exchange, the other in Covent Garden, offered their students a four-year course, 'and to avoid such Inconveniences as might happen by promiscuous Teaching, different times and separate Apartments will be appointed to distinguish the Learners according to their Age and Sex'. There were to be 'extern' students who received three teaching sessions of three hours each per week, and boarding 'academicks' paying an annual thirty-pound fee, with an extra twenty for keeping a servant. King William himself had volunteered to contribute a thousand pounds to encourage the project as soon as the war was over. The whole scheme looks fascinating on paper, and might have revolutionized English higher education, which had to wait another two centuries before the opening of new universities and the establishment of technical colleges. Alas, potential subscribers in 1695 were put off by the proposed lottery method and the idea quickly sank without further trace.

Some of those who might have subscribed to the Academy were doubtless also enthusiastic collectors of Purcell's songs, whose diversity and inventiveness continued to attract buyers of the various collections issued by Playford and Carr. In 1694 the latter had issued the fifth volume of *Comes Amoris*, featuring the duet 'What can we poor females do?' and the beautiful 'I loved fair Celia', in which the free flowing style of declamatory song-writing from an earlier generation tugs at Purcell's memory. Now, in 1695, Playford's *Deliciae Musae* set off a new songbook series with a Purcell selection including 'She that would gain a faithful lover', a breezy little number with a vocally testing melisma in its final bars, the harmonically arresting 'Who can behold Florella's charms', and 'Love, thou canst hear', one of Purcell's miniature cantatas, its four sections, one of them over a ground bass, concluding with a reprise of the opening. The poetry here was by Sir Robert Howard, a free paraphrase of a Horatian ode.

The summer campaigning season in Flanders brought King William a spectacular success with the capture of Namur after a two-month siege. By no particular irony, the fall of the hotly contested fortress made him a hero to the French – 'he is a man of genius, a great King and worthy to be so', said the Duchesse d'Orleans, Louis XIV's sister-in-law but much more partial to her Dutch cousin. British military glory had received a tremendous fillip, and this was calculated to sound an echo in London theatrical productions that autumn. In September, soon after the capitulation of the citadel at Namur, the Drury Lane company mounted an adaptation of John Fletcher's tragedy *Bonduca*, based on the historical Queen Boadicea – or Boudicca or Buddug – of the Iceni and her struggle against the invading Romans. The new version by George Powell laid far greater stress on the play's patriotic aspect than on Fletcher's by no means contemptible handling of the seventeenth century's favourite love–honour–friendship theme. The majority of Purcell's outstandingly effective music, after the ruggedly turbulent overture (there are some sprightly act tunes too), is concentrated on the temple scene in Act III, where the opening numbers 'Hear us, great Rugwith' and 'Divine Andate, president of war' (did Powell, by the way, make up these names?) are given greater urgency by the fact that the gods on whom they call are initially reluctant to respond. When a flame at last is kindled on the altar, the assembled chorus of priests, led by two soloists, breaks into the extended 'Sing, sing, ye Druids', a striking example of the composer's formal originality in developing his material through carefully welded episodes – a string introduction leading into a duet, which then becomes a chorus, all over a ground bass.

The oracle consulted by the Druids finally breaks silence with the predictably ambiguous declaration that 'much blood will be spilt'. Even 1690s gung-ho patriotism was not going to pervert the course of history by making this into Roman blood, but a misreading of the omens produces sufficient confidence in the Britons to demand martial music, and Purcell rises splendidly to the occasion. The alto and bass duet 'To arms, to arms', with its stirring trumpet ritornello, is followed up by 'Britons, strike home', a straightforward call to the flag which became one of his best-loved pieces, sung in London theatres throughout the eighteenth century, and particularly opportune on the many occasions when the nation happened to be at war and morale required a boost.

For a complete contrast, Purcell summoned up his unfathomable skill in exploiting the tender-pathetic manner so indelibly imprinted on the musical memory by airs such as Dido's 'When I am laid in earth' or 'O Solitude, my sweetest choice'. In the last act, when the play's other main female figure, the confusingly named Princess Bonvica, is about to commit suicide, she is given the song 'O lead me to some peaceful gloom' as an accompanying mood piece: this was not in fact sung by the character herself, as played by the actress Mrs Knight, but performed instead by Letitia Cross, evidently gaining in importance to Purcell as a versatile and expressive interpreter of his work. Several commentators on this bleakly mournful air have noted the cunning with which its poignancy is wrung out of the repeated three notes – C, D, E – of the bass, the implicit irony in the vocal allusion to 'shrill trumpets' and the overall sense of life-disdaining exhaustion which provides the dramatic *raison d'être*.

Purcell himself was not in the least exhausted, as it seemed, by the demands the theatre made on him. For the company's production of Richard Norton's tragedy *Pausanias* he furnished a gorgeous essay in sustained eroticism, the song 'Sweeter than roses', a sophistication of those earlier recitative or cantata-like pieces he had written during the 1680s, while for a revival of Dryden's *The Spanish Friar* he chose to set a poem 'While I with wounding grief did look', whose music had originally been composed by Gottfried Finger as a homage to Mrs Bracegirdle's

271

performance as Marcella in *Don Quixote*. The latest of Southerne's plays, his brilliantly perceptive and sardonic adaptation of Aphra Behn's novel *Oroonoko*, was adorned with a dialogue by D'Urfey on the theme of infant sexuality, sung by Jemmy Bowen and Letitia Cross, to music which Purcell loads with insidious charm.

Whatever their dubious investment potential, 'operas' or plays with extensive operatic episodes continued to be a favourite feature of the Drury Lane–Dorset Garden programme. Until recently it was believed that Purcell had supplied the music for the 1695 revival of Shadwell's version of *The Tempest*, but apart from his song 'Dear pretty youth' it seems likely that most of what used to be accepted as his work, including the famous 'Come unto these yellow sands' and 'Halcyon days', was actually written by John Weldon in 1712. For another revival of a play from the days of King Charles however, an authentic Purcell score does survive, but in a highly garbled state among its different manuscripts, which has left scholars puzzled as to exactly where some of the various numbers belong in the play.

Nobody is quite sure of the precise date in 1695 when *The Indian Queen* was performed. It may have been given as early as March, before the two companies went their different ways; it may belong to that autumn; or, since the fifth-act masque was set by Daniel Purcell, it could have been presented after the composer's death. The original play was written by John Dryden and Sir Robert Howard in 1664, a highly exotic confection set in Mexico on the eve of its conquest by the Spaniards and concerned with an unhistoric, geographically impossible war between the 'neighbouring' empires of the Aztecs and the Peruvian Incas. Montezuma, we are required to believe, was really an Inca who went over to the enemy after his bid for the hand of the Princess Orazia had failed, though such treachery brings little comfort to the Aztec Queen Zempoalla, whose sad passion for him provides the tragic core of the play.

Both Dryden and Howard, connected through the former's marriage to the latter's sister, were still alive, and both had direct personal acquaintance with Purcell. Some of the superlative quality of *The Indian Queen* music must surely derive from a sense of friendly obligation, an idea on the composer's part that he would give their work the very best embellishment of his genius. The result is one of his most vitally inspired dramatic scores, shot through with an awareness of Zempoalla's lovesick predicament which gives much of the music an additional ironic tension, cunningly at odds with its surface glamour.

A prologue prophesying the arrival of the Spanish invaders offered Purcell the chance to write a through-composed operatic exchange between its Indian boy and girl protagonists, divided into miniature aria and arioso sections whose distinctive character gives a sense of real personal engagement in the dialogue. We should bear in mind that Dryden himself was to create a sequel to the play, entitled *The Indian Emperor*, in which Cortez and his conquistadors appear, and the 1695 audience must certainly have grasped the ominous import of these opening exchanges in the earlier tragedy.

The masque of Envy and Fame, forming the next significant musical intervention, belongs either to the second or third acts, and is heralded by a transposed version of the trumpet symphony from *Come, Ye Sons of Art*, whose festal pomp is carried over into Fame's air with the chorus 'I come to sing great Zempoalla's glory'. Surely the foursquare simplicity of melodic outline here is intentionally designed for subversion by Envy and his brace of minions, who burst in with a trio supported by fretful violins repeatedly ascending and descending in thirds, while 'the followers of Envy' reinforce the words 'this' and 'hiss' with their own hissing. The malign spirit, sung by a bass, is electric with eagerness to blast the lofty tenor-voiced Fame, resolute in C major, and Purcell cleverly dovetails the envious riposte 'I fly from the place where Flattery reigns' with a reprise of the lethally effective hissing trio.

Again we feel that a warning note has been sounded, notwithstanding Fame's cheerful conclusion to the masque. It is in the Act III conjuring scene however that Purcell excels himself as a purveyor of supernatural doom and shadowy portentousness. Summoned to interpret Zempoalla's disturbing dreams, the magician Ismeron calls up the god of Sleep in an incantation, some of whose lines the composer seems deliberately to have poached from the acting dialogue in order to bolster the effectiveness of what turns out to be among the finest-wrought of all Baroque dramatic arias (Dr Burney, in the eighteenth century, insisted that it was a recitative, which is technically correct, but doesn't do justice to the true nature of the piece).

'Ye twice ten hundred deities' begins with a gaunt-boned arioso, tinged with patches of foreboding chromaticism, before moving into a rhythmic incantatory catalogue, 'By the croaking of the toad/ In their caves that make abode . . . By the crested adders' pride/ That along the cliffs do glide' with passages for strings, before ending in a series of falling sequences evoking the 'bubbling springs' that 'use to lull thee in thy sleep'. When the god does appear, it is to a dignified symphony for oboes which reminds us of their more solemn dramatic uses in an earlier theatrical age, that of Shakespeare and his contemporaries, for ghosts, visions and cortèges, as opposed to their more familiar 1690s' context as festal, 'sprightly', military instruments. Sleep having told Zempoalla nothing she really wants to hear, in a singularly neutral, even pallid musical idiom, she is admonished by a pair of aerial spirits in an almost mocking rondeau, bidding her 'cease to languish', with the reminder that 'greatness clogg'd with scorn decays'.

For the rites which occur in Act V, Purcell consciously returned to the world of similar scenes in *Circe* and *Oedipus*, with perhaps a recollection also of the devils in *The Libertine*, using male soloists and a chorus in appropriately sombre vein. The positioning of this music in the play is clear enough, but musicologists still seem undecided as to where to put the most openly engaging number in the score, another rondeau song commenting on Zempoalla's passion but this time less sardonically, since it is written as if sung by the Queen herself. In fact the actress who played her, Mrs Knight, was not noted as a singer, so as in *Bonduca*, the music was entrusted to Letitia Cross. 'I attempt from love's sickness to fly' is song at its most airborne and unfettered, its structures like crystalline cases to a rapturous eroticism, and all Purcellians must wish that they had been present on the night of its first performance in 1695.

If this was, as has sometimes been suggested, during the early autumn, then perhaps Purcell was already starting to sicken of the illness which at length proved fatal to him. The causes of his death have been much discussed down the centuries, and every biographer has his or her theory. One idea which carries some credibility relates to *Bonduca*, where he had written a most 'ingeniose' catch, whose words run as follows:

Jack, thou'rt a toper, let's have t'other Quart:
Ring, ring, ring, we're so sober, 'twere a shame to part.
None but a Cuckold, bully'd by his wife
For coming late fears a Domestick strife:
I'm free and so are you too, call and knock
Boldly, tho' Watchmen cry past two o Clock

Sir John Hawkins, writing in the late eighteenth century, tells us that Purcell caught a cold as a result of being locked out of the house by his wife when he came home reeling drunk after an evening at a tavern called the Hole In The Wall in Baldwin's Gardens. This may be true, given what his works suggest as to his convivial habits, especially some of his catches or the full-blooded hymn to booze in the highly enjoyable duet ''Tis wine was made to rule the day' one of whose verses runs:

Let my Queen live for ever
And let's still drink French wine;
Let my rage be immortal
And my liquor divine.

Though a tavern called the Purcell's Head apparently existed during the composer's lifetime, ideas more charitable to both husband and wife imply either tuberculosis or influenza as the ultimate cause of death. Whatever the case, we know that by the time Part III of *The Comical History of Don Quixote* was mounted at Dorset Garden in November, he was already ill, since the *Orpheus Britannicus* volume appends a note to Altisidora's 'From rosy bow'rs' which tells us that it was 'The last SONG the Author Sett, it being in his Sickness'. On 21 November 'Henry Purcell, of the City of Westminster, gent. being dangerously ill as to the constitution of my body, but in good and perfect mind and memory' made his will, leaving everything to 'my loveing wife Frances Purcell' and appointing her sole excutrix. It was drawn up by his brother-in-law John Baptist Peters and witnessed by two neighbours William Eeles and John Capelin. By that same midnight Purcell was dead.

Through the most mournful of coincidences, the next day was the feast of St Cecilia, for which John Blow had written a Te Deum and an ode, *Great Choirs of Heaven*, and the musicians gathered at St Bride's, Fleet Street, as in the previous year. The news of Purcell's death, however prepared they were for the shock, must have been devastating, and its effect on the world of the arts in London at the time is preserved for us by an elaborate and quite remarkable work consecrated to the composer's memory by Jeremiah Clarke. *Come, Come Along for a Dance and a Song* begins with a sense of cheerful festivity which is suddenly and drastically interrupted by the entrance of a messenger, announcing the arrival of the terrible news, whereupon joy changes to deepest sorrow. That this was what the London musical community felt is symbolized by the august funeral rites with which the composer was honoured. A London newspaper *The Flying Post* told its readers that 'Mr Henry Pursel one of the most Celebrated Masters of the Science of Musick in the Kingdom, and scarce Inferior to any in Europe' was to be buried in Westminster Abbey, by unanimous resolve of the Dean and Chapter, 'with all the Funeral Solemnity they are capable to perform for him'. Frances, his widow, given the choice of whereabouts she wished 'to Reposite his Corps', selected the area at the foot of the organ he used to play.

On the evening of 26 November, 'the whole Chapter assisting with their vestments, together with all the Lovers of that Noble Science, with the united Choyres of that and the Chappel Royal', Henry was laid in earth to the sound of his own music. His colleague at William and Mary's coronation, Stephen Crespion, led the funeral procession, 'when the Dirges composed by the Deceased for her late Majesty of Ever Blessed Memory' were played by 'Trumpeters and other Musick'. As at that earlier royal service, Morley's Funeral Sentences, encasing Purcell's 'Thou Knowest, Lord', were sung, the last of them, 'I heard a voice from heaven', as earth was cast upon the coffin. His monument, a small Baroque cartouche decorated with a flaming lamp, a mask and the Purcell coat of arms, was paid for by his pupil Annabella Howard.

Its inscription, said to have been composed by John Dryden, runs as follows: 'HERE LYES HENRY PURCELL Esq. Who left this Life and is gone to that Blessed Place where only his Harmony can be exceeded. Obiit 21mo die Novembris Anno Aetatis suae 37mo Anno Domini 1695.'

In its notice of the funeral *The Flying Post* had announced that Purcell's 'place of Organist is disposed of to that great Master Dr Blow'. Henry's old friend, teacher, competitor and creative kindred spirit was one of many musicians now moved to commemorate him with such skill as they could muster. While he set Dryden's *Ode on the Death of Mr Henry Purcell* as a cantata for two countertenors, recorders and continuo, Daniel Purcell provided the music for an elegy on his brother by an equally faithful associate, Nahum Tate, and Gottfried Finger's setting of a poem by Purcell's Westminster schoolfellow James Talbot 'Upon the death of H.P.' was performed at one of the public concerts now regularly taking place at York Buildings. For Clarke's *Come, Come Along*, the company at Drury Lane, where the dead composer's music had so often disarmed a critical audience, assembled a large orchestra, including trumpets and drums, and among the soloists were those who had sung for him in past years, such as Jemmy Bowen, Letitia Cross and John Freeman.

The poetry of these and other tributes witnessed to an authentic sense of loss, transcending the standard decorum of early Augustan elegiac verse and imbued with an awareness of Purcell as a dearly loved friend or, quite simply, as the most remarkable English musical talent of his age. Dryden's memorial of him, with a rueful wit, releases 'the Godlike Man' from likely damnation in the line, 'we beg not Hell our Orpheus to restore,' sending him instead to Heaven along a file of angels to whom he gives lessons on the way, and the poem ends with a cynical assurance to his fellow musicians that they can

> live secure and linger out your days
> The Gods are pleas'd alone with Purcell's Layes,
> Nor know to mend their Choice.

More intimate was the elegy by his friend Robert Gould, a protégé of Lord Dorset, whose tragedy *The Rival Sisters* was among the last for which Purcell wrote the music.

Gould praised:

> Such wondrous goodness in a life so young,
> That I, ev'n I, was number'd with the rest,
> Prest in his arms and kneaded to his breast.

He recalled too that alert, intelligent face which John Closterman painted and Godfrey Kneller drew:

> So justly were his soul and body join'd,
> You'd think his form the product of his mind,
> A conqu'ring sweetness in his visage dwelt,
> His eyes would warm, his wit like lightning melt . . .

Was this the man Frances Purcell and their two children Edward, a musician like his father, and Frances, who married the minor poet and journalist Leonard Wellstead, knew and loved? The widow lived on until 1706, moving first to a house in Dean's Yard, Westminster, thence to Richmond, and publishing several of her husband's manuscripts in the years immediately following his death, including his collected theatre music, the songs gathered together in *Orpheus Britannicus*, and a scattering of keyboard pieces, as well as the so-called *Ten Sonatas of IV Parts*.

We should surely not have to view this as simply a cynical exercise in money-spinning on Frances's part. The age wanted whatever of Purcell's it could hang on to, because it knew that there was nobody to take his place. When Charles Gildon, who had accommodated *Dido and Aeneas* to *Measure for Measure* in 1700 with the help of Daniel Purcell, told him, apropos another project, that his music 'was so admirable, that the best Judges tell me . . . that there is the true Purcellian Air through the whole', the thrust of such praise must have been obvious. By the beginning of the eighteenth century, when King William, perhaps recalling its associations with Queen Mary, was recorded at having wept openly on hearing his music played, Purcell had achieved that eminence posthumously for which, as Tudway tells us, he had striven so hard during his life. He had become, in the consecrating memories of those who survived him 'the Delight of the Nation

278

and the Wonder of the World', 'our all-pleasing Britain's Orpheus', 'Harry the Great, the Blest!' Though much of his music subsequently sank out of view, he never lost his iconic significance among English composers, but it is only now, at the end of the twentieth century, that we have begun to accept the multiplicity of his achievement as something quite astonishing, the reflection of an artistic personality almost supernatural in its gift for being everything at once, abundant and three-dimensional. Since a true biography of Henry Purcell is impossible to fashion, it is in what he made, and in the world within which he felt, experienced and imagined, that we must look for our English Orpheus.

Notes

Prologue: The Unfriendly Time

1 *Thomas Tomkins*: Denis Stevens, *Thomas Tomkins, 1572–1656*, London, 1957, p. 65.
   Some Parliamenters: Stevens op. cit., p. 63.

2. *Very elaborate and artful*: Thomas Tudway, ms. remark quoted in Stevens op. cit., p. 94.
   Broke down the rayl: Records of church desecration by the Puritans are quoted in Percy A. Scholes, *The Puritans And Music In England And New England*, Oxford, 1934, p. 323. Scholes acknowledges that his source, Bruno Ryves's *Mercurius Rusticus*, 1646–7, is highly prejudiced.

4 *Some there are*: For Whitelocke on dancing see Scholes op. cit., pp. 62–4.

7 *I went to visit*: John Evelyn, Diary, 5th May, 1659.
   The Siege of Rhodes: For a full discussion see Edward J. Dent, *Foundations Of English Opera*, Cambridge, 1928.

9 *John Jenkins*: Complete account of his career in Andrew Ashbee: *The Harmonious Musick Of John Jenkins*, Vol. I, Surbiton, 1992.
   Roger North on Jenkins: Ashbee op. cit., p. 96.

10 *When most other good arts*: John Wilson, *Roger North On Music*, London, 1959. p. 294.

Chapter One: A Peculiar Readiness of Fancy

14 *Shropshire Purcells*: Maureen Duffey, *Henry Purcell*, London, 1994, pp. 13–15.
   This last week: F.P. & M. Verney, *Memoirs Of The Verney Family*, London, 1907, Vol. ii, p. 39.

16 *Westminster*: For Purcell's Westminster, see Mackenzie E.C. Walcott, *The Memorials Of Westminster*, London, 1851.

19 *The Chapel Royal*: Best accounts are in Christopher Dearnley, *English Church Music 1650–1750*, London, 1970 and David Baldwin, *The Chapel Royal, Ancient & Modern*, London, 1990.

20 *he had lived some considerable time*: Wilson, *Roger North On Music*, op. cit., p. 299.

21 *Some of the forwardest*: Thomas Tudway quoted in Dearnley op. cit., pp. 25–6.

25 *For each of them*: Baldwin, *The Chapel Royal*, op. cit., p. 191.
    Had the arrogance: Samuel Pepys, Diary, 13 February 1667.

26 *Purcell at Westminster*: I am grateful to Dr Peter Holmes, Westminster School archivist, for information regarding the Abbey Treasurer's accounts. He points out that the spelling 'Pursell' used in the records from 1677 changes to 'Purcell' when Robert South becomes Treasurer in 1680. In each case it remains consistent whether referring to the Bishop's Boy or the musician.

30 *Pelham Humfrey*: For Humfrey, see Peter Dennison, *Pelham Humfrey*, Oxford Studies of Composers, 1986.

32 *A great Critick*: *The Works Of Sir George Etherege*, ed. H.F.B. Brett Smith, Oxford, 1927, Vol. ii, pp. 225–33.

35 *Two suits of plain cloth*: quoted in Dearnley, op. cit., p. 37.

37 *The 1674 Tempest*: see Dent, *Foundations*, op. cit., Ch. 4. Also Dennison, *Humfrey*, op. cit., Ch. 7.

39 *A magnifick consort*: Wilson, *Roger North*, op. cit., p. 349.

43 *The so much cry'd up*: quoted in Franklin B. Zimmerman, *Henry Purcell, A Guide To Research*, New York 1982, p. 64.

48 *Only upon Sundays*: Christopher Hogwood, *Thomas Tudway's History Of Music*, in (with Richard Luckett ed.) *Music in Eighteenth Century England, Essays in Memory of Charles Cudworth*, Cambridge, 1983.

Chapter Two: Court, Chapel and Stage

51 *Restoration theatre*: Full accounts of literary and social background in Allardyce Nicoll, *A History of Restoration Drama 1660–1700*, Cambridge, 1923 and Montague Summers, *The Restoration Theatre*, London, 1934.

52 *The place where they act*: Francois Brunet, unpublished ms. quoted in Summers op. cit., p. 63.

54 *Restoration theatre music*: Curtis Price, *Music in the Restoration Theatre*, Ann Arbor, Michigan, 1979.

62 *Birthday odes*: A full study in Rosamond McGuinness, *English Court Odes, 1660–1820*, Oxford, 1971.

65 *Frances Purcell's family*: Duffey op. cit., pp. 61–70.

66 *Orpheus Britannicus preface*: quoted in Zimmerman, *PRG*, op. cit., pp. 141–3.

72 *Charterhouse motets*: Nigel Fortune, Purcell, *The Domestic Sacred Music*, in *Essays on Opera and English Music in honour of Sir Jack Westrup*,

ed. Sternfeld, Fortune & Olleson, Oxford, 1975, pp. 62–78. Also Samuel Herne, *Domus Carthusiana*, London, 1677.

Chapter 3: After the Italian Way

88   *Here came over*: Wilson, *Roger North*, op. cit., p. 302.

90   *North on Matteis*: Ibid, pp. 307–10, 355–8.

93   *Colista and Lonati*: Peter Allsop, 'Problems of Ascription in the Roman Sinfonia of the late Seventeenth Century', *Music Review* 50, pp. 34–44. Also Michael Tilmouth 'The Technique and Forms of Purcell's Sonatas', *Music & Letters* 40, p. 115.

95   *Sonnatas of III Parts*: preface quoted in Zimmerman, *PRG*, op. cit., pp. 75–77.

100 *The Reverend Mr Sub-dean*: Sir John Hawkins, *A General History of the Science and Practice of Music*, 1875 edn., Vol. ii, p. 745.

101 *I had not assum'd*: Zimmerman: *PRG*, op. cit., p. 75.

104 *Purcell and the Test Act*: documents in Franklin B. Zimmerman, *Henry Purcell, 1659–1695*, London, 1967, pp. 100–1.

106 *He had the Danish*: John Evelyn, Diary, op. cit., 25th July, 1683.

109 *Yet it was wonderful*: Ibid. 13th July, 1683.

111 *St Cecilia festivities*: See W.H. Husk, *An Account of the Musical Celebrations on St Cecilia's Day*, London, 1857.

116 *Frost fair*: Evelyn, Diary, op. cit., 24th Jan 1684.
     Playford's Choyce Ayres: Zimmerman, *PRG*, op. cit, p. 80.

119 *They that go down*: Hawkins, *General History* op. cit., p. 744.

122 *I can never forget*: Evelyn, Diary, op. cit., 6th February, 1685.

Chapter 4: Fools and Fanaticks

123 *She showed herself*: Abbate Rizzini quoted in Mary Hopkirk, *Queen Over The Water*, London, 1953, p. 85.

128 *For my part*: Evelyn: Diary, op. cit.
     Duke of Modena's oratorio: Victor Crowther, *The Oratorio in Modena*, Oxford, 1992, p. 66.

129 *Being the King's birthday*: Evelyn: Diary, op. cit., 15th October, 1685.

130 *Evelyn on Lord Keeper North*: Ibid, 23 January, 1683.

132 *Roger North on Lord Keeper North*: Wilson, *Roger North*, op. cit., pp. 33–48.

136 *My wishes are*: Hilton quoted in *The Catch Book*, ed. Paul Hillier, Oxford, 1987, p. xi.

137 *Organ choosing*: Zimmerman, *Henry Purcell*, op. cit., pp. 137–8.

141 *The Bishop in his mire*: Evelyn, Diary, op. cit. 29th December, 1686.

142 His holding out: Ibid, 19th April, 1687.

145 *Letter to the Dean of Exeter*: quoted in Zimmerman, *Henry Purcell*, op. cit., pp. 139–40

152 *Playford's introduction to Harmonia Sacra*: Zimmerman: *PRG* op. cit., pp. 98–9.

156 *Her being so positive*: Hester W. Chapman, *Mary II, Queen of England*, London, 1953, p. 142.

158 *Battle of the organs*: Best account is in J.A. Westrup, *Purcell*, London, 1965 (fifth edn.), pp. 51–3, quoting Burney, Hawkins and ms. sources.

162 *By my last Pacquet*: *Letters of Sir George Etherege*, ed. Frederick Bracher, Berkeley, Calif. 1974, p. 96.

164 *The King's birthday*: Evelyn, Diary, 4 October, 1688.

Chapter 5: Wayward Sisters

165 *God knows my heart*: Chapman, *Mary II*, op. cit., p. 167.

167 *Coronation perks for musicians*: documents in Zimmerman, *Henry Purcell*, op. cit., pp. 165–9.

170 *Reappointment of musicians*: Lists in ibid. pp. 163–4.

171 *Lewis Maidwell*: see *Westminster Elizabethan XII*, pp. 214–5.

175 *Verney on japanning*: *Verney Memoirs*, op. cit., Vol. ii, pp. 312–3.

178 Dido & Aeneas *dating*: Bruce Wood & Andrew Pinnock, 'Unscarr'd by Turning Times: The Dating of Purcell's *Dido & Aeneas*'. *Early Music* 20, pp. 373–90. Also Curtis Price: '*Dido & Aeneas*, questions of style and evidence', Ibid. 22, pp. 373–90.

186 *Lady Dorothy Burke*: W.H. Grattan Flood: 'Purcell's *Dido & Aeneas* – who was Lady Dorothy Burke', *Musical Times* 59, p. 513.

187 *Mrs Buck's letter*: Mark Goldie, 'The earliest notice of Purcell's *Dido & Aeneas*, EM 20, pp. 393–400.

190 *Frances Purcell's dedication*: Zimmerman, *PRG*, op. cit., p. 139.

195 London Gazette *on Yorkshire Feast*: Westrup, *Purcell*, op. cit., p. 66.
      Much of it seems to have been written: Ibid, p. 66.

198 *Mary in William's absence*: Chapman, *Mary II* op. cit., Ch. 3.

Chapter Six: Bringing Home the Indies

202 *I shall content myself*: Colley Cibber, *An Apology For His Life*, Everyman edn. London, 1914, p. 62.

204 *Set out with Coastly Scenes*: John Downes, *Roscius Anglicanus*, London, 1708, p. 42.

206 *Musick is yet*: Dedication in Zimmerman: *PRG*, op. cit., p. 107.

208 *Ridiculous ... that scene*: Anon, *A Comparison Between the Two Stages*, (1702) ed. Staring B. Wells, Princeton, NJ. 1942, p. 30.

214 *Charlotte Butler*: Olive Baldwin & Thelma Wilson, 'Purcell's Sopranos', *MT* 123, pp. 602–9.

220 *I remember*: Wilson, *Roger North*, op. cit., p. 217.

222 *An audacious study in irony*: For political overtones in *King Arthur*, see Curtis Price, *Henry Purcell and the London Stage*, Cambridge, 1984, pp. 289–95.

      There was so much: Wilson, *Roger North*, op. cit., p. 218.

224 *Her youth and lively aspect*: Cibber, *Apology*, op. cit., pp. 90–2.

228 *The Queen, having a mind*: Hawkins, *General History*, op. cit., p. 564.

229 *Arabella Hunt*: Baldwin & Wilson, *Purcell's Sopranos*, op. cit.

231 *Every branch*: Cibber, *Apology*, op. cit., p. 99.

234 *The Court and the Town*: Downes, *Roscius Anglicanus*, op. cit., p. 43.

Chapter Seven: The Last Song

242 *Durfey has brought*: *Letters Of John Dryden*, ed. Charles E. Ward. Duke University, Durham NC, 1942, pp. 52–3.

245 *Playford's Harmonia Sacra II*: Zimmerman, *PRG*, op. cit., p. 118.

248 *In guilty night*:Basil Smallman, 'Endor Revisited, English Biblical Dialogues of the Seventeenth Century', *ML* 46, pp. 137–46.

250 *Dublin celebrations*: J.W. Stubbs, *The History Of The University Of Dublin*, Dublin, 1889.

255 *Letitia Cross*: Baldwin & Wilson, *Purcell's Sopranos*, op. cit.

257 *Tudway on the Te Deum*: Peter Holman, *Henry Purcell*, Oxford Studies of Composers, 1994, p. 141.

259 *Queen Mary's death*: Chapman, *Mary II* op. cit., pp. 249–60.

261 *Flat trumpets*: Bruce Wood, 'The First Performance of Purcell's Funeral Music For Queen Mary', in Michael Burden, *Performing The Music Of Henry Purcell*, Oxford, 1995.

262 *Compos'd by Mr Henry Purcell*: Hogwood, *Thomas Tudway's History Of Music*, op. cit., p. 65.

264 *The unjust oppressions*: Allardyce Nicoll, *Restoration Drama*, op. cit., p. 330.

265 *The house was very full*: Cibber, *Apology*, op. cit., p. 163.

268 *Who Can From Joy*: Olive Baldwin & Thelma Wilson, 'Who Can From Joy Refraine? Purcell's Birthday Song For The Duke of Gloucester', *MT* 122, 596–9.

276 *Purcell's funeral*: Documents quoted in Margaret Campbell, *Henry Purcell, Glory Of His Age*, London, 1993, pp. 236–8.

278 *Was so admirable*: quoted in Eric Walter White, 'New Light on *Dido & Aeneas*', in *Henry Purcell 1659–1695, Essays On His Music*, London, 1959.

277 *Purcell elegies*: Full texts of all these in Zimmerman: *Henry Purcell*, op. cit., pp. 339–59.

Suggestions for Further Reading

The Purcell literature is currently expanding as a result of interest shown in him during the tercentenary celebrations, but its scope is still fairly narrow. Two recent biographies, by Robert King and Maureen Duffey, have usefully enhanced our awareness of the composer's creative and professional life, the former with the help of handsome illustrations and practical performing experience, the latter through a remarkable intuitive sympathy with the spirit of Purcell's era.

Individual studies of the artist, containing detailed analyses of many major works, are best represented, at the time of writing, by Martin Adams's *Henry Purcell: The Origins and Development of his Musical Style* (Cambridge, 1995) and by Peter Holman's volume in the *Oxford Studies of Composers* series (1994), a book which must surely rank as the best single essay on Purcell ever written. An excellent collection of single-topic studies has recently been gathered together under Michael Burden's editorship in *The Purcell Companion* (London, 1995). We are promised a further volume from the same editor, *Performing The Music Of Purcell*.

Details of editions and manuscripts, as well as a complete catalogue of Purcell's compositions, may be found in two volumes by Franklin B. Zimmerman, his earliest serious biographer. *Henry Purcell: A Guide to Research* (New York, 1989) contains, in addition, the texts of all the various prefaces and introductory matter to the early published editions, besides giving details of relevant musicological literature. *Henry Purcell: An Analytical Catalogue Of His Music* (London, 1963) examines the manuscript sources and early copies, with notes as to background and current location.

For a broader overall view of the musical milieu in which Purcell worked, the newest volume in the *Blackwell History Of Music In Britain: The Seventeenth Century*, edited by Ian Spink (Oxford, 1993), is highly recommended. Those interested specifically in Purcell's work for the theatre will find Curtis Price's exhaustive survey *Henry Purcell and the London Stage* (Cambridge, 1984) an invaluable companion. The context of the sacred works is lucidly portrayed in Christopher Dearnley's *English Church Music, 1650–1750* (London, 1970).

Index of Works of Henry Purcell

Index of Works of Henry Purcell

General Index